Dr. Abravanel's Body Type Diet and Lifetime Nutrition Plan

Dr. Abravanel's Body Type Diet and Lifetime Nutrition Plan

Revised Edition
Elliot D. Abravanel, M.D.
and Elizabeth King Morrison

Illustrations by Vivien Cohen
and Alan Sanborn

BANTAM BOOKS
New York   Toronto   London   Sydney   Auckland

This or any other diet and fitness program
should be followed under a doctor's supervision.

DR. ABRAVANEL'S BODY TYPE DIET AND LIFETIME NUTRITION PLAN:
REVISED EDITION
A Bantam Book
PUBLISHING HISTORY
Bantam hardcover edition published March 1983
Bantam paperback edition / March 1984
Bantam revised trade paperback edition / July 1999
Grateful acknowledgment to *Tufts University Health & Nutrition Letter* for
permission to reprint a portion of the article "Keeping Fat Off the
Middle" that appeared in the October 1997 issue.

ISBN 0-7394-0424-5

Published simultaneously in the United States and Canada

Bantam Books are published by Bantam Books, a division of Random
House, Inc. Its trademark, consisting of the words "Bantam Books" and the
portrayal of a rooster, is Registered in U.S. Patent and Trademark Office and
in other countries. Marca Registrada. Bantam Books, 1540 Broadway, New
York, New York 10036.

PRINTED IN THE UNITED STATES OF AMERICA

ACKNOWLEDGMENTS

A new edition of a book that has been in print for more than fifteen years necessarily incorporates the suggestions and help of many people. We would like to thank in particular the many thousands of readers with whom we have corresponded; your questions and comments have driven us to think harder and create clearer explanations, and have added greatly to our knowledge of the Body Type System in action.

Our thanks also to all the Body Type Counselors, and in particular the Counselor Trainers: Gail Rembisz, Kevyn Van Lehn, Judith Levy, Veronica Haitsma, Celene Gunther, and Jan Scecina. For their insightful comments on the revised Body Type Checklist, our special thanks to Body Type Counselors Bonnie Mickelson, Kate Lynch, Wendy Just, and Jane Cone. The support of our office staff, especially Laura Tregoning and Paula Gooley, and our knowledgeable advisers Barbara Kramer-Tralle and Lea Morrison, has been invaluable. We'd also like to thank our wonderful agent, Rosalie Heacock.

CONTENTS

FOREWORD TO THE
1999 EDITION

In 1983, when I first introduced the concept of Body Type Dieting, the idea that people were different and needed different diets was exciting and very new. I was able to offer a unique system for finding a diet that was right for each individual, based on his or her own type of metabolism, as revealed by the body itself. As I traveled the country speaking about body types, I found that most people had a surprised "aha" reaction. They said, "I see! That explains a lot! Why hasn't anyone told me that before?"

Now, as this new edition is being published, I'm delighted to find that the body type idea has taken large strides toward general acceptance. Once you've entertained the notion that a diet that's right for one person may not be right for someone else, it's hard to go back to the old one-size-fits-all way of looking at things. A large number of doctors, nutritionists, exercise instructors, and others with whom I have worked have made body types very much a part of their own view of human diversity.

Yet there are still many people who don't recognize their own body type. And many (indeed, most) nutrition experts have yet to learn how to take each person's type of metabolism into account when making dietary recommendations. I invite them to take a close look at the material in this new edition, to weigh the recommendations, and to contact the Body Type Institute at 1-888-263-9897 if they would like any more information on implementing them in their own practice.

Glandular Body Typing
and Your Good Health

I feel today, as I did in 1983, that Body Typing based on the glandular system has medical validity and a strong history of predictive success in terms of determining the right diet for you as an individual. It also has implications for your overall health. One of the main reasons for bringing out a new edition at this time is to give a fuller emphasis to the health benefits of knowing your body type. You may have chosen this book to lose weight, but your health should be the overriding consideration.

There are other reasons for a new edition as well. I knew I could give you more help in determining your body type than I did in 1983. The Body Type Checklist in the first edition has worked quite well, on the whole, and many people have been able to find their body type and have gone on to follow my recommendations very successfully. But I have been concerned over the past ten years or so at the significant number of readers who have not been able to determine their body type to their own satisfaction.

At the Body Type Institute, Elizabeth King Morrison and I have worked with a large number of people who have had this problem, and have improved our understanding of what is needed for this vital first step in Body Type Dieting. We have revised the Body Type Checklist and added a way for you to get additional help finding your body type if you need it.

I have also updated my diet recommendations, or rather, I have updated the form in which they are made. The recommendations themselves have not changed except in a few minor details, because the physiology of the four body types has not changed—each one has the same needs it had in 1983, and those needs must be met by the same diet.

But the scientific understanding of diet in general has changed greatly since 1983. There is much more knowledge of how the right diet can promote health and minimize the risk of various diseases, including obesity, heart disease, and diabetes. I have put my recommendations into this context so that you can clearly see how the Body Type Diets meet today's scientific nutritional standards.

I have also extensively updated my exercise recommendations for each Body Type. Researchers today consider the importance of

regular physical activity to be equal to, or even greater than, the importance of good nutrition in promoting physical and mental
health. In fact, not exercising is now considered a risk factor equal
to smoking! But if you're like most people, you're still not as active
as you wish you were. You may have tried a dozen diets for every
one time you've started an exercise regimen. This edition has a practical exercise program for your body type, including cardiovascular,
strength, and flexibility training, with hints on how to ease into it
comfortably.

I also wanted to give you some insight into the nutritional supplements that are right for your body type. As a physician, I have
watched the medical view of supplementation change radically
since the eighties. In the 1983 edition I followed the then-current
medical thinking and did not recommend nutritional supplementation. Today, I understand the value of supplementation that takes
the needs of each body type fully into account. I'm giving you my
recommendations and urging you to use them—you can add
greatly to your health, and reach your best weight more efficiently,
with the judicious use of just the right supplements for your body
type.

There are other areas where particular health measures can add
greatly to the effectiveness of the Body Type Program. Yoga positions
for each body type and my Long Weekend of Rejuvenation are examples. This new edition adds these and other recommendations,
and I think you'll find them very helpful.

It's possible to think of the Body Type Diet as mainly a way to
lose weight. But I have seen over and over in my practice that its importance goes far beyond weight alone. It provides a paradigm for
thinking about health that should be at the very heart of medicine—
namely, a concern for the particular needs of each individual. I invite you to learn your body type for whatever reasons seem most
important to you, but you should also know that this knowledge can
greatly improve your health and your prospects for a longer life, with
a better quality of life to the very end. That is my wish for you and
my primary reason for this new edition.

Elliot D. Abravanel, M.D.
Los Angeles, California
June 1998

FOREWORD TO THE
1983 EDITION

I live in Southern California, and it seems to me that nowhere is the connection between health and beauty more obvious than it is here. The intense light of the desert, the year-round warmth and perpetual sunshine invite a style of life that is lived largely out of doors. It is impossible for anyone to hide an unhealthy, out-of-shape body under layers of heavy, concealing clothing.

In my medical practice I see many intelligent, health-conscious people who are concerned about their weight. They want to look good, but they are well aware that good health is the key ingredient to true beauty. My Body Type Diet and Lifetime Nutrition Plan is designed with this kind of person in mind. This program is not just a way of losing weight, but an entirely new set of *principles of dieting,* based on the most modern theories of the biochemical interaction of foods with the body.

A diet should transform your body, not just change it in a superficial way. A body is not a static entity from which fat can be peeled away like layers of an onion. The transformation must come from within, for only a healthy, balanced body can maintain its ideal weight. Overweight itself indicates imbalance in the system. Defining exactly what imbalances exist, and then correcting them through diet while you are losing weight, is precisely what the Body Type Diet and Lifetime Nutrition Plan accomplishes.

No Single Diet
Works for Everyone

The most important principle of Body Type Dieting, which I have evolved in the course of treating thousands of overweight patients, is that *there is no one diet that works for everyone, and there never will be.* Rather, there are four very different body types—that is, four types of metabolism—defined by which of the body's four major glands (the gonads, the adrenal glands, the thyroid gland, and the pituitary gland) is dominant in the system. Each of these four body types has its own, very specific dieting requirements.

Discover Which of the
Four Body Types You Are

The Body Type Diet has an essential preliminary step that no other diet has: the step of determining your body type. You'll learn how to do it in Chapter 5. Knowing your body type tells you a great deal about your overweight. It explains, first, how you became fat— which foods you felt irresistible cravings for, and ate too much of, in the past. It also explains how you look in an overweight condition— where you have fat deposits, and which parts of your body remain relatively slim despite your overweight.

Even more important, your body type determines your strategy for getting, and staying, slender. It determines which foods you must eliminate from your diet, even though other people just as overweight as you are can safely eat them and still lose weight. It determines which foods you *must* eat while dieting in order to free yourself from cravings and achieve metabolic balance. It even determines *when* you should eat—whether you will lose weight more easily by eating your biggest meal early, in the middle, or late in the day.

In short, your body type determines what type of diet will work for you. It provides you with a guide through the confusing muddle of diets available everywhere today, and lets you custom-tailor a weight loss program to fit *your* metabolic needs.

The Body Type
Diet Program

Once you know your body type, you start on your Body Type Weight Loss Diet and follow it for a week. What happens after that depends on how much you want and need to lose. If you have only a few extra pounds, you change at this point to the Last Five Pounds Diet for your body type. If you have more excess weight, you follow your Weight Loss Diet for up to three weeks before changing to the Last Five Pounds Diet for a week. This four-week program can then be repeated, if necessary, until you have reached your weight goal.

When you do reach your weight goal (and you will!), you move on to the Health and Weight Maintenance Diet for your body type. This is a flexible and easily followed eating program for a lifetime of good health at your ideal weight.

What Is Your
Ideal Weight?

Your ideal weight is not defined by tables or numbers. It is, very simply, the weight at which you look your best and feel wonderful. It is the weight at which you are free from "pockets" of fat and cellulite, at which your body is well proportioned and attractive. It is the weight at which you have abundant energy, both mental and physical, and at which you rest well and get full value from your rest.

A table of heights and weights cannot tell you what this weight is for you, because no table or chart has ever taken into account the fact that the ideal weight differs, among people of the same height, according to body type. You will see when we look at the four body types why the Adrenal and Gonadal Types are always slightly heavier, at their ideal weight, than the Thyroid or Pituitary Types. Because of this natural variation, the only way to be sure of determining your ideal weight is to reach it—through Body Type Dieting.

The Most Effective Weight Loss Diet—
and the Best of Health

Modern medicine has a good idea of what sorts of things shorten life. Obesity, smoking, poor diet, lack of exercise, lack of sufficient rest, and environmental pollution—all are contributors to shorter life expectancy. But it is still not entirely clear how long a person might live if all circumstances were completely right.

Some experts in genetics believe that our bodies are programmed to die after a certain number of years, or breaths, or heartbeats. Others believe that our lives are not limited by time alone, but by other factors that cause our systems to begin to decline. Some of these limiting factors are under our control and can be eliminated; wrong eating habits are certainly one factor that we can control.

The Body Type Diet and Lifetime Nutrition Plan is intended, ultimately, as a contribution toward slowing—and reversing—the body's decline. It is for weight loss, yes. My experience has shown me over and over again that the Body Type Diet produces the fastest, safest, and most effective weight loss for each of the body types. But it is also designed for improvement in the quality of life. My aim has been to help all who follow these diets make the most of their potential to enjoy life in all its fullness. After all, life is not just a salted cracker or a scoop of cottage cheese. It's a banquet.

Elliot D. Abravanel, M.D.
Los Angeles, California
September 1982

Dr. Abravanel's Body Type Diet and Lifetime Nutrition Plan

FINDING THE RIGHT DIET FOR YOU

Most people today believe that to be slim is necessarily to be healthy. They are mistaken: Most diets are so unhealthy as to be useless in the long run. In fact, most diets aren't even useful in the short run, even for weight loss, because the lost weight invariably comes right back.

Occasionally, a diet will work for some lucky dieter. But for every dieter who loses weight, there are hundreds more who fail. And no one ever explains why a diet works, when it does, or why it fails.

The Body Type Diet answers these questions. Body Type Dieting is not just another peel-away-the-pounds fad. Rather, it is a systematic medical program relating different types of diet to different types of body, in order to enable each individual to find the diet that will be effective, safe, and healthy for him or her.

HOW I DISCOVERED THE IMPORTANCE OF BODY TYPES

I developed the concept of the Body Type Diet and Lifetime Nutrition Plan more than twenty years ago, when I was a young doctor with a busy general practice. Unlike medical specialists, who focus their attention on one system of the body or another, I was a generalist, accustomed to looking at my patients as whole people in whom all parts of the body have to work together for health. Naturally one of the problems often presented to me was the problem of overweight, and I was often asked for advice about diet. Since the importance of maintaining one's ideal weight is, from a health standpoint, beyond dispute, I determined to find a way to help my patients achieve this goal.

But I was not fully satisfied with any of the diets available at that time. What struck me was that while one or two patients would lose weight on one or the other of the many popular diets that exist in the marketplace, most of them either failed to lose, or lost weight and quickly gained it back.

I decided to take a closer look at those of my patients who did lose weight successfully, and to isolate those factors that were the keys to success.

Two patients who happened to come to my office on the same day, illustrated clearly what I discovered. The two were both women, good friends who had decided to diet together for mutual reinforcement. Both had managed to lose about nine pounds; one wanted to lose six more, the other sixteen more pounds. Both had been on a popular diet that was low in protein and fats and high in complex carbohydrates. But there the similarity ended.

The first patient, whom I will call Anna, was the one within six pounds of her weight goal, and she looked very well. She had lost her weight from the right places—her hips and thighs, rather than her face, which had never been fat. She told me that she felt healthy and vigorous even though she was dieting, and she looked that way, too.

The second patient, Joanne, was a contrast to Anna in almost every way. She retained "pockets" of fat on her outer thighs, which, she told me, she'd been unable to lose. Her face was gaunt and she had a pasty, unhealthy color. Moreover, she was having difficulty sticking to her diet, and was constantly suffering from an intense craving for sweets.

What was particularly interesting to me was that both women had followed exactly the same diet. I knew them both, and was confident that Joanne had not been "cheating"; she was highly motivated to lose weight. Obviously, the difference was not in the diet but in the dieter, or rather in the *interaction* of dieter and diet. The way the diet worked for Anna was obviously not the way it worked for Joanne.

Examining the two women, I discovered that their bodies were indeed very different. Anna had a very steady, strong metabolism. She had excellent digestion, was active all day, and had relatively little variation in her energy level. Joanne was a very different type; she was livelier than Anna, but more given to ups and downs in energy. She had intense nervous energy, but tended to "crash" in the late afternoon if she wasn't careful. She drank a lot of coffee and diet cola to keep herself going. In short, she was more high-strung and more delicate than Anna.

I decided to put Joanne on a completely different diet from the high-carbohydrate one that had seemed to work for Anna. The diet I selected was high in protein, lower in carbohydrates, and eliminated all caffeine drinks. The idea of this diet was to provide a steadying balance for her delicate, high-strung system. Meanwhile, I told Anna to continue as she had been, until she had lost the rest of her excess weight.

To my delight, Joanne responded beautifully to her changed program. After just a week on the diet she began to look healthier. Her face, which had been so gaunt, filled out and her cheeks were rosy. But more important to her, she began to lose the pockets of fat on her thighs. Within four weeks she had lost the entire sixteen pounds. *Five years after that memorable month, she was still at her ideal weight.*

Anna, meanwhile, continued on her high-carbohydrate diet and by the end of the next week she had lost her remaining six pounds. Now both women had dieted successfully—but on diets that, like their metabolisms, were diametrically different.

The conclusion reached from Joanne, Anna, and thousands of other patients over the years was that success in dieting depends on the particular character of the dieter's metabolism. If this vital factor is not considered, the diet will inevitably fail. Without a system for determining what type of body a dieter has, dieters and their physicians alike are at the mercy of chance and guesswork.

THE FOUR BODY TYPES

Individuals process foods differently—this much is common knowledge. We have all observed that some people can eat much more than others without gaining weight. Also, some people need more of different kinds of food—more protein, more carbohydrates, or more fats. And some people are affected adversely by foods that other people tolerate well.

These facts are indications of a vitally important truth: Each person has his or her body type, based upon how food is metabolized in the body. There are a number of traditional systems for classifying individuals according to body type. Perhaps the best known is the classification into *ectomorph* (the slim, rangy person), *endomorph* (the rounder, plumper person), or *mesomorph* (the thicker, more muscular person), developed by Dr. William Sheldon in his book *The Atlas of Man.* The limitation of this system is that it is purely descriptive; it doesn't tell *why* a person is slim, round, or muscular.

Another system is that used in classical Chinese medicine, which classifies bodies according to which of the five "elements" (earth, water, fire, air, or ether) predominates. While this system has a good deal of value and is useful in certain courses of treatment, I wanted to find one that would be both highly accurate and easier to use. The same consideration applied to the Ayurvedic or classical Indian system, in which individuals are classified into types according to their balance of *doshas,* or elements: *vata, pitta,* and *kapha.* Again, Ayurveda is a highly refined and developed system of medicine, but it requires years of study to use correctly. I wanted a system that would use recognizable Western terms, be in full agreement with my scientific and medical knowledge about the body, and be readily understandable by lay person and physician alike. In short, I wanted a system that would *prescribe* the right diet while accurately *describing* the body type.

I set about to develop such a system. I began to classify individuals according to which of their four major glands—the pituitary gland, the thyroid gland, the adrenal glands, and the gonads or sex glands—was most active, or dominant, in their metabolism. According to this system, I could then classify a person as a "Pituitary Type," a "Thyroid Type," an "Adrenal Type," or a "Gonadal Type."

The inspiration for my system of body types came from Henry Bieler, M.D., a great physician and nutritionist, and author of *Food Is Your Best Medicine.* Dr. Bieler shows in this book how it is possible to distinguish between individuals with a dominant thyroid and a dominant adrenal gland on the basis of fairly obvious physical characteristics. Dr. Bieler's "thyroid type" is slender, fine-boned, long-limbed—much like the classic ectomorph. His "adrenal type" is squarer in shape, thicker and more solid, and closely resembles the classic mesomorph. Dr. Bieler also suspected that there might be a third body type, the pituitary type, but he was not certain of this and did not fully define what this type would look like.

I took Dr. Bieler's original work as my point of departure. I went on to make a full description of the Pituitary Type. I also found that, while three types are sufficient to classify men, women require a fourth classification, which I named the "Gonadal Type."

I also realized that although Dr. Bieler's suggested system of body types was useful descriptively, he had not done any work relating the types to their best diet for weight loss. This was to be my task. I studied carefully the relationships between foods and the glands, and on this basis was able to develop for each type the precise diet to enable people with that body type to lose weight most effectively.

Once you know your own body type you will know, first, what type of metabolism you have—that is, how quickly or slowly, efficiently or inefficiently, your body processes food. Second, you will know how your body reacts to each of the three classes of food: proteins, carbohydrates, and fats. Third, you will know which foods within the three classes are most useful to your type of metabolism. Finally, you will know the characteristic weaknesses of your metabolism that must be offset by diet. On the basis of this information I will help you to select the precise Body Type Diet that will work for you.

It is important for you to realize that your Body Type Diet is not a crash diet that you will follow until you reach your desired weight, and then forget. *It is a lifetime eating program designed for improved health, energy, and vitality at your ideal weight.*

For this reason I do not want you to follow your Body Type Diet blindly. I want you to really understand your body type, to see what your metabolic strengths are and what potential weaknesses you may have.

In the next chapters we are going to look at the Body Type Diet Program in detail. You will learn what body type you are, and you will see how your metabolism can be strengthened and balanced through the foods proper for *your* body type.

You will then be ready to take control of your health and your weight, and to use the tool of your Body Type Diet to create the ideal body *for you.*

THE BASIC FEATURES OF
THE BODY TYPE DIET

There are certain basic guidelines for healthy, balanced eating that apply to all of the body types, and that you must understand whether you turn out to be a Gonadal, Adrenal, Thyroid, or Pituitary Type. These are the guidelines that all good nutritionists would give you, and which would be absolutely correct from a scientific point of view. Everything in the Body Type Diet supports these general truths.

Then, there are special guidelines for your particular body type. These are guidelines that are yours alone, which will enable you to fine-tune the rules of good nutrition so that they are exactly right for your type of metabolism. Understanding the special rules of Body Type Dieting you will encounter in this chapter will enable you to appreciate your own Body Type Diet more fully, and to follow it more intelligently.

We'll start with the basic rules of healthy eating, then go on to the special Rules for Body Type Dieting.

BASIC RULE #1: ALWAYS EAT A BALANCED, HEALTHY DIET WITH PLENTY OF VARIETY

Experts agree: A balanced, healthy diet is based on whole, natural foods, and includes a wide variety of foods eaten in moderation. There is no place in a healthy diet for an extreme emphasis on one food or group of foods at the expense of balance and variety. It should not ask you to eat grapefruit for a month.

It also necessarily meets the standard of low-fat eating, drawing 30 percent or less of its calories from fat, and only 10 percent or less of its calories from saturated fat. Along with this small amount of fat, a balanced diet includes protein, carbohydrates, and lots of fresh produce.

As you go through the Body Type Diets, you'll see that each one more than meets these criteria for healthy balanced eating.

BASIC RULE #2: WHEN DIETING TO LOSE WEIGHT, NEVER LOSE SIGHT OF HEALTH AND BALANCE

"Yes, a healthy diet is the main thing," people often think, "and I'll be very certain to eat that way after I've lost weight, but right now I'm going to go on the _____ (cabbage soup, grapefruit-and-cottage-cheese, no-carbohydrate, etc.) diet. I've just got to get rid of these pounds!"

If you ever start to think this way, stop! Losing weight at the expense of balance and health will not do you any good in the long run. In fact, it won't even do you any good in the short run, because you will lose more energy than weight. Any weight that you do lose will not come off from the right places, and it will definitely not stay off for long.

The only way to reach and keep your best weight is to increase your balance with every pound you lose in weight. And you can only do this by beginning correctly with your Body Type Diet.

BASIC RULE #3: WHEN THINKING ABOUT ANY DIET, KEEP YOUR BODY TYPE IN MIND

If you keep up with current books and articles on dieting, you know that there are two major schools of thought in nutrition today. These are the "high-carbohydrate, low-fat, less protein" school and the "high-protein, lots of meat, carbohydrates make you fat" school.

The first is clearly the "official" position and the one with far more scientific backing. The government supports it and so does the

Food Guide Pyramid
A Guide to Daily Food Choices

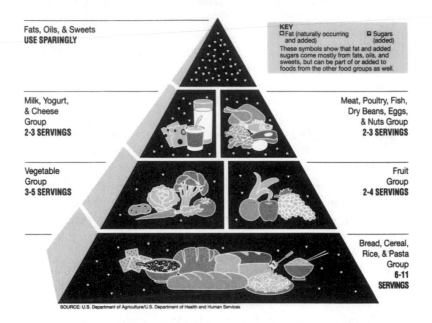

SOURCE: U.S. Department of Agriculture/U.S. Department of Health and Human Services

American Heart Association. It is clearly laid out in the U.S. Department of Agriculture "Food Pyramid," published in 1992 (see above). The pyramid replaced the "four basic food groups" of 1956 as the government's official nutritional guidelines.

The American Heart Association states the same idea in terms of percentages: We are told to get 55–60 percent of our calories from carbohydrates, just 15 percent from protein, and 30 percent or less from fat.

The meat and dairy industries were rumored at the time of publication to be unhappy with the pyramid, and to have delayed its publication for about a year. You can see why this might be so. Meat and dairy foods and their products are demoted from equal status with fruits, vegetables, and grains, which they had under the old "food groups" plan, and given decidedly secondary status on the pyramid.

But other experts (for example, nutritionists at the Center for Science in the Public Interest) say that the pyramid does not go far enough to discourage consumption of meat and dairy foods. In their opinion, meat and dairy should be at the very top of the pyramid—the "use sparingly" level—or even removed from the pyramid completely. But in general, the majority of nutritionists and dietitians support the Food Pyramid.

The competing view, by contrast, says that eating too much carbohydrates is not helpful and can even be harmful, leading to insulin resistance and other medical problems. However, the idea that the pyramid tells us to eat far too much grains and not enough protein has little official backing and is frequently denounced as unscientific and unsafe by mainstream nutritionists. Nevertheless, it is a popular view and has enthusiastic proponents.

Faced with these conflicting views, how do you decide which is correct? How do you keep from losing faith in *any* nutritional recommendations, if they can't even get closer together than that? And which view is actually in your long-term best interests? The underlying controversy, of which this is just today's version, is about what you should eat to give you sufficient protection from cardiovascular disease and cancer to maximize your longevity. However, these tendencies differ for each body type. Therefore, I believe that the only way to resolve this particular conflict is through a thorough understanding of the different metabolic needs of the body types.

For two of the body types, I have found that the Food Pyramid does indeed put too much emphasis on carbohydrates. Thyroid and Pituitary Types *do* need to get a larger proportion of their calories from animal protein than is recommended in the pyramid (although the Atkins diet is not right for these body types, either—it's much too high in saturated fat). Adrenal and Gonadal Types, on the other hand, do better with even *less* protein than the pyramid recommends.

My view of the pyramid is that it is a good starting point, and certainly an improvement over the 1956 recommendations. But just as there isn't any one diet that is right for everyone, a single Food Pyramid won't work for everyone, either. So I've worked out a Food Pyramid for each of the four body types (you'll find it in the chapter on your Body Type Diet).

BODY TYPE DIETING: MOVING
BEYOND THE BASICS

The only way to find your way through the conflicting claims of today's experts is to be aware of your body type and its requirements. Yet, you should keep in mind the essentials to a really healthy diet—the basics that are known and respected by all real nutrition experts. Never stop eating a wide variety of good-tasting, enjoyable, real foods; don't ever give up eating plenty of fresh produce; always eat protein and carbohydrates in the right proportion for your metabolism; and be sure to eat just enough fats and oils for health and taste, and to make it mostly vegetable oils, with a minimum of saturated fats such as that found in fatty meats.

The Body Type Diets do more than meet these criteria of modern nutritional theory—they embody their very essence. When you turn to the chapter on the diet that's right for your body type, you'll see exactly how these principles are applied and personalized for you. But now we need to go beyond these basic truths, and look at the important differences in nutritional requirements among the four body types. These are what I call the "Rules of Body Type Dieting."

BODY TYPE RULE #1: USE FOOD TO CREATE
HARMONY IN YOUR GLANDULAR SYSTEM

Each Body Type Diet is an individualized application of the same basic strategy: a strategy of utilizing foods that are in harmony with the metabolic needs of your body type. To do this, you need to appreciate the fact that everything you eat has an effect on your glandular system. When you understand how this works, you can use food to create a state of metabolic balance in which your body can reach and maintain its ideal weight.

For each of the four body types, the particular combination of foods is different; but in each case the *approach* to selecting foods is the same. The approach is, fundamentally, to *restrict* foods that are stimulating to the dominant gland of your body type (these are your body type's "danger foods"), and to *encourage* foods that strengthen and support your less active glands.

You'll discover in Chapter 3 precisely which foods perform

these functions for your own body type, and how this approach works so effectively to enable you to reach your ideal weight.

BODY TYPE RULE #2: FOLLOW THE BODY TYPE DIET SEQUENCE

Each body type has a four-week sequence of diets, consisting of three weeks of the Body Type Weight Loss Diet and a fourth week on the Last Five Pounds Diet. This four-week sequence can be repeated as many times as necessary to reach your ideal weight. The Body Type Diet sequence has been worked out with the needs of your body type in mind.

If you have only a small amount of weight to lose, you may only need to follow a part of the four-week sequence. See your own Body Type Diet for details.

The Weight Loss Diet for each body type uses the strategy described in Rule #1 to produce fast, effective weight loss. The Last Five Pounds Diet takes the basic strategy one step farther: It restricts your body type's "danger foods" still further, and provides special dieting helps that are used for this phase of the sequence only.

The purpose of the Last Five Pounds Diet is to help your body deal with the most stubborn of all dieting problems: the tendency of your body to reach "plateaus" in dieting, at which weight loss unaccountably slows or stops. I have found that it is possible to overcome the problem of plateaus by using a special diet every fourth week, the interval at which plateaus most often occur.

The diet is called the Last Five Pounds Diet to distinguish the most difficult of all plateaus, the one that occurs when you are down to your last five pounds of excess weight. As everyone who has dieted knows, these pounds are far harder to lose than the five, fifteen, or fifty pounds that come before, because they are often made up of a special kind of fat called "cellulite."

Cellulite is the wrinkly, "cottage cheese" fat that is visible on almost every woman, and present though not visible on most men. In women, it is found most often on the hips, thighs, abdomen, and upper arms. The special strategies of the Last Five Pounds Diet are designed to facilitate the mobilization of the toxins in cellulite, the burning of cellulite itself, and the elimination of plateaus that occur regularly during a weight loss program.

BODY TYPE RULE #3: EAT THE RIGHT AMOUNT OF FOOD FOR EACH PHASE OF BODY TYPE DIETING

Each Weight Loss Diet contains about 1,200 calories per day, and each Last Five Pounds Diet, about 1,000 calories. Experience has convinced me that the 1,200-calorie-per-day level is the safest, most effective one for long-term, permanent weight loss. Reducing calories below this level for any extended period runs the risk of nutritional deficiencies. However, a temporarily lower caloric intake can be used to break plateaus.

The caloric level is not the most important aspect of the diet by any means. Reducing the number of calories consumed is a necessary ingredient in losing weight, but is not enough in itself to ensure success. The laws of physics cannot be changed; you cannot lose weight unless you eat fewer calories than you burn up in activity. If you eat *more* calories than you burn up, you will gain weight. This is true even if every bite you put in your mouth is in itself a healthy, low-fat food.

But the body is not a machine, requiring only energy to run. It is an organic, spiritual system with many requirements, nutritional and otherwise, all of which must be met in order for you to achieve balance—the only way the weight you lose will stay away.

BODY TYPE RULE #4: KNOW THE RATE OF WEIGHT LOSS THAT'S RIGHT FOR YOU

Weight loss on this diet sequence occurs at the maximum safe rate for each individual. You can determine the weight *you* will lose by a simple formula. If you follow the recommendations carefully, maintaining approximately 1,200 calories per day, most people will lose between two and four percent of their body weight in the first week and one to two percent of their body weight in each of the following weeks.

For example, suppose you weigh 150 pounds. You will probably lose three to six pounds the first week (two to four percent of 150), and one and a half to three pounds in each week following (one to two percent of 150). The larger loss in the first week is not truly significant, as most of it is water.

Keep a couple of factors in mind, however. One is that the rate of weight loss is quite variable. In general, Adrenal and Gonadal Types tend to lose weight more slowly than Thyroid and Pituitary Types, at least at the beginning. If you're an A or a G, don't despair—take comfort in the reason, which is that you have a steadier metabolism than a T or P. Thyroid Types, particularly, tend to bounce around in their weight loss, losing five pounds in a few days but then gaining three or four back the next day. A's and G's may lose just a pound, but that pound will stay off and be followed by another pound the next week.

Also, remember that in losing weight, slower is better. If you lose a pound a week, you are doing *well,* not badly. You may have been gaining weight slowly but steadily for a long time. If you simply *do not gain,* you should consider that to be progress. Yes, I know that most people are eager and anxious to lose weight. But try not to obsess about it. The real goal is balance. If you learn to understand your body, discover how to feed it for maximum energy and health, and encourage all your glands to work in harmony, be assured that your ideal weight will follow naturally.

RULE #5: TIME YOUR EATING ACCORDING TO YOUR BODY TYPE

When you eat is nearly as important in dieting as *what* you eat. Each of the body types has a rhythm; a time of day when the dominant gland is most active and a time of day when it is least active. It is easy for a dieter *not* to eat during the time of maximum activity of the dominant gland; conversely, it is hard to avoid snacking during the time of least activity. The actual burning of fat takes place more efficiently during the gland's active times.

Understanding the metabolic rhythms of each body type resolves an old dieting controversy about breakfast. Some dieting experts say that a big breakfast is a must, others that it's a "must not." The truth is that for some body types, a substantial breakfast is essential to efficient dieting; for others, it's the surest way to sabotage a diet.

Pituitary and Thyroid Types diet more easily and lose weight more quickly if they eat a substantial breakfast with protein. Adrenal and Gonadal Types, while they do need something for breakfast, do better if they eat more lightly in the morning and more substantially later in the day.

BODY TYPE RULE #6: USE YOUR HERBAL HELPS

There are many doctors who believe that medicine began with the discovery of modern drugs, and overlook the older, less well studied medicaments, such as herbs. I believe, however, that traditional herbal remedies have a great deal to offer, even to modern medicine. I've tested the use of herbs with my diet patients, and have found that there is an herbal tea for each body type that provides invaluable help in promoting dieting effectiveness.

Precisely how these herbs produce their effects is not entirely clear. Traditionally, fenugreek tea, which I use for Pituitary Types, is an intestinal lubricant and is used to relieve fevers, headaches, and irritation of the mucous membranes. Raspberry leaf tea (my tea for Thyroid Types) is used as an antacid. Parsley tea (the Adrenal Type herbal help) is used for diseases of the kidney and for jaundice, and red clover tea, which I use for Gonadal Types, is a blood purifier and diuretic that is also said to stimulate the liver and gallbladder.

Whatever their precise interaction with the glandular system, what the teas do for their respective body types is to produce a general systemic soothing effect that can probably be attributed to a soothing of the dominant gland. I have patients drink a cup of their herbal tea at the point in their day when their dominant gland is most likely to be irritated or fatigued—again, the time of day when the temptation to snack is greatest. The result: Dieting is easier, cravings are less bothersome, hunger is easier to deal with, and "dieting nerves" are soothed and comforted.

BODY TYPE RULE #7:
USE YOUR SNACKING STRATEGY

Sometimes, even while you're dieting, you will feel a craving and you will take a snack. This is not supposed to happen, but it does. Most diets ignore this fact of life, but the Body Type Diet takes a more constructive approach: It deals with the biochemical reality underlying the so-called sin.

The desire to snack is not a random occurrence; it is related to the rhythm of the dominant gland. Each of the four major glands has a time of day when it is at its lowest ebb, and this produces a "danger" time of day when energy is low and the desire for an energy "lift" the hardest to resist. It is all too easy at this time to reach for one of the foods containing a stimulant for your dominant gland. But if, instead, you know of a food to eat that will support another of your glands in a gentle, healthy way, you will get the energy lift your body is crying for, with a minimum of harm to your diet.

The Body Type Snacking Strategy provides you with a snacking food for those danger times, one that is in harmony with your metabolic needs and that you can eat safely without destroying your diet. The actual snack that works differs according to body type, but the Body Type Snacking Strategy is used (with great success) by all the body types. You will find your best snack in the section on your Body Type Diet.

IRRESISTIBLE CRAVINGS: WHAT THEY TELL YOU ABOUT YOUR BODY TYPE

"What are the foods that you find yourself craving when you are on a diet?" I asked a woman patient who was about twenty pounds overweight. Her extra pounds were distributed all over her body, like baby fat.

"Oh, just the usual things," she said. "Yogurt, apples, cottage cheese."

Intrigued by this reply (since I don't think I've ever craved any of these foods in my life), I asked the next patient which foods she had cravings for when dieting. This patient happened to be a woman with a slim face and slender legs, arms, and hands, who was carrying her fifteen extra pounds around her hips and thighs. "Cookies and cake, especially with coffee," she said promptly, looking surprised that I should bother to ask. "Doesn't everyone?"

The next overweight patient that day happened to be a stocky, thickly built man with a paunch and a good deal of extra weight across his back. I asked him which he craved more strongly, yogurt or cookies. He looked at me as if I must be suffering from a touch of the sun. "I'm not a dessert person," he said, "and I hope I never find out what yogurt tastes like. I crave meat. Give me a good thick steak, and you can keep the rest of it."

I was fascinated by the diversity of these replies, and thought I'd heard everything, but there was more to come. Right after the stocky meat-lover came a woman who, from a sitting position, didn't look overweight at all. When she stood, however, I could see that she had all of ten extra pounds on her rear end.

"I crave anything fried," she replied promptly to my question, "or creamy or spicy. The richer and hotter a food is, the less able I am to resist it."

Since that day I have asked this question of literally thousands of patients, and a pattern of cravings has long ago become clear. Cravings differ greatly from person to person, and it takes an understanding of body types to find a pattern in this diversity. In fact, the diversity of cravings is one of the most important clues to the necessity of designing different diets for different body types, for in each body type the particular craving tells us exactly what is going on in the metabolism.

Cravings are irresistible desires for food, usually fattening food, which are the leading cause of dieting failure. The onset of a craving in the course of a diet is a definite sign that you are not following the right diet for your body type. It's also a sign you're about to crash and burn.

A craving is the body's way of saying that it needs something your diet is not supplying. Unfortunately, a craving is not specific. It's more like a baby's cry—a way of communicating a need, but not of saying what the need is. The body doesn't have a way of saying, "I need more protein!" or "Give me more Vitamin C!" or "I can't take all this coffee!" All it can do is say, "I need something!"

Almost invariably, we interpret the craving incorrectly. We feed ourselves potato chips when we need milk, or ice cream when we need eggs. The underlying need remains unsatisfied, and the craving continues though we stuff ourselves with food.

Neither a psychological nor a behavioral approach to cravings is truly effective in controlling cravings. You can follow all the rules, eat slowly, chew everything a hundred times, eat only in the dining room with the television off; you can find more love and approval and go through years of therapy—and all this may improve your life a great deal. But if your *body's vital nutritional requirements* aren't satisfied, you will still have the physical needs that send you to the refrigerator. The only way to truly eliminate cravings is to get on a diet that meets your needs—that is, your Body Type Diet.

This doesn't mean that on your Body Type Diet you will never feel the slightest desire for something you shouldn't eat. Desires can always arise. But there is a big difference between a desire and a craving. A desire can be resisted, or it can be satisfied with a bite or two of what you want. A craving, because it is a sign that you are not giving your body what it needs, can by its nature never be satisfied until the actual need is satisfied.

FOODS THAT ARE GLANDULAR STIMULANTS

Many patients have told me that when they've had cravings, they've felt instinctively that their bodies must be signaling that they have some requirement or other. But the object of the craving is almost never identical with the body's requirement; rather, the object of a craving has to do with the type of metabolism one has—that is, one's body type.

The explanation of why the four body types have cravings for different classes of foods lies in the biochemistry of how foods interact with the different glands. A number of discoveries, some recent and some of long standing, indicate that different foods actually stimulate different glands to become more active and to produce more of their particular chemicals, or hormones. In each of the four types, foods are craved that have a stimulating effect on the dominant gland.

In the Pituitary Type, cravings are invariably for dairy products, which recent research indicates are stimulating to the pituitary gland. In the Thyroid Type, cravings are for sweets and starches, which have long been known to stimulate the thyroid gland. The Adrenal Type craves animal products and salty foods, which stimulate the adrenal glands, and the Gonadal Type craves fats and spices, which are stimulating to the sex glands.

THE NATURAL AFFINITY FOR STIMULATING FOODS

In each body type, a natural affinity exists for the food group that stimulates the dominant gland. Because we each derive energy most easily from the gland that is strongest in our metabolism, the food that stimulates that gland naturally gives us the most effective energy "lift." We learn very early that foods that stimulate our dominant gland are the foods that will revive us most effectively whenever we feel tired, stressed, or run-down.

An important part of this picture is the fact that the hormones that are secreted by each of the glands have very specific feelings associated with them. Each of us forms an association, also very early in life, with the feeling that comes from our dominant gland's hormones. Thyroid hormones give an "up," zippy feeling, and T-Types love that lively feeling. When a T-Type feels stressed, she wants to feel more like herself—lively and creative. She's actually longing for an upsurge of thyroid hormone. Adrenal hormones, by contrast, give a feeling of unlimited power. We've all felt the surge of adrenaline in a fight-or-flight reaction, but to an Adrenal Type, this feeling feels comforting and right. Each of the body types feels most at home, most like herself or himself, when the body is enjoying an abundance of hormones from the dominant gland.

We are all subject to many stresses—physical, mental, psychological, or any combination of these. If we have any nutritional deficiencies in the diet, this in itself is stressful. In addition, modern life imposes stresses of all kinds every day. When under stress, we want to feel more centered, more calm, more like ourselves. So we react to stress by *overeating* those foods that appear to relieve our stress, increase our energy, and make us feel more centered—that is, those foods that stimulate our dominant gland.

This is the way in which cravings develop from our natural affinity for certain foods. What we are actually craving is not the nutritional value of what we crave, but its value as a *stimulant to* the dominant gland, which results in a particular feeling. We think we crave a food, but it's a feeling that we are actually craving. The feeling is not bad in itself—what is bad is the way we come to rely too much on that feeling, overeat the food that gives it to us, and thus exhaust our dominant gland.

NATURE OR NURTURE?

Which comes first, the affinity for certain foods, or the body type? If a mother feeds her baby thyroid-stimulating foods, does she make that baby a Thyroid Type? Or was the baby born with a strong thyroid gland that would become dominant no matter what he might be fed?

The answer is that the body type is inborn, which means that it is genetically determined. All infants begin their lives with the same diet—milk—yet evidence of body type can be seen very early, before differing diets would have had a chance to "force" an individual into one or the other of the body types.

So our body types come from nature, not nurture. The role of nurturing is not to make a child into a certain body type or change his nature from one body type to another. That is simply not possible. Yet nurture can play a role in helping children grow up balanced and craving-free (more about this in Chapter 10). The key is to understand which foods stimulate each of the glands, and how this stimulation leads to cravings.

Dairy Foods: The Pituitary Stimulators

Research on the pituitary gland has recently uncovered an intimate association between dairy products and pituitary gland activity. It appears that in infants, the pituitary hormone known as prolactin, a milk-stimulating hormone in the mother, is present in high concentrations in the baby's body and in the mother's milk that the baby drinks. The indications are that one function of milk is to stimulate pituitary activity in the baby and so promote brain development, since the hormone prolactin is critical in brain development and intellectual functioning.

If an infant is bottle-fed, he still receives significant amounts of prolactin from formula or milk. Studies have also shown that prolactin appears in higher-than-usual concentrations in the blood of adults who drink milk as well. Milk and milk products are thus clearly pituitary-gland stimulators, and people with dominant pituitary glands develop an affinity for milk and milk products very early. When under stress of any kind, they reach for milk products for their energy "lift," and thus come to actually crave these foods and to overeat them.

Starches: Stimulating the Thyroid

The connection between stimulation of the thyroid and carbohy-drate intake has long been established. Eating carbohydrates triggers a complicated series of events with two main results. One is that the thyroid is stimulated to produce more thyroid hormone, and the other is that the cells of the body, due to the presence of fructose in the blood, become less responsive to the presence of the thyroid hormone. The brain overreacts to the fructose and secretes still more thyroid-stimulating hormone (TSH). The thyroid gland is actually given a double dose of stimulation: the first from the initial direct stimulation when the carbohydrate food is eaten, the second, some hours later, from TSH.

For a Thyroid Type, there seems to be no more effective energy lift than the one provided by a carbohydrate—either a sweet food like a candy bar or a starch such as bread or pasta. Yet the danger of depending on these foods for stimulation, and so overeating, is very real.

Meat, Butter, Eggs, and Salt: The Adrenal Stimulators

In the case of the adrenal glands, the biochemistry of food interaction has been the subject of intensive study lately, due to the association of cholesterol (found in adrenal hormones) with heart disease. Cholesterol—the same cholesterol that is found in butter, meat, and eggs—is the core molecule of several adrenal hormones, such as cortisone and aldosterone. Eating cholesterol-rich foods stimulates the adrenal glands to produce their hormones in greater quantities.

Adrenal Types derive stimulation from their adrenal hormones in several ways. For one, cortisone gives a feeling of energy and eu-phoria. It also helps Adrenal Types burn up tremendous food energy, one reason why A-Types have such excellent digestions. Adrenal hormones also raise blood pressure, and there is a peculiar feeling of fullness and power associated with a rise in blood pressure, a feeling that Adrenal Types come to enjoy without really knowing what it is.

Unfortunately, high blood pressure is associated with heart disease, to which Adrenal Types are particularly prone.

Salt also contributes to high blood pressure, and for this reason Adrenal Types often use it as a stimulant, with results that can be very damaging.

Spices, Fats, and Oils:
The Gonadal Stimulators

It has long been known that spices have an effect called vasodilation that affects the gonads, or sex glands, in particular. Vasodilation is, simply, the effect of dilating the blood vessels and producing a state of passive congestion. When a G-Type woman eats spicy foods, the blood flow to the pelvic organs—uterus, vagina, and ovaries, as well as to the lower bowel—increases, resulting in stimulation of function in these areas. There are two results: The area becomes more active and sensitive, and the production of hormones is increased. Eating fats also has an engorging effect on the pelvic organs; again, the result is stimulation of the sex glands.

This does not imply that Gonadal-Type women are sexually stimulated by eating these foods or that they necessarily experience a craving for sex as a result (although they might). Sexual stimulation is a complex phenomenon and depends on many physical and psychological factors, not simply on stimulation of the sex glands per se. G-Type women tend to feel a craving for spicy or creamy foods as a way of reviving their energy, in just the same way that Thyroid-Type women crave sweets and Adrenal-Type women crave salty food. But since the rich, creamy foods that G-Type women crave are very dense calorically, overweight is quite common among exhausted women with this body type.

Overstimulation and Cravings:
Your "Downfall Foods"

For each of the four body types, then, there is a particular class of foods that is stimulating to the dominant gland—one which causes the gland to produce more than usual of its particular hormones, and which gives to that body type a feeling of stimulation and energy resulting from the increased activity of the gland. Again, it is the *feeling* that is craved, not the food per se.

As with any stimulant, the foods that stimulate the dominant gland come to be needed in ever-greater quantities. At first, for example, a Thyroid Type may get an effective lift from one candy bar. Later it takes two or three, or a dozen, to produce the same effect. An Adrenal Type will need increasing quantities of rich, salty meats, a Gonadal Type more and more spicy foods, a Pituitary Type greater and greater amounts of cheese and ice cream.

What is happening within the body is a *gradual weakening of the dominant gland*. As the dominant gland becomes weaker, we need to eat more and more of our stimulating foods to get the same "lift." The result is an ever-increasing cycle of overeating and its concomitant overweight. If you are overweight, you are suffering from a weakened condition of the dominant gland.

This condition can be corrected by either eliminating or drastically reducing foods that are stimulating to the dominant gland. Foods that stimulate your dominant gland are the "downfall foods" for your body type, for they are the ones with the greatest power to undermine and sabotage your dieting efforts.

The condition of a weakened or exhausted dominant gland can be seen most clearly in Thyroid Types, because the thyroid is the most easily worn out of the glands. I have seen countless T-Types in my practice who were born with strong thyroid glands (this is apparent from their body type) but who have so exhausted their thyroid by overeating sweets or starches that their thyroid hormone level is extremely low. They have been put on Synthroid, or other forms of thyroid hormone, and told they must take it for life.

But it is not only T-Types who weaken their dominant gland by overeating their "downfall foods." All the body types do the same thing to their own dominant gland, and the results are clearly seen in their reduced energy, their rampant cravings, and, of course, their unwanted pounds.

When I say that you must reduce or eliminate foods that overstimulate your dominant gland, I am referring to those foods that have the strongest and most obvious effect on the system. Not all carbohydrates, dairy products, meats, or fats are strongly stimulating, and even those that are stimulating may have nutritional value as well. (I'll discuss specific foods from these categories when I give you your Body Type Diet.) They all may be part of your diet once your system is in balance.

But you will need to tune in to your true *danger foods*—the ones that you crave and consume in quantities much beyond what you actually require. *You are using these foods as drugs, not as foods.* This is why you must restrict them in your diet until you have reestablished metabolic balance and eliminated the cravings, and use them only very circumspectly after you have reached your ideal weight.

On the other hand, it is not necessary for you to be as concerned about foods that are not danger foods for your body type. In diets designed without your specific body type in mind, certain foods may be restricted or eliminated that are not danger foods for you at all. Adrenal Types may be told to eliminate starches, or Thyroid Types told to cut out red meat or eggs—restrictions that are not just unnecessary but actually wrong for their type of metabolism. These foods are not addictive to these body types—on the contrary, they are balancing and helpful.

However, careful control of danger foods is necessary, and it is very difficult unless you first succeed in eliminating your cravings for them. Overcoming cravings is the essential key to becoming and remaining balanced, slender, and healthy. You can only do this on a diet that satisfies your body's nutritional needs, as opposed to its needs for stimulation. Your Body Type Diet will strengthen your entire system, using foods that are not stimulating to your dominant gland. It will also help you handle the normal stresses of living by strengthening your body's less-active glands, so that you do not need to rely on your dominant gland so exclusively for energy.

CRAVINGS AND FAT LOCATION

Before leaving the subject of cravings, there is one more remarkable aspect that I want to touch on: the strong connection between which foods you crave and overeat, and the location of extra pounds on your body.

If you weren't aware of the differences among body types, you might have supposed that where your fat was located was random—one person just "happens" to gain weight primarily in the thighs, someone else mainly in the stomach. Or you might have thought it was "genetic" in a vague, nonspecific way, with a thought like "My mother always gained weight in her rear, and so do I," or "I have love handles just like my Dad's."

It's often true that fat location runs in families, but there's much more to it than that. Your main fat location, which may be your back, stomach, hips, thighs, rear end, or all over your body, is specifically related to your body type and thus to the activity of your dominant gland.

Fat location is not a random event, because fat is not the same on different parts of your body. Fat is a distributed organ, which means that it is an organ, like your heart or lungs or liver, but one that is distributed around your body and not located in one specific place. Like all of your organs, fat responds to the hormones circulating in your blood; but the fat in different parts of your body responds primarily to different hormones. That's why each of the body types puts on weight in its own special locations when the dominant gland begins to weaken from overstimulation.

Here's how it works. Let's say you're a Thyroid Type. You were born with a strong thyroid gland but began stimulating it with sweets and starches as a child. Throughout your childhood your healthy thyroid gave you a quick metabolism, and you could eat whatever you wanted without putting on a pound—and of course, you were burning up calories in growth as well. By the time you were twenty, though, your thyroid was starting to get tired.

Now, fat on the upper hips, lower tummy, and thighs is responsive to thyroid hormones. For as long as your thyroid is strong, these areas remain fairly free of fat. But when your thyroid starts to wear out, it can no longer keep fat from accumulating in these areas. The more sweets you eat, the more tired your thyroid becomes, and the more fat builds up in the typical T-Type areas. So when you say, "This candy bar is going straight to my hips," it is almost literally true.

Your Shape Is Your Metabolism Writ Large

A growing body of evidence today indicates that there is a relationship between fat location and certain health risks. Fat on the stom-

ach is associated with increased risk of both heart disease and diabetes. This is an important insight because it indicates that your body
shape is an indicator of what's going on inside, in your metabolism.

But the evidence needs to be interpreted correctly. It is not the
fat itself that creates the risk, but the type of metabolism that gives
rise to that particular fat location. If your abdomen is your main fat
location, you are probably an Adrenal Type. A-Types crave meat,
high-fat cheeses, salty foods, butter—all the cholesterol-laden foods
that stimulate the adrenal glands. When you eat these foods, the
adrenals are stimulated to produce even more adrenal hormones,
flooding your system with adrenal-related activity.

But the adrenal glands do not become exhausted as quickly as
the thyroid gland does. Rather than gradually wearing out, they just
keep pumping out hormones, which also have the effect of stimulating your appetite. Between your appetite and your cravings, you
continue eating high-cholesterol foods, and fat accumulates in the
area most responsive to adrenal hormones, which is the stomach. Not
only is this fat very near the heart and the other internal organs, it is
also very metabolically active, since it responds to the adrenal hormones that are continuing to flood the system. So it doesn't just sit
there; it comes and goes in the bloodstream, where it can collect in
the arteries and increase your risk of heart problems.

You can see from this analysis that abdominal fat is associated
with heart disease for two reasons: because it indicates the kind of
metabolism that craves cholesterol-rich foods, and because fat in this
location is highly responsive to adrenal hormones and thus more
likely to move in and out of the bloodstream, where it can cause
harm.

Fat Must Be Removed Metabolically

Thyroid, Pituitary, and Gonadal Types all have their own typical fat
locations where the fat responds to the hormones of their dominant
gland. But these body types do not deposit fat in as dangerous a location as Adrenal Types. It's not that hip, thigh, or rear fat is "good,"
as some studies have stated. Fat in these locations indicates an exhausted thyroid or overstimulated ovaries, and is a sign of imbalance
just as stomach fat is.

But it is worth noting that liposuction on these areas *may* have the effect of causing fat to return higher up on the body, where it is more dangerous. In liposuction, fat cells are actually removed from the area. So a T-Type, for instance, who has had liposuction on her thighs has actually lost fat cells from that area. If her cravings cause her to continue overeating, fat will not be able to accumulate in the (lost) fat cells, and it may be forced into her stomach area. This has not been established definitely but it is a possibility.

The most important point is that fat can be lost from your body type areas only when your cravings are controlled and your dominant gland recovers. Removing fat metabolically means creating a state of balance in your entire system. When all your glands function strongly, your metabolism can function as it is designed to and your entire body can be kept in balance at your ideal weight.

In the next chapter I will go through the four body types one by one, and show you in more detail the way your cravings come about and how they can be controlled. I want you to understand this perfectly *before* you start to focus completely on your own body type.

BODY TYPE DIETING: HOW IT USES YOUR STRENGTHS AND CORRECTS YOUR WEAKNESSES

Before we go about finding your body type, let me give you some case histories from my medical files, illustrating how patients of each body type have responded to the diet that is right for their body type and their body type alone. These studies illustrate how the Body Type Diet works, by making use of the biochemical realities of the metabolism. In every case the diet has been designed to support the strengths and correct the weaknesses that are found in each of the four types of metabolism.

It is fascinating to observe in this connection the way the body type concept clarifies understanding of complex, interrelated problems. For example, the first patient I want to tell you about is a woman named Tina M. When she originally came to me, she just wanted a checkup to try to find out why she felt so tired all the time.

Tina was a thoroughly exhausted Gonadal Type. She worked in public relations, and although she was well trained for her job and good at it, at the time she walked into my office she felt totally burnt out. She was about twenty-five pounds overweight, and of course in typical G-Type fashion, it was all on her rear and her outer thighs.

Nature has not intended G-Type women to have a flat rear. The gonads (or sex glands, which in women are the ovaries) dominate this type of metabolism, so they have a strong supply of female sex hormones in their system. These hormones are the chemicals responsible for the development of sexual differences between men and women. Under their direction, women acquire thicker hair, softer skin, finer features, more rounded bodies, shorter stature, higher voices, and more developed breasts. They also develop a more pronounced rear end—and in G-Types this is the primary location of any extra pounds. However, it is *not* necessary for G-Type women to be overweight or out of proportion, as Tina now was.

TINA'S STORY

I asked Tina to tell me about herself, starting with her diet. It turned out she was living on Mexican and Thai food, and was drinking two to three alcoholic drinks per day. She also told me that she exercised on a step machine and took a vitamin supplement.

I asked about stress, and she mentioned that she was under a lot of pressure at work. She felt she wasn't performing well and that her boss wasn't pleased. A moment later she added that she was also having sexual problems in her relationship with her boyfriend—another source of stress.

I now knew the basis of Tina's problem. All the influences she had described—food, job and relationship pressures, even her exercise plan and her vitamin pill—had led Tina down the garden path of G-Type imbalance. Every single influence I've mentioned turned out to be contributing to her exhaustion because of the structure of her Gonadal-Type metabolism.

Tina's diet was the first thing to change. All the Thai and Mexican foods were overstimulating her dominant gland, her ovaries, which are much affected by spice, by grease, and also by alcohol. I put her on the G-Type Weight Loss Diet right away, knowing that this change alone would go a long way toward taking care of her fatigue. It is also important as preventive medicine for Gonadal Types. A low-fat diet has been associated with decreased risk of breast and uterine cancer, and this is something I want to see G-Types take full advantage of.

Next I looked at her vitamin pill to see precisely what she was taking. It turned out to be a good start; but as a G–Type, she needed more antioxidants, especially vitamins A and E, to offset her toxic tendencies. I put her on the G–Type Nutritional Supplement Program (see Chapter 13) and made sure she was getting just what she needed.

Her exercise was the next thing to scrutinize. I told Tina that a step workout was just about the worst exercise for her. It is mainly a lower-body exercise, and what she needed was both an aerobic program and an exercise that would improve upper-body/lower-body coordination. I suggested a program in which she would alternate brisk walking with kung fu (see Chapter 12 for more on Body Type Exercise Plans).

Tina's relationship problems were also contributing to her exhaustion and weight gain problems, especially the sexual aspect. Her inner conflicts over sex were probably causing congestion in her uterus and ovaries. However, I only mentioned this point to her lightly because it was already a subject of stress between Tina and her boyfriend, and I didn't want to add pressure to her life at this point.

I asked her about her job stress and found that she was going in to work very early and leaving early, because this was the way her boss liked to work. However, G–Types tend to have more and better energy in the later portions of the day. I suggested Tina try adjusting her hours and see what happened. This one simple change was very helpful. She began arriving at ten and leaving at six, and the quality of her work improved dramatically. She got better rest and had much better energy.

A month later I had Tina try the Long Weekend of Rejuvenation for Gonadal Types. This is a special weekend I've designed with the specific needs of each body type in mind, a sort of spring cleaning to make the metabolism more balanced and efficient (see Chapter 15). The results were a revelation to Tina, and she was inspired to continue reordering her life in accordance with her needs as a Gonadal Type.

I was thrilled to see how Tina looked after about ten weeks. She appeared fully ten years younger, with the fat gone from her hips and the bags vanished from under her eyes. She told me that with her improved performance at work, she'd been given a raise, and then added that even her sex life had smoothed out. It turned out that when she started feeling better about herself, Tina was able to communicate her own wishes more easily to her boyfriend. And she discovered to her amazement that he was quite willing to adjust, too. They had both become much happier.

The Scope of Change

One of the most interesting points about Tina's case is how *little* she actually had to do to make such great and positive changes. I think we often imagine that to improve our lives we must revamp them from top to bottom. We shrink from such great effort, and end up doing nothing. Actually, it often turns out that the changes we need to make are relatively small and involve only *adjusting* what we are doing anyway to the exact needs of our body type.

Tina was already taking vitamins—she just needed to take a little more of the *right* vitamins to make a major difference. She was exercising—but needed to change to the right exercise for her particular metabolic needs. She didn't need to change her job or her boyfriend—just make some adjustments in the way she related to them. She only had to change her diet, and there again it was more a question of emphasis than of total change. Once the metabolism is in better balance, even a G-Type can eat *some* spicy food!

This is an excellent example of the way the body type concept works. Tina's example shows the way you can use the knowledge of your body type to make dramatic improvements in your life as well. It's a matter of *personalizing* what you do and adjusting your actions to the needs of your body type.

If Tina had been a Thyroid Type, we might have looked at the same areas, but the program we would have come up with would have been entirely different. What worked for Tina won't necessarily work for you—but the principles that Tina and I used will help you set up the exact program that will give you the results you want.

The "Aha!" Experience

One interesting experience of Tina's I've found applies to almost everyone. Once she understood her body type, she herself was able to begin making the right changes in her life to give her the results she wanted. In fact, knowing about her body type gave her a way of using a lot of information she already had about herself, but hadn't put together in quite that way.

Like Tina, you'll probably find that the moment of discovering your body type is a real "aha!" experience. You discover that you're a Thyroid Type or a Pituitary Type, an Adrenal Type or a Gonadal Type, and suddenly all kinds of perceptions you've had about yourself fall into place. You think, so *that's* why I always need to sleep two hours less than my husband! Or, no *wonder* I crave potato chips at four in the afternoon! Or, now I know why I feel so good all morning when I jog and eat yogurt for breakfast! Whichever your type, there's always a shock of recognition—yes, right, that's me, that's how I am.

Knowing your body type helps you trust your intuition about yourself. For example, it's part of good nutrition for T-Types to eat eggs for breakfast regularly. Some T-Types I've had as patients have already discovered this about themselves and tell me that the eggs make them feel much better. But they go on to ask anxiously, "*Should I* have them? Aren't they bad for me?" They have the experience of their own better feeling but aren't confident enough to trust it in the face of expert advice to the contrary. So I tell them that their perception is valid and explain the value of eggs by describing the dynamics of their T-Type metabolism.

There are many things you know about yourself in this way, and when you know your body type, you find the reasons they are so and learn to work with your body with assurance that what you're doing is right.

The Model's Problem

Occasionally I see a Gonadal Type who has only a small amount of fat to lose. Barbara was and is a top model; you have seen her picture many times in magazines, wearing bikinis and other revealing bits of clothing. (Surprisingly, many top models and actors are G-Types: Clothes look very good on a balanced G-Type body, because the look of a slightly accentuated rear end shows the lines to advantage.)

But Barbara had a real problem, considering her profession: Her thighs and her rear end had begun to spread and to show cellulite. Although women of all body types are susceptible to cellulite, Gonadal-Type women are the most susceptible of all. Barbara admitted that she had been on an extended spree of rich and creamy food, which had started at a photo shoot in the Bahamas. Now, for the first time, she was having trouble getting work. The camera never lies, and in her line of work cellulite is a bitter truth.

I saw my treatment of her as an acid test of the Gonadal Type Diet. The cellulite removal had to be absolutely complete. Barbara didn't want liposuction—she was afraid of it and wanted to *clean* her body completely. But while other people can get away with a trace of wrinkly fat, she couldn't. Since she had only twelve pounds to lose, she went on the Weight Loss Diet for two weeks and then the G-Type Last Five Pounds Diet for a week. I had her lose fifteen pounds, just to make sure all the cellulite would be gone. It did disappear. The benefits of the G-Type Diet are not just for models like Barbara, of course, but her case illustrates the way the diet works for someone with the motivation to follow it religiously.

THE ADRENAL TYPE: IS FAT INEVITABLE?

There are certain phrases, meant to be comforting, that actually hurt more than they comfort. Phrases like "Don't worry about your weight, you carry it so well." "You're not fat, you're muscular." "You're athletic looking." "You're built like your father" (especially depressing if you happen to be a woman). And, perhaps worst of all, "You're just big-boned."

The object of these remarks is invariably an Adrenal Type, the person whose dominant gland is the powerful adrenal gland. Or, I should say, adrenal glands, for there are two of them, one located on top of each kidney. No bigger than two lima beans, the adrenals are the most powerful glands of the body and the ones with the most diverse functions.

Chemicals secreted by the adrenals, which go by the general name of adrenal hormones, assist the liver in the manufacture of glycogen, the blood sugar that is later distributed throughout the body by the thyroid. They assist the kidneys to purify the body's fluids. They control the formation of both muscle and fat, and affect the balance between them. They also stimulate the appetite, so that we eat and keep our bodies supplied with food. The adrenals are the glands of balance, power, and steadiness of energy, and contribute these qualities to many functions of the metabolism.

The Adrenal-Type metabolism shares the characteristics of its dominant gland. A-Types are the most powerful and steadiest of the four body types. Adrenal Types even look powerful: They are solidly built, have square or round faces, strong, squarish hands and feet, broad shoulders, and thick waists; bodies shaped for power rather than speed.

In their cravings, A-Types are the amazement of other body types in that they truly do not care about dessert. The adrenal glands are stimulated by rich and salty foods, especially meat, cheese, and butter, which have the effect of increasing the production of adrenal hormones. One of their effects is to raise the blood pressure, which produces a feeling of pressure and energy in the body, and this is the feeling to which A-Types are unconsciously addicted. The quick energy "rush" of carbohydrates does little for them, and this is why sweet desserts have no appeal. When A-Types want energy, it is the powerful stimulation of fats that turns them on.

The adrenals are powerful glands, and A-Types do not tire easily. They like to keep that powerful feeling going, and it is not unusual for an A-Type to eat three hearty, protein-laden meals per day, with salty snacks such as nuts, salami, or aged cheese in between.

The combination of the powerful, strongly built body, the strong frame that carries weight well, the strong digestion that Adrenal Types always enjoy, and the healthy appetite that adrenal hormones produce, makes overweight a very real possibility in A-Types. But it is a mistake to imagine that an A-Type *must* be fat. There is great potential for a slender, well-balanced, and much healthier body, but it requires very different eating habits from the ones I have just described.

An overweight A-Type may acquire a figure of truly Falstaffian proportions. Take Robert S. I heard his booming voice in the waiting room before I saw him, and he had all the other patients laughing. He was a good-looking man, with great energy, verve, and an infectiously charming personality—and eighty extra pounds. I knew at once he was an Adrenal Type, for this body type has its own typical fat distribution. Where Thyroid Types balloon around the middle and remain slim in their arms and legs, A-Types thicken all over, though they do put a great deal of their excess weight in front, in a potbelly.

Robert was a high-powered salesman who put in long hours and often had to share meals with customers as part of making a sale. I saw from his high energy level that although he was in the habit of overstimulating his adrenals, he had not exhausted them. (The adrenals, fortunately, are much harder to exhaust than the thyroid or the pituitary, and can stand a great deal of overstimulation.)

Adrenal Types sometimes have a hard time getting started with weight loss, because their bodies are so steady and have a very definite weight set-point. But in Robert's case, weight loss came fairly easily, despite the fact that he had never before tried to curb his appetite. Even as a child, he told me, his mother had never discouraged him from eating, since he was eating "healthy" meat and potatoes rather than "unhealthy" sweets.

Thanks to his strong adrenals, his energy remained high on the A-Type Weight Loss Diet despite the reduction in adrenal stimulators. The first week Robert weighed in to find he had lost seventeen pounds! Imagine! He proceeded to lose the rest of his eighty extra pounds in only twelve weeks, and he kept laughing the whole time. On the twelfth week of his diet he brought in with him the trousers he had been wearing the first day. He put them on over his new clothes, and they were yards too big.

Increased Creativity:
The A-Type Diet Bonus

In about the third week of his diet Robert reported that he seemed to be becoming more creative and spontaneous in his work. I explained that this was due to the increased pituitary and thyroidal activity in his metabolism. These glands give lightness and quickness to the system, and these qualities are reflected in a more creative mental and emotional state.

Robert's last five pounds came off as easily as the others, on the A-Type Last Five Pounds Diet. He is now on the A-Type Health and Weight Maintenance Diet, and tells me that he feels great and is an even more successful salesman than before. His cheerful gusto is now balanced with greater creativity and flexibility—an unbeatable combination.

We tend to associate the "meat, no dessert" craving only with men, but there are many Adrenal-Type women in this world as well. The A-Type woman also gains weight across the middle and is prone to acquire a potbelly and to lose her waist when overweight. She is also what Jane Russell used to call a "full-figured gal," and puts on weight very readily in her breasts.

Sonya J., a teenager, was already thirty pounds overweight at the age of sixteen. With her stocky, full-figured body she looked a good deal older than her years. I could see that her adrenals were going full blast and that this was allowing very little activity to her thyroid or pituitary. So I suggested that she might want to try a completely vegetarian diet, and get her protein from legumes and dairy products rather than meat.

I did not see her again for several months, and when I did I barely knew her. The transformation was both stunning and delightful. She was slim and her body had much more lightness and grace. Her face now showed a fine bone structure that had previously been lost in a jowly accumulation of fat.

A vegetarian diet is by no means ideal for everyone. Many, many Thyroid and Pituitary Types have come to me severely out of balance from trying (sometimes for years) to stay with a vegetarian or even a vegan diet. Although I sympathize with the desire to be a vegetarian, it's completely the wrong diet for these body types.

But for Adrenal Types, particularly A-Type women, the nearly vegetarian diet is ideal. Lacking a pronounced sweet tooth, they are not tempted to eat too many sweets, or to try to live on only pasta, as T-Types do. Their strong adrenals do not suffer in the least from the lack of stimulation. At the same time, the stimulation this diet gives to the pituitary and thyroid provides an excellent degree of balance to their metabolism. In Sonya's case and in many other A-Type patients, the results have been very gratifying.

THE THYROID TYPE: WHEN A THIN PERSON GETS FAT

The overweight Thyroid Type is among the commonest sights in a doctor's life. The Thyroid Type is intended by nature to be slim— every line of the body calls out to be lithe, shapely, and delicate. Yet this is a metabolic type highly vulnerable to overweight, with a dominant gland easily exhausted and particularly susceptible to the inducements of our sweets-oriented eating habits. T-Types really took a big hit when we started eating refined sugar three hundred years ago.

The thyroid, located at the base of the throat just above the notch you can feel in the front of the breastbone, is in charge of the function of the metabolism called oxidation—the burning of food in the tissues. Like all the glands, it works by secreting hormones into the bloodstream. The amount of thyroid hormone this gland secretes determines the rate at which the body burns its food. Thyroid hormones also control the flow of energy from the liver to the blood. The liver is our storehouse of glycogen, or blood sugar, and it releases this energy supply into the blood when directed by the thyroid. In addition, the thyroid affects heart rate and muscle tone.

With the thyroid as dominant gland, the Thyroid Type has, ideally, an abundant supply of thyroid hormones, which in turn produce a metabolism that burns food rapidly and efficiently. It also produces a body that has a streamlined, "greyhound" look—slender arms and legs, long, slim hands and feet, a long neck, a neat, slim torso. Even in an overweight T-Type, traces of this basically slender body type always remain. They get fat around the middle, but fat seldom goes below their thighs—the calves and feet always look as if they belonged to another, slimmer person, and their hands and face remain thin until they become very overweight indeed. An overweight T-Type never looks like a "fat person," but rather like a slim person who has, unaccountably, become fat!

Balanced T-Types whose thyroids are still strong are the ones who are the envy of their friends for their ability to eat and eat and not gain weight, an ability that lasts only if they do not overstimulate their thyroid to the point of exhaustion. More typically, they burn out their thyroid by the time they are in their twenties (early thirties at the latest), and weight gain follows.

While balanced, they are wiry, speedy, and energetic, and they never need to rest—or so they think. Unfortunately, they generally overrate their staying power. The truth is that T-Types do need to rest, because of the nature of the thyroid itself. The gland is designed to provide the body with "bursts" of energy, but it needs time to recover after a release of thyroid hormones. T-Types do have great energy bursts, but they should intersperse these bursts with periods of rest.

Instead, what they tend to do—and I have seen this over and over in both my medical and my weight-control patients—is to take a quick-acting thyroid stimulant like sugar, coffee, cola, or tea whenever they begin to feel tired. Of course, all body types tend to take foods that stimulate their dominant gland whenever they feel tired, pressured, or stressed, but T-Types are unusually vulnerable to this tendency.

The result is predictable. The thyroid, constantly stimulated, begins to become less efficient. In extreme cases it may even collapse and stop functioning altogether. The T-Type, used to eating whatever she or he wants and not gaining weight, now finds that the pounds start to collect, and the transformation from slim to fat can be dramatically sudden.

The Sudden Onset of T-Type Fat

Sally H. is a typical Thyroid Type. I'd seen her about a year before, when she'd needed a minor surgical procedure. At that time she'd been very slender—in fact, she was working as a model. But this time when she walked into my office I nearly didn't recognize her. She weighed almost two hundred pounds. Her former striking looks were almost totally buried in the fat—although even at this point she still had trim ankles and feet. She looked extremely unhealthy and her whole body was covered with cellulite.

I learned that she had gone through a divorce a few months after her surgery. These two events, coming so close together, had added up to a great deal of stress. But instead of taking things easy for a time, she'd reacted in typical T-Type style and taken on a heavy work schedule. Then, feeling tired, she'd started drinking quantities of cola and eating thyroid-stimulating sweets. She even had to have a cola drink and a sweet before she could get up in the morning! In this way she had gained over ninety pounds, and her modeling work had evaporated.

I put her immediately on the Thyroid Type Diet—a higher protein diet with eggs for breakfast, chicken, fish, or meat at lunch and dinner, a minimum of carbohydrates in the form of whole grain, plenty of vegetables, and no caffeine whatsoever. I wanted to rest her highly overstimulated thyroid, and I also wanted to give some support to her adrenals. For T-Types who have been relying on thyroidal energy to get through their days, stimulating the adrenals is an important part of dieting. By bringing into action the steadier energy of the adrenals, the thyroid is relieved of a great deal of its burden.

Sally had trouble following her diet at first, because of the severity of her thyroidal exhaustion. In her run-down state, she imagined she couldn't function without stimulants, but after about a week she began to feel the strengthening of her adrenals. She continued dieting and lost weight at a steady rate until she had lost fifty pounds. At this point she suddenly began looking radiant again, and I knew that her thyroid was starting to recover.

From this point on her weight loss became more rapid, the result of her more efficient thyroid. She lost her last pounds of excess weight on the T-Type Last Five Pounds Diet, and by the end of her diet she looked and felt completely herself again.

I warned her, however, that she would have to continue to pay attention to her diet for the rest of her life. Although she was now much stronger, she would always have the delicate Thyroid-Type metabolism. It responds beautifully to a healthy, high-protein, low-carbohydrate diet, but disastrously to overstimulation through sweets and caffeine.

The T-Type Energy Connection

Jerry S., a young and ambitious professional man who worked long hours, was another interesting Thyroid Type. When he came to me for help he was only about fifteen pounds overweight, every pound of which was in a "roll" around his midsection. But his real problem was the unsteadiness of his energy.

I asked for his dietary history, and it was a thyroidal nightmare. Breakfast was coffee and toast with jelly. Next came a coffee break with a doughnut, at midmorning. Lunch was a sandwich, a Coke, another coffee, and a dessert, and he told me that often by the end of the day he was too tired to make dinner, and just had coffee and cookies.

When I told him he was going to have to eliminate caffeine and sweets, his eyes flashed angrily (this was his addiction to thyroid stimulants making itself known). He'd imagined I was going to prescribe some kind of diet pills, which T-Types love because they are also thyroid stimulants and give them a temporary feeling that they have their old energy back. I told him diet pills were the last thing he needed in his condition—I doubted his thyroid could take much more strain.

He was an intelligent man, and when I explained to him what he was doing to his metabolism, he agreed to try to change his eating habits. I had him reduce his caffeine intake gradually over the course of a week, until he was down to just one cup of decaffeinated coffee in the morning.

He lost his fifteen pounds in three weeks. The roll of fat around his middle gave way to firm flesh, and his complexion, which had been dull-looking, became smoother and more luminous. He reported that he was no longer getting tired in the middle of the day. He needed less sleep, and was able to put in the long hours his work required without a break.

The Temptations of the T-Type

I emphasized to both Sally and Jerry, and to all my T-Type patients, the importance of continuing attention to diet and to rest. Given the constant availability of sweets and starches, and the social lures of a cup of coffee, tea, or cola, this warning is necessary. T-Types who have lost their excess weight and balanced their metabolism can enjoy caffeine in moderation, can even eat some sweets, but should always be attentive not to rely on these stimulants for energy when what their bodies really need is a period of rest.

THE PITUITARY TYPE: "I'M TOO OLD TO HAVE BABY FAT!"

Sarah K. said she was thirty-seven, but from her looks she could have been in her late twenties. I noticed first that her head gave the appearance of being slightly too big for her body, a sure sign of a Pituitary Type. She also had a round, childlike face and a bright, interested expression. Her thirty or so extra pounds were in the typical "baby-fat" all-over distribution of the P-Type: She had some fat on her hands and arms, her back and chest were rather pudgy, and her stomach was rounded like a child's. She did not have one particular area of fat, such as hips, thighs, or rear; all were rounded but no one area stood out noticeably. All in all, a classic overweight Pituitary Type.

Sarah told me that she was a vegetarian. The reason, she said, was that her digestion was weak, especially for heavy foods like meat, so she generally avoided animal foods and obtained most of her protein from dairy products. "In fact," she said, "I almost live on yogurt and cheese sandwiches. I didn't think it would be possible to get fat on yogurt, but it looks like I've done it!"

When I gave her the Pituitary Type Diet, she looked nonplussed. The diet contains the highest proportion of protein of any of the diets. It also allows no dairy products at all, and has meat at every meal, including breakfast.

Sarah was reluctant to try the diet at first, but I was able to persuade her that while a vegetarian diet is suitable for Adrenal and Gonadal Types, it is not at all appropriate for the P-Type metabolism. She promised to try it for a week, but her parting glance told me she thought I was out of my mind.

When I saw her the following week she was beaming over a five-pound weight loss. She was now ready to hear an explanation of how and why the diet works. I told her that being a Pituitary Type means that of her body's four major glands, the pituitary was the strongest and set the tone of her metabolism.

Located within the skull behind the eyes, the pituitary gland is known as the "master gland" because it is responsible for controlling and regulating all glandular activity. The pituitary works by secreting chemicals, called pituitary hormones, into the bloodstream. These hormones regulate the activity of the thyroid and the adrenals, and have general control over the functioning of the sex glands as well. They are responsible for the body's growth and sexual maturation. They also govern the body's response to changes in the external environment. Through a complex series of chemical reactions, the pituitary reacts to such aspects of the environment as the weather and the time of day, and conveys these changes to the rest of the body so that it can respond in an appropriate way.

A metabolism that is dominated by this master gland has, by nature, very good coordination among the different parts of the body. But there is no one aspect of the body's metabolism that works more strongly than any other. This explains why, in the P-Type, fat accumulates all over the body. Each of the other glands has a particular area where it directs fat to be stored. In the Pituitary Type, no one area is emphasized, so fat is stored everywhere more or less equally. The particular fat location is, technically speaking, "diffuse subcutaneous fat," more commonly known as baby fat.

Sarah had already told me that her digestion was somewhat weak; I now learned that her sexual function also was not strong. She said she'd never been able to understand what all the "fuss about sex" was about. Both these weaknesses can be traced to the typical weakness of the P-Type metabolism: lack of strength in the adrenals (digestion) and the gonads (sexual function). She'd been overstimulating her pituitary with dairy products, and giving some stimulation to her thyroid with carbohydrates, but her very light vegetarian diet gave no stimulation or support to her lower glands.

To offset these weaknesses, the Pituitary Type Diet employs a high proportion of animal protein, which is stimulating to the lower glands. Without this stimulation, the metabolism remains sluggish in the essential adrenal and gonadal functions. And without strong support of the lower glands, Pituitary Types easily become fatigued and stressed and feel uncontrollable cravings for dairy foods. On the Pituitary Type Diet, these cravings are drastically reduced, and entirely eliminated after a few weeks.

I saw Sarah every week for the next ten weeks. She lost weight steadily until she reached her weight goal of 120 pounds. What impressed her was how easily she dieted; she was free of cravings and felt more energetic than before she started dieting. What impressed me, on the other hand, was observing her metabolism's balance improve as the weeks went by. She lost her baby fat and began to look more like an adult. And as she slimmed down, she developed a more sensual shape. At the same time her digestion improved, and she told me with some surprise that she was starting to understand why people were so interested in sex! For Sarah, the Pituitary Type Diet is the *only* diet that would produce the positive and holistic benefits that so delighted us both.

Another Way P-Types Can Go Wrong

A P-Type I saw about three years ago was an attorney who felt that he would be more effective in front of juries if he were slimmer. So he'd (unwisely) eaten nothing for the past two weeks but grapefruit and cottage cheese. He was now worried about his health, and well he might be—he had lost some weight, but felt weak and was suffering from headaches and irritability.

Since he was a Pituitary Type, his problem was easily explained. The diet he'd been on couldn't have been worse for his body type. Pituitary Types need plenty of animal protein and must avoid dairy products completely—the exact opposite of what he'd been doing.

I changed him at once to the P-Type Weight Loss Diet. Two weeks later he was back with a glowing report. He'd lost five more pounds and was now at his ideal weight. But of greater importance was the fact that his weakness and headaches were gone. His very appearance proclaimed the increased metabolic balance produced by his Body Type Diet.

NOW IT'S YOUR TURN

Now the time has come for you to start applying these principles to yourself. In the next chapter I take you through the steps of finding your body type. Once you have done this, you will be ready to start the Weight Loss Program for your body type.

THE BODY TYPE CHECKLIST: FINDING YOUR BODY TYPE

To select your Body Type Diet—the diet that will work for your own type of metabolism—you must first know what type of body yours is. Your "body type," as you have seen, is simply a shorthand way of describing your metabolism—its strengths and weaknesses, its needs and requirements—in terms of which of the four major glands dominates your body chemistry.

This chapter will show you the steps involved in discovering whether your dominant gland is the gonads, the adrenals, the thyroid, or the pituitary, by means of close observation of your physical characteristics, without costly or time-consuming laboratory tests.

What makes it possible to determine your body type by observation is the pervasive influence of the dominant gland on many aspects of your makeup. The most important influence of your dominant gland is in your body's basic shape—that is, the proportions of your limbs, your head, and your torso. The next most important are the location of your extra pounds and, in particular, the location of your wrinkly fat, or cellulite. Part 1 of the Body Type Checklist focuses on these areas. The illustrations that accompany the Checklist will also help you to answer these questions.

Other influences of the dominant gland are in the areas of food cravings (which are reflections of brain chemistry), energy level (which reflects glandular biorhythms), health (which reflects the degree of integration of the glandular system), and the broad outline of your personality (because chemistry is destiny, even for the mind). These areas are also covered in the Checklist, in Part 2.

There are separate Checklists for Women (page 50) and Men (page 57). This is because there are four body types in women and only three types in men. Also, of course, the questions are somewhat different because men and women have different basic shapes, regardless of body type.

Body Type Determination:
How Hard Is It, Really?

One of the changes between this edition and the 1983 edition is my assessment of the difficulty of finding your body type. Then, I stated that after completing the Checklist you would definitely know your body type. Now, I feel that I need to expound on some of the difficulties involved, so that if you do have trouble determining your own body type you will not feel discouraged and will know what to do.

I well remember a story I heard shortly after this book was published, from three readers who wrote to me about their Checklist experience. They were coworkers in an office and had decided to try the Body Type Program together. All three of them bought copies of the book and took the test. One, Mary J., saw immediately that she was a Thyroid Type. She barely had to even answer the questions— she just looked at the illustrations and, pointing to the T-Type woman, said, "That's me." When she went through the questions on the Checklist, she had almost every check in the T-Type column.

The second and third women, sisters named Laura and Jillian, weren't so sure. Laura said she thought she was Adrenal, but wasn't sure, and Jillian was extremely uncertain whether she was a Thyroid or a Gonadal Type.

So they took my advice from the book. Let me repeat it here: If you have any doubt about your result after doing the Checklist, go through the questions again with the aid of a friend or spouse in answering the questions. I said that you should be sure that the person you ask to help you is the kind who will feel comfortable answering questions about your body. In finding your body type, there's no place for being shy about helping you decide if your hips are round or flat, your breasts are small, medium, or large, or whether you have cellulite on your stomach, hips, or thighs.

The reason I suggested you get this help was that it is quite difficult to be objective about our own bodies. In fact, most of us are far too hard on ourselves. We believe our rears are "huge" and our thighs are "gigantic" when in fact our rears are rounded and our thighs just a bit padded. We may also have fat locations we're simply not aware of, because we can't see them very well. A helper can see us from angles we can't, and can also provide perspective we may not have.

And in fact that's what happened when Laura and Jillian did the Checklist together. Laura looked at Jillian from the back and side, noting that from the back, her widest point was low rather than high on her hips and that the "saddlebags" on her thighs were clearly defined in outline (a G-Type characteristic).

Laura was also able to help Jillian pinpoint her cravings. Jillian said that she thought her main craving was for sweets. Laura told her, "It's true that you almost always stop for a cookie on the way back from lunch, but are you sure it's the sugar you're craving? I've noticed that you usually say no to hard candy and only like the really greasy cookies from the mall. Maybe it's the fats you're craving, not the sweets." When she thought about it, Jillian decided it was true.

So by the end of their session together, Laura and Jillian both felt quite certain that Jillian was a G-Type. But they could not decide about Laura. She had some characteristics of an Adrenal Type, Jillian agreed, but not all. She didn't really look like the illustration. Her energy pattern didn't seem to fit. Her cravings (apple pie, frozen yogurt) were confusing. They just couldn't be sure. It was at this point that they wrote to me, wondering what to do next.

"Classic," "Moderate," and "Unusual" Body Types

The three women above illustrate the variable difficulty of Body Typing. I have found that about 35 percent of the population are *classic* examples of a body type. Mary was one of these. You could have picked her out as a Thyroid if you saw her going up an escalator while you went down. She was tall, long-boned, with a long face and hands. She lived on sweets and caffeine. Her energy was up and down all day long. Her mind was quick and creative. She had every classic T-Type characteristic.

These "classic" people almost just have to hear about the body type concept to know what they are. Although I should add that occasionally they resist their body type—they don't like the idea that they can be categorized so easily. I remember a woman at a lecture who was quite upset with me when I determined her body type immediately from the podium. She was a classic Adrenal Type, but for some reason she didn't want to be. So even classic people can present a body-typing problem.

Then, another 40 percent of the population are *moderately clear* examples of a body type. Their type doesn't just leap out at you, but if you look at them closely, preferably in their underwear or a swimsuit, and are reasonably careful in doing the Checklist, you will be able to find their body type, even without a lot of training. Jillian was an example of a moderately clear Gonadal Type.

Finally, the last 25 percent of the population are, at least to the untrained eye, just plain hard. They are somewhat *unusual* examples of their body type. They have characteristics of more than one type; they have many cravings or no cravings at all; their energy patterns aren't clear; their personalities aren't characteristic. Laura, it turned out, was one of these. Adrenal, with a strong secondary Thyroid? Pituitary, with a secondary Adrenal? Jillian, Mary, and Laura herself just couldn't tell.

Why It Can Be Hard

I have been able to pinpoint at least five reasons why you might find yourself in the "unusual" or hard-to-Body-Type group. They are:

1. You are very well balanced. If you're close to your best weight, and in good health, it's likely that all four of your glands are working well. So your body will show *some* features of all their glands. It won't have the features of gross dominance that make body-typing easy.
2. You are more than forty or fifty pounds overweight, so the distinguishing features of your body type may be obscured. For

instance, you may be a Gonadal Type, and your first thirty extra pounds went mainly onto your rear and thighs. But then you began to put on weight in other places as well—and your body type will be more difficult to see. (In these cases, a picture taken when you were slimmer will tell the story of your body type more clearly.)

3. You have a genetic background from which you derive particular features. For example, some women with Scandinavian ancestors have a genetic disposition to rather curvy rears, but they are not necessarily all Gonadal Types. Or, for another example, some Asian women may appear slighter than women of European ancestry, but they are not necessarily Pituitary Types, as I mistakenly supposed at one time. The genetic factor does not usually cause confusion, but it's worth mentioning because your perception of your features may have to be modified by taking your genetic background into account.

4. You have had cosmetic or reconstructive surgery. In this case, you'll need to think back to how you looked *before* your surgery. If you're a Gonadal-Type woman who has had breast implants, or a Thyroid-Type woman who has had liposuction on your thighs, you have erased some of the markers of your body type. Again, pictures taken before the surgery can be helpful.

5. You are over fifty or sixty, and age has covered up some of the characteristics of your body type. For example, whatever your body type, your legs may have become thinner or you may have lost musculature. If you're a Gonadal-Type woman who has gone through menopause, you're a special case of this—I'll discuss you in a separate section (see page 98).

How to Get Help

If you've been through the Checklist by yourself and then again with a helper, and still are not sure of your body type, it's very possible that you belong to the "unusual" group. And you're the reason that I began several years ago to train people in body type determination.

The certified Body Type Counselors have all gone through a training course in which they studied the characteristics, including those of the more unusual examples of their own body type, in detail. Elizabeth King Morrison and I function as backup support for the counselors; if they cannot be sure of the body type they can ask one of us. If you are stuck in determining your body type, you can call 1-888-BODYTYPE for information on locating a trained counselor.

THE BODY TYPE
CHECKLIST FOR WOMEN

PART 1: YOUR APPEARANCE

1. First, turn to the drawings that begin on page 62. Use the heavier or lighter version depending on which one corresponds more closely to you at your present weight. Comparing your body with the drawings, which one do you most resemble?
   A. G-Type
   B. A-Type
   C. T-Type
   D. P-Type

2. This question has three versions. Use the one that best fits your weight.
2–1. Use if you are within twenty pounds over or under your best weight.
   A. You are significantly smaller above the waist than below. Lower body is in fairly good shape, but still appears more substantial and stronger than your upper body.
   B. You appear strong and sturdy, with strength deriving from strong bones rather than necessarily from muscle. More substantial above the waist than below.
   C. You are fine-boned and graceful, with a good balance of weight and strength above and below the waist.
   D. You are somewhat childlike and undeveloped in appearance, more like a young girl than like a woman.
2–2. Use if you are twenty to fifty pounds overweight.
   A. You are definitely disproportionate above and below the waist. Stomach is relatively flat, but your rear and outer thighs carry extra weight.
   B. You appear square and sturdy. Weight is visible on the front of your body and above the waist, especially in your stomach and upper back. Face, hands, and feet show extra pounds.
   C. You are curvy, with weight both above and below the waist, but with a defined waist. Face, hands, and feet are fairly slim.
   D. You are pudgy all over, like a child who has put on weight.

2–3.   Use if more than fifty pounds overweight.
   A.   You are disproportionate above and below the waist, with a very substantial rear end. Weight in stomach, but less than the weight on your rear.
   B.   You have a prominent stomach, with substantial weight on your back. Rear end has weight, but less than the weight in front.
   C.   You are curvy, with extra weight above and below the waist, but still maintain a waist. Your face, extremities (hands and feet), calves, and lower arms have put on weight, but less than the weight you have around your middle (chest to thighs).
   D.   You are undefined in outline, with fat all over and not much curve at waist. Breasts have put on weight and there is substantial weight on your knees.

3. Viewing yourself from the front, which of the following best describes your basic shape?
   A.   Disproportionate between upper and lower body: small head, shoulders, breasts, and chest; long waist; heavier lower body; and strong legs.
   B.   Square, sturdy, and strong-looking both above and below the waist. Full-figured, without much of a curve at the waist.
   C.   Fine-boned and with arms and legs appearing long in proportion to the torso. A pronounced waist, and equal curves above and below the waist.
   D.   Rather childish-looking, without many curves anywhere.

4. Viewing yourself from the side, which best describes your shape?
   A.   Back is slightly swayed, rear end prominent.
   B.   Back straight, with rear end either quite flat and tucked under, or having a low, flat appearance.
   C.   Lower back straight, neck coming forward somewhat, rear end rounded but not extremely pronounced.
   D.   Shoulders quite rounded, head coming forward from the line of the back, rear end small and childlike.

5. Viewing yourself as best you can from the back, which best de-
scribes your shape?
   A.   Narrow at the shoulders and through the back, greatest
        width below waist is low (lower hips to upper thighs).
   B.   Square-looking from shoulders to hips, shoulders not ex-
        tremely broad but strong-looking, not much waist curve.
   C.   About as wide at shoulders and hips, waist curves inward,
        greatest width below waist is high (upper hips).
   D.   Childlike curves, not much waist or hips.

6. Your face is:
   A.   Small for body size, and may have downward-slanting eyes.
   B.   Square or round.
   C.   Long, slender.
   D.   Large for body size.

7. Your hands are:
   A.   Longer in palms than fingers, fingers blunt on ends.
   B.   Square, blunt fingers.
   C.   Long, tapering fingers.
   D.   Small, delicate, tapering fingers.

8. Your chest and breasts are:
   A.   Small chest, small breasts.
   B.   Large chest, large breasts.
   C.   Small chest, medium to large breasts.
   D.   Medium chest, small breasts.

9. Looking at yourself from the back, where is most of your extra
weight?
   A.   Quite low on your body: lower hips, outer thighs.
   B.   High on your body: across the shoulders and back.
   C.   In the middle of your body: spare tire, wide hips, heavy up-
        per thighs.
   D.   All over, no single location.

10. Looking at yourself from the side, where are most of your extra pounds?
   A.   In the back, in a prominent, shelflike rear end.
   B.   In the front, in a prominent stomach.
   C.   Both front and back, with your waist remaining distinct.
   D.   In a rounded, childlike stomach and rounded rear end, with waist not remaining distinct.

11. Check your body for cellulite (wrinkly, cottage-cheese fat). If you have cellulite, where is it *mainly* located?
   A.   On your rear and saddlebags.
   B.   On your stomach, back, or upper arms.
   C.   On your thighs.
   D.   On your knees.

PART 2: CRAVINGS, HEALTH, AND PERSONALITY

12. Which would you consider your main food craving?
   A.   Rich and spicy food.
   B.   Greasy, salty food.
   C.   Sweets or starches.
   D.   Dairy products.

13. Which would you be most likely to succumb to if you found yourself in a fast-food restaurant at the end of a long, tiring afternoon?
   A.   A taco.
   B.   A cheeseburger.
   C.   A sweet roll or cookies.
   D.   A milk shake.

14. How many caffeinated coffees, teas, or colas do you drink each day?
   A.   One or two cups.
   B.   Three or four cups.
   C.   Five or more cups.
   D.   None.

15. Which of these best describes your energy pattern?
    A.   Good in the morning, better in the evening.
    B.   I feel fairly energetic all day, but wear out in the evening.
    C.   Up and down all day.
    D.   I'm a morning person.

16. If you exercise, why do you do it?
    A.   Because moving feels good.
    B.   Because I'm supposed to.
    C.   So I can eat more later.
    D.   To get an exercise "high."

17. Which is your most typical small health problem?
    A.   Bladder infections.
    B.   Constipation.
    C.   Fatigue.
    D.   Colds.

18. Do you have any of these larger health problems?
    A.   Breast lumps.
    B.   High blood pressure.
    C.   Ulcers.
    D.   Chronic allergies.

19. Do you tend to have cramps during your menstrual period?
    A.   First day only.
    B.   Rarely.
    C.   Often.
    D.   Don't know, never noticed.

20. If you could work in any situation, which would suit you best?
    A.   In my home.
    B.   In a well-run corporation with room to move up.
    C.   Out in the world, traveling.
    D.   In a serene, well-designed office.

21. If you could have any job in the world, which would you choose?
   A.   Teaching something I love.
   B.   Marketing something I believe in.
   C.   Creating something I feel passionate about.
   D.   Designing something people don't even know they need yet.

22. Which best describes your disposition?
   A.   Sensuous, warm, and comfortable.
   B.   Friendly, open, and practical.
   C.   Lively and temperamental.
   D.   Intellectual, detached, idealistic.

23. When you're "up," you're
   A.   Radiant and loving.
   B.   Friendly and outgoing.
   C.   Sparkly and funny.
   D.   Giggly.

24. When you're "down," you're
   A.   Weepy.
   B.   Angry.
   C.   Depressed, irritable.
   D.   Withdrawn, obsessed.

25. Which best describes your temper?
   A.   Quick-tempered but easily distracted by flattery or apologies.
   B.   Slow to get angry, but when you do, you stay mad for a while.
   C.   Impatient, inclined to get depressed when thwarted.
   D.   Feel upset after the event, have a hard time communicating about it.

Now add up your points for each letter.
   A._____   B. _____   C. _____   D. _____

If your highest number of answers is A, you are a Gonadal Type. Turn to Chapter 6 for the G-Type Weight Loss Program.

If your highest number of answers is B, you are an Adrenal Type. Turn to Chapter 7 for the A-Type Weight Loss Program.

If your highest number of answers is C, you are a Thyroid Type. Turn to Chapter 8 for the T-Type Weight Loss Program.

If your highest number of answers is D, you are a Pituitary Type. Turn to Chapter 9 for the P-Type Weight Loss Program.

SPECIAL INSTRUCTIONS IF YOU HAVE A TIE

A tie indicates that you are close between two body types. However, you do have a dominant gland, even if it is not strongly dominant. To break your tie, use only your answers from Section 1. If you are still unsure or if you also have a tie in Section 1, consider consulting a Body Type Counselor for professional body type determination.

SPECIAL INSTRUCTIONS FOR GONADAL TYPE WOMEN

If your score indicates that you are a Gonadal Type, and you feel confident in this determination, this indicates that your dominant gland is your ovaries. You need to be aware that yours is the only body type that actually changes in the course of your lifetime, because your ovaries wind down at menopause and eventually stop dominating your system. How quickly this happens—whether it happens immediately at menopause or does not happen for many years—depends on several individual factors that I'll tell you about in your own chapter, Chapter 6.

THE BODY TYPE
CHECKLIST FOR MEN

PART 1: YOUR APPEARANCE

1. First, turn to the drawings that begin on page 70. Use the heavier or lighter version depending on which one corresponds more closely to you at your present weight. Comparing your body with the drawings, which one do you most resemble?
   A.   A-Type
   B.   T-Type
   C.   P-Type

2. This question has three versions. Use the one that best fits your weight.
2–1.   Use if you are either at your desired weight, or within about twenty pounds over or under your best weight.
   A.   You are strong and sturdy, with a basically muscular appearance even if you are out of shape. You have a large chest and sturdy arms and legs.
   B.   You are longer boned, with a more streamlined appearance. Your chest and hips are narrower, and you have long arms and legs.
   C.   You are boyish, more like a young boy than like a man.
2–2.   Use if twenty to fifty pounds overweight.
   A.   You are square, sturdy, and heavy-looking. Weight has accumulated on the front of your body in a potbelly. Face, hands, and feet show extra pounds.
   B.   You are saggy, out-of-shape-looking, with weight all around your middle. Face, hands, and feet are still relatively slim.
   C.   You are pudgy all over, like a child who has put on weight.
2–3.   Use if more than fifty pounds overweight.
   A.   You have a very prominent stomach, with substantial weight also on your back. Rear end is round and weight extends down legs to feet.
   B.   You have extra weight all around your middle, in a large spare tire. There is also a potbelly but it is not confined mainly to the front—it extends all around the middle. Your

face, calves, and lower arms have put on weight, but less than the weight you carry around your middle (chest to thighs).
C.   You look undefined in outline, with fat all over the body.

3. Viewing yourself from the front, which of the following best describes your basic shape?
   A.   Square, sturdy, and strong-looking both above and below the waist.
   B.   Fine-boned, with arms and legs appearing long in proportion to the torso.
   C.   Childish-looking, without much definition anywhere.

4. Viewing yourself from the side, which best describes your shape?
   A.   Back slightly swayed, rounded rear end.
   B.   Lower back straight, neck coming forward somewhat, rear end flat or slightly rounded.
   C.   Shoulders quite rounded, head coming forward from the line of the back, rear end small and childlike.

5. Viewing yourself from the back, which best describes your shape?
   A.   Square-looking from shoulders to hips, shoulders not extremely broad but strong-looking, not much waist curve.
   B.   Wider at shoulders than hips.
   C.   Narrow shoulders and hips.

6. Your face is:
   A.   Square or round.
   B.   Long, slender.
   C.   Delicate, and your head appears large for body size.

7. Your hands are:
   A.   Square, with blunt fingers.
   B.   Long, with long, tapering fingers.
   C.   Small, with delicate, tapering fingers.

8. Your skin is:
   A.   Oily, slightly coarse, ruddy.
   B.   Smooth, even-colored.
   C.   Dry, delicate.

9. Your teeth are:
   A. Large, slightly yellowish, strong (few cavities).
   B. Small, white, weak (prone to cavities).
   C. Large, especially front center.

10. Looking at yourself from the back, where have you put on most of your extra weight?
   A. High on your body: across the shoulders and back.
   B. In the middle of your body: spare tire, wide hips, heavy upper thighs.
   C. All over, no single location.

11. Looking at yourself from the side, where have you put on most of your extra pounds?
   A. In the front, in a prominent stomach.
   B. Both front and back, in a spare tire.
   C. In a rounded, childlike stomach and rounded rear end.

PART 2: CRAVINGS, HEALTH, AND PERSONALITY

12. Which would you consider your most important food craving?
   A. Greasy, salty food.
   B. Sweets or starches.
   C. Dairy products.

13. Which would you be most likely to succumb to if you found yourself in a fast-food restaurant at the end of a long, tiring afternoon?
   A. A cheeseburger.
   B. A sweet roll or cookies.
   C. A milk shake.

14. How much coffee, tea, or cola with caffeine do you drink each day?
   A. Three or four cups.
   B. Five or more cups.
   C. None, one, or two cups.

15. If you exercise, why do you do it?
    A.   Because I'm supposed to.
    B.   So I can eat more later.
    C.   To get an exercise "high."

16. Which is your most typical small health problem?
    A.   Constipation, minor aches.
    B.   Fatigue.
    C.   Colds.

17. Do you have any of these larger health problems?
    A.   High blood pressure, hardening of the arteries.
    B.   Ulcers or colitis.
    C.   Chronic allergies.

18. If you could have any job in the world, which would you choose?
    A.   Marketing something I believe in.
    B.   Creating something I feel passionate about.
    C.   Designing something people don't even know they need yet.

19. If you could work in any situation, which would suit you best?
    A.   A well-run corporation with room to move up.
    B.   Out in the world, traveling.
    C.   In a serene, well-designed office.

20. Which of these jobs would you choose?
    A.   Production type (salesperson, engineer, executive).
    B.   Creative type (writer, artist, entrepreneur).
    C.   Technical type (computer programmer, accountant).

21. Which best describes your disposition?
    A.   Friendly, open, and practical.
    B.   Lively and changeable.
    C.   Intellectual, detached, idealistic.

22. When you're "up," you're
    A.   Friendly and outgoing.
    B.   Sparkly and funny.
    C.   Happy and full of wonder.

23. When you're "down," you're
    A.   Angry.
    B.   Depressed, irritable.
    C.   Withdrawn, obsessed.

24. Which best describes your temper?
    A.   Slow to get angry, but when you are, you stay mad for a while. You get over it by talking.
    B.   Impatient, inclined to get depressed when thwarted. You get over it by resting.
    C.   Get upset after the event, have a hard time communicating about it. You get over it by thinking.

Now add up your points for each letter.
    A._____   B. _____   C. _____

If your highest number of answers is A, you are an Adrenal Type. Turn to Chapter 7 for the A-Type Weight Loss Program.
    If your highest number of answers is B, you are a Thyroid Type. Turn to Chapter 8 for the T-Type Weight Loss Program.
    If your highest number of answers is C, you are a Pituitary Type. Turn to Chapter 9 for the P-Type Weight Loss Program.

SPECIAL INSTRUCTIONS IF YOU HAVE A TIE

A tie indicates that you are close between two body types. However, you do have a dominant gland, even if it is not strongly dominant. To break your tie, use only your answers from Section 1. If you are still unsure or if you also have a tie in Section 1, consider consulting a Body Type Counselor for professional body type determination.

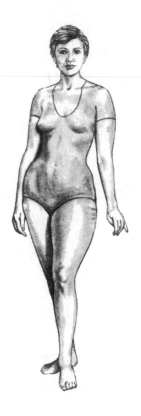

Figure 1: The G–Type woman with extra pounds. Note the difference in size between her upper and lower body, her small waist, and the "saddlebags" on her outer thighs.

Figure 2: The G–Type woman in profile, with extra pounds. Note that almost all of the extra weight is behind her. Her stomach is relatively flat, and her lower back appears swayed.

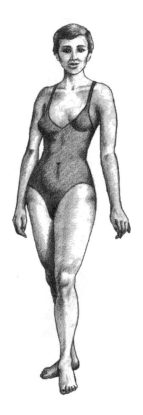

Figure 3: The G–Type woman at her best weight, seen from the front. Note that she does not look very much different in this view from the way she looked with extra pounds.

Figure 4: The G–Type woman at her best weight, from the side. Here you see the changes: Her rear is now in proportion to her body, although a G–Type woman will never have a flat, boyish rear—it is not her nature.

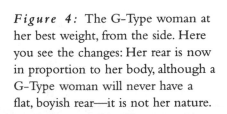

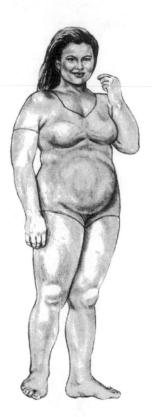

Figure 5: The A-Type woman from the front, with extra pounds. Note the straight, sturdy line of her body, the square face, the large breasts.

Figure 6: The A-Type woman from the side, with extra pounds. Note the straight back, the flat, tucked-under rear, and the extra weight in the front of her body.

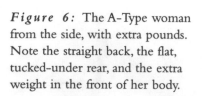

Figure 7: The A-Type woman at her best weight, from the front. Note her strong, athletic shape, full figure, and shapely legs.

Figure 8: The A-Type woman at her best weight, from the side. Note her straight back and neck and her trim stomach.

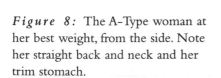

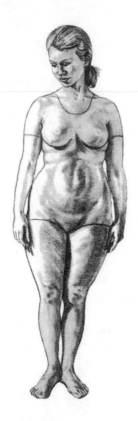

Figure 9: The T-Type woman from the front, with extra pounds. Note the extra weight on thighs and upper hips, the curvy waist, and the tapering lower arms and legs.

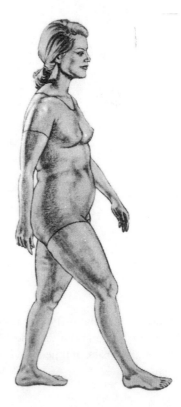

Figure 10: The T-Type woman in profile, with extra pounds. She has a rounded, but not pronounced, rear end, and fat on her stomach, mainly below the navel.

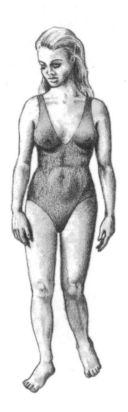

Figure 11: The T-Type woman from the front, at her best weight. Note the curvy torso, long legs, long head, and delicate facial features.

Figure 12: The T-Type woman from the side, at her best weight. Note the flatter stomach, rounded rear, and slimmer thighs.

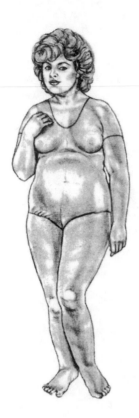

Figure 13: The P–Type woman from the front, with extra pounds. Note her childlike, undeveloped look, baby fat all over, small breasts, and angelic expression.

Figure 14: The P–Type woman from the side, with extra pounds. Note her rounded shoulders, her head coming forward from her back, and her rounded, childlike tummy and rear.

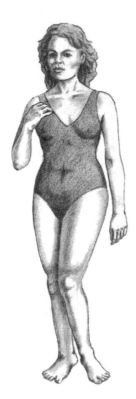

Figure 15: The P-Type woman at her best weight, from the front. Note her more adult-looking figure and more focused expression.

Figure 16: The P-Type woman from the side, at her best weight. Note her straighter neck, her trimmed-down tummy, and the more defined shape to her rear.

Figure 17: The A-Type man from the front, with extra pounds. Note his strong, sturdy appearance, his broad chest, and his thick, straight arms and legs.

Figure 18: The A-Type man from the side, with extra pounds. Note his classic pot or "beer" belly, his rounded rear end, and thick neck.

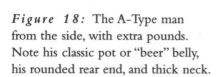

Figure 19: The A-Type man from the front, at his best weight. Note that he still looks strong and sturdy, and maintains a good musculature with little effort.

Figure 20: The A-Type man from the side, at his best weight. Note the trimmed-down stomach, which greatly reduces his risk for several health problems.

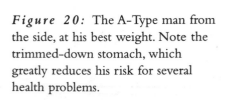

Figure 21: The T-Type man from the front, with extra pounds. Note his long limbs, fat accumulation in thighs, and his "love handles" (a roll of fat around the middle).

Figure 22: The T-Type man from the side, with extra pounds. Note his flat rear, fat around his waist, and delicate neck.

Figure 23: The T-Type man from the front, at his best weight. Note his trimmer thighs and the weight loss around his waist.

Figure 24: The T-Type man from the side, at his best weight. Note his improved posture, trimmer waist, and generally more streamlined appearance.

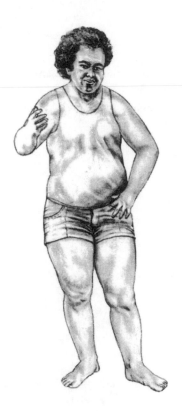

Figure 25: The P-Type man from the front, with extra pounds. Note his boyish, relatively undeveloped look, his small chest, sloping shoulders, and "baby fat" all over.

Figure 26: The P-Type man from the side, with extra pounds. Note how he differs from the A-Type man: a softer-looking, more childlike tummy, a head that comes forward from the line of his back, and less developed muscles.

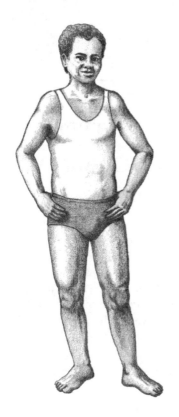

Figure 27: The P-Type man from the front, at his best weight. Note his still-boyish but more defined shape, coming from the loss of his diffuse subcutaneous fat ("baby fat").

Figure 28: The P-Type man from the side, at his best weight. Note his straighter neck, trim body, and still-rounded rear.

THE GONADAL BODY TYPE WEIGHT LOSS PROGRAM

The weight loss program you are about to learn is much more than a "diet." It's a whole new way of thinking about food, one that will ultimately put you in complete charge of your body—not just your weight, but your energy level, your physical endurance, your mood, your health, and much more. It's called a "weight loss program" because reaching your best weight is the first step, and it's the one you're probably most interested in right now. But while you're working on that goal, the other benefits will be coming along, too, automatically, as part of the package.

As a G-Type, you have gained weight in the past by eating foods that stimulate your ovaries (gonads): greasy and spicy foods such as rich sauces, creamy dips, dishes made with cheese or butter, or spicy dishes like Thai and Mexican food. This is the origin of G-Type weight problems. The overstimulation of your ovaries creates a state of exhaustion and imbalance that allows fat and/or cellulite to accumulate on the areas of your body controlled by ovarian hormones: your rear and outer thighs.

The G-Type Diet works on the underlying cause of the problem in order to reestablish balance in your system. What you do is cut back on ovary-stimulating foods, and increase foods that are supportive and stimulating to your pituitary and thyroid glands.

You accomplish this by cutting down on or eliminating red meat and eating a minimum of fats and oils and no stimulating spices—these are the ovary-stimulating foods. Equally important, you must eat plenty of fruit and fresh vegetables, low-fat or nonfat dairy products, a small amount of sugar and caffeine, and a moderate amount of carbohydrates—these are the foods that stimulate your pituitary and thyroid.

The results for you will be a lighter, less sluggish metabolism, more energy, faster weight loss than you've ever experienced, and (especially during your Last Five Pounds Diet), a dramatic loss of the cellulite (the wrinkly fat commonly found on hips, thighs, buttocks, or upper arms) that virtually all G-Types over the age of fifteen are so prone to acquire.

THE BASIC STRATEGY
FOR G-TYPES

The key to weight loss for you as a Gonadal Type is to create balance in your system by simultaneously decreasing stimulation to your gonads and increasing it to your thyroid and pituitary. All of the problems you encounter in losing weight can be traced directly to overstimulation of the gonads on the one hand and the lack of support you give to your thyroid and pituitary glands on the other.

The best way to accomplish this is to cut out red meat, creamy foods, and fatty foods. While on your Basic Weight Loss Program do not eat any red meat *at all*. Even the lighter proteins found in chicken, fish, and eggs are reduced. All creamy, buttery dishes are also completely eliminated. For the necessary fat in your diet you are allowed a small amount of vegetable oil.

Eliminate Spices
(Herbs Are OK)

On the G-Type Weight Loss Program spices are eliminated in favor of nonstimulating herbs. Many popular diets urge dieters to spice up their foods, since spices add variety and have no calories. This is acceptable for other body types, but not for G-Types. The idea is to rest the sex glands, not to continue overstimulating them. Herbs such as dill, parsley, basil, tarragon, and thyme are fine. You can use a tiny bit of salt (see "Recipes for Gonadal Types"), but go easy.

Concentrate on Chicken, Fish, and Dairy Foods

For your protein requirements, eat plenty of chicken, fish, and light dairy products instead of red meat. Yogurt and cottage cheese are excellent foods for you, not only for their protein but for the stimulation they give to the pituitary gland. I also have given you a glass of nonfat milk at both lunch and dinner. The protein in the milk is light and nonstimulating to the gonads, but gives you enough staying power so you will not feel hungry in the afternoon or evening.

Take Carbohydrates in Moderation, Even a Little Caffeine

Your system benefits from a moderate intake of carbohydrates, partially from whole grains, partially from ordinary refined grains. Eat lots of fruit. Fruit is an excellent food for you; it provides natural stimulation to the thyroid gland.

You may have a small amount of caffeine (coffee or tea) as well, with a little sugar in the morning. Allowing even half a teaspoon of sugar is unusual for a diet, but in your case it is an effective part of the strategy of thyroid and pituitary stimulation.

G-Types as Vegetarians

A vegetarian diet can be very suitable for the G-Type metabolism. Since you generally lack a strong sweet tooth, you usually are not tempted by too many sweets. The pituitary and thyroid stimulation that a vegetarian diet provides can give a great degree of balance to your G-Type metabolism.

If you do choose to be vegetarian, you'll do best if you get your protein from eggs, legumes, tofu, and light dairy products. The G-Type Weight Loss Diet is a partially vegetarian diet anyway, having some meatless or dairy meals and some meals with lighter animal protein from poultry and fish. To adapt the diet to be fully vegetarian, simply make the nonmeat choices or substitute an equivalent quantity of tofu or legumes for the meat.

The Total Strategy

Summarizing your total dieting strategy: no red meat, a minimum of fats and oils, lots of fruit and fresh vegetables, plenty of light dairy products, a small amount of sugar and caffeine, a moderate amount of carbohydrates, mostly from whole grains, and no stimulating spices.

In addition to the lighter, less sluggish metabolism, the increased energy, and the smooth, fast weight loss, you will also be delighted with the lighter, more creative feeling you have inside—a direct result of creating more balance and harmony among your glands by enlivening your underactive thyroid and pituitary.

THE G-TYPE MEAL SCHEDULE

Eat Very Lightly in the Morning

Most important is that you start the day with a *very* light breakfast. What works for G-Types is to eat for breakfast only a small piece of fruit and a cup of coffee or tea (either regular tea or red clover tea).

Many successful, slender G-Types give credit to their light breakfasts for losing and keeping off their fat. If they start the day with a heavy meal, they eat all day long. Starting with a light breakfast keeps them light all day.

The gonads are more active at night than in the early hours of the day, which means that your metabolism handles food better later in the day than early.

Eat Lightly at Lunch

Your lunch is also fairly light, so that your body continues on a fat-burning metabolism throughout the afternoon. My patients tell me how well it works for them to stay with light food throughout the day. Not only is weight loss faster, they actually feel lighter and get more accomplished than if they burden themselves with a heavy meal at lunchtime.

Dinner Is Substantial

Your most substantial meal comes in the evening. This is not only most effective in terms of burning fat; it will also help you avoid snacking at night, a time when many G–Types respond to the increased activity of the dominant gland with what I call "sensual" eating (eating for sensual enjoyment, as opposed to eating for stimulation).

Observe the Intervals Between Meals

You *must* observe the intervals that I specify between meals. These are four hours between breakfast and lunch and five hours between lunch and dinner on the Basic Weight Loss Diet; and five hours between breakfast and lunch and six between lunch and dinner on the Last Five Pounds Diet. Even though the G–Type breakfast is very light, and lunch not very heavy, either, the intervals remain important. It is during these periods that the body burns fat.

Your Danger Periods

You have two danger periods for snacking: late morning and late evening. These are times when your metabolism is at a low ebb. The morning "low" is due to a lessening of thyroidal activity following the thyroid-stimulating breakfast, and the evening "low" relates to increased late-evening activity of the gonads, which produces an impulse toward sensual eating.

Your Best Snack

Despite your two danger periods, it is not physically necessary for you to eat anything at all at either of these times. Your thyroid gland has not been exhausted by overstimulation, and will revive after a short "low" in the morning without any intervention.

A G–Type patient once commented that she'd been very apt to snack in the late morning once she'd given up her former giant breakfasts. She was experiencing a momentary thyroidal lag. When she tried sitting down for ten minutes with a cup of red clover tea, instead of having a snack, she found that at the end of the ten minutes she felt good again, and the desire to snack had passed of its own accord.

If you absolutely must have a more substantial snack, take a small portion of fruit—for example, a few grapes or a couple of strawberries. They will stimulate your thyroid gently and get you through to the next meal. A small amount of fruit is also the snack of choice if you find yourself doing "sensual eating" late at night. If this is a pattern for you, you may save your dinner fruit and eat it instead later in the evening.

The G-Type Herbal Help:
Red Clover Tea

Red clover tea is a "must" for G-Type weight loss—it makes dieting not only much easier but much more efficient as well. Red clover is a tea that is traditionally used to ease menstrual problems, and your overstimulated and overtired gonads benefit tremendously from its restorative powers. You make it like this: Bring water to a full boil and add a teaspoon of red clover tops for every cup of tea you want. Allow to steep for five minutes, strain, and serve. If you can find red clover tea bags, you may find them easier to handle than loose tea. You may use a half-teaspoon of honey or sugar with your tea if you wish. Red clover tops are available in most health food stores.

Rules for G-Type Dieting

In the following pages are both general guidelines for G-Type dieting (a complete list of exactly what you are to eat for each meal, both for the Basic Weight Loss Diet and the Last Five Pounds Diet) and a week of sample menus for each of the diets. You may use the sample menus or substitute your own, as long as you use the same foods and follow the guidelines closely.

You may substitute freely *within the boundaries allowed for each meal,* but do not rearrange the food among meals, as the order and distribution is important. Poultry and fish should be broiled, grilled, or baked (see guidelines for each meal). Vegetables may be steamed, boiled in a small amount of water, or sautéed in the permitted vegetable oil only. Seasonal fruit may be substituted for the suggested fruit at any meal. Poultry should be eaten without skin. *Do not omit anything; every food is there for a reason.*

THE COMPLETE GONADAL-TYPE WEIGHT LOSS PROGRAM

Begin with one week of the Basic G-Type Weight Loss Diet. How long you follow it depends on how much weight you want to lose.

TO LOSE FIFTEEN POUNDS OR MORE:

Follow the Basic G-Type Weight Loss Diet for three weeks, and then the G-Type Last Five Pounds Diet for a week. Then go back to the G-Type Basic Weight Loss Diet, changing to the Last Five Pounds Diet every fourth week for as long as needed. When you are within five pounds of your ideal weight, change to the Last Five Pounds Diet and finish your weight loss with it.

TO LOSE FIVE TO FIFTEEN POUNDS:

Follow the G-Type Basic Weight Loss Diet for two weeks, then the G-Type Last Five Pounds Diet for a week (or less, if you reach your ideal weight before the end of the final week).

TO LOSE FIVE POUNDS OR LESS:

Follow the G-Type Basic Weight Loss Diet for one week, then the G-Type Last Five Pounds Diet for a week (or less).

WHEN YOU REACH YOUR IDEAL WEIGHT:

Change to the Health and Weight Maintenance Program for G-Types.

Dishes that are marked with a star are those for which a recipe is provided in Appendix 1.

THE G-TYPE WEIGHT LOSS DIET: GENERAL GUIDELINES

Breakfast

1 small piece of fruit—you may choose any available fruit, from apples, cherries, and peaches to mangos, kiwis, and star fruit. The quantity of fruit is 1 piece, or 1 cup of fruit like grapes or berries. To make the best fruit choice, look for fruits that are locally grown and in season. The more flavorful and fresh the fruit, the better it is for you.

Coffee, tea, or red clover tea (with a small amount of sugar or honey if desired)

WAIT FOUR HOURS

Lunch

A large green salad, with any combination you like of lettuce or other fresh greens (the darker the better), cucumber, mushrooms, celery, sprouts, radishes, bell pepper, tomato, and onion

1 teaspoon of any *clear* diet dressing (Note: not a creamy or spicy dressing—even a "reduced fat" blue cheese or ranch will be too stimulating to your dominant gland)

1/2 cup of a cooked sweet vegetable such as beets, carrots, pumpkin, squash, or turnip

A choice of 1 egg (boiled, poached, or scrambled) OR a small serving of low-fat dairy (3 ounces of low-fat firm cheese such as reduced-fat mozzarella or string cheese OR 1 1/2 cups of nonfat yogurt OR 1 cup of low-fat or nonfat cottage cheese)

1 serving of grain—your choice of a slice of whole-grain bread (rye bread is particularly recommended) OR 1/2 cup of cooked grain such as brown rice or bulgur wheat OR 1/2 cup of pasta

1 glass of skim milk

1 piece of fruit, from the same choices as offered at breakfast

Coffee, tea, or red clover tea (with a small amount of sugar or honey if desired)

WAIT FIVE HOURS

Dinner

Your choice of 4 ounces of white meat poultry or fish OR 2 eggs (boiled, poached, scrambled, or fried in 1 teaspoon of vegetable oil). Do not choose the eggs if you had an egg for lunch, and don't choose the eggs for dinner more than twice a week.
1 teaspoon of vegetable oil (you may use it in preparation of your poultry or fish, on your vegetables, or to cook your eggs)
Steamed vegetables, your choice, as much as you like
A serving of grain, your choice, whole or refined (but give preference to whole grains such as brown rice, whole wheat, or whole-grain pasta). As at lunch, a serving is $^1/_2$ cup.
1 piece of fruit, from the same choices as breakfast
1 glass of skim milk
Red clover tea (with a small amount of sugar or honey if desired)

THE G-TYPE WEIGHT LOSS DIET: A WEEK OF SAMPLE MENUS

Monday

BREAKFAST:
1 large nectarine (or other fruit in season)
Coffee, tea, or red clover tea (sugar or honey if desired)

LUNCH:
Large green salad with clear diet dressing★
$1^1/_2$ cups of plain yogurt
1 slice of rye toast
1 plum (or other fruit in season)
1 glass of skim milk
Hot tea (sugar or honey if desired)

DINNER:
Stir-Fried Chicken★ (or substitute your own chicken recipe, as long as the chicken is cooked without skin and without additional fat or oil)
$^1/_2$ cup of brown or white rice

Cucumber salad dressed with 1 tablespoon of yogurt
1 glass of skim milk
1 peach (or other fruit in season)
Red clover tea (sugar or honey if desired)

Tuesday

BREAKFAST:
1 mango (or other fruit in season)
Coffee, tea, or red clover tea (sugar or honey if desired)

LUNCH:
Large green salad with clear diet dressing*
1 hard-boiled egg
1 slice of whole-wheat toast
1 glass of skim milk
$^1/_2$ papaya (or other fruit in season)
Iced tea (regular or red clover, sugar or honey if desired)

DINNER:
4 ounces of Chicken Salad with Yogurt* (or use your own chicken
    recipe, prepared without skin or added oil)
Steamed spinach, as much as you like
2 pieces of rye Krispbread
1 cup of strawberries (or other fruit in season)
1 glass of skim milk
Red clover tea (sugar or honey if desired)

Wednesday

BREAKFAST:
2 red or black plums (or other fruit in season)
Coffee, tea, or red clover tea (sugar or honey if desired)

LUNCH:
3 ounces of low-fat string cheese
1 slice of whole-grain bread

Large green salad with clear diet dressing*
1 glass of skim milk
1 apple (or other fruit in season)
Coffee (sugar or honey if desired)

DINNER:

Greek-Style Eggs* (or use your own egg recipe, prepared with 1
    teaspoon of vegetable oil only)
Steamed zucchini and string beans
1 cup of green grapes (or other fruit in season)
1 glass of skim milk
Red clover tea (sugar or honey if desired)

Thursday

BREAKFAST:

1/2 banana (or other fruit in season)
Coffee, tea, or red clover tea (sugar or honey if desired)

LUNCH:

1 cup of low-fat cottage cheese
Large green salad with clear diet dressing*
2 pieces of rye Krispbread
1 mango (or other fruit in season)
1 glass of skim milk
Tea (regular or red clover, sugar or honey if desired)

DINNER:

Marinated Fish with Vegetables* (or use your own fish recipe, using
    no breading and 1 teaspoon of vegetable oil only)
1/2 cup coleslaw (made with cabbage and 1 tablespoon of diet may-
    onnaise)
1/2 cup of bulgur wheat*
1 cup of fresh cherries (or other fruit in season)
1 glass of skim milk
Red clover tea (sugar or honey if desired)

Friday

BREAKFAST:

2 apricots (or other fruit in season)
Coffee, tea, or red clover tea (sugar or honey if desired)

LUNCH:

1½ cups of yogurt
1 cup of strawberries (or other fruit in season)
Large green salad with clear diet dressing★
1 slice of rye toast
1 glass of skim milk
Tea (regular or red clover, sugar or honey if desired)

DINNER:

Lemon Chicken Kabobs★ (or use your own chicken recipe, prepared
    without skin or added oil)
½ cup of millet★
1 apple (or other fruit in season)
1 glass of skim milk
Red clover tea (sugar or honey if desired)

Saturday

BREAKFAST:

½ cantaloupe (or other fruit in season)
Coffee, tea, or red clover tea (sugar or honey if desired)

LUNCH:

1 hard-boiled egg
1 slice of whole-grain toast
Large green salad with clear diet dressing★
1 glass of skim milk
1 banana (or other fruit in season)
Tea (regular or red clover, sugar or honey if desired)

DINNER:

Salmon Steak Florentine★ (or use your own fish recipe, prepared
    without breading or additional oil)

$^{1}/_{2}$ cup of white or brown rice
1 pear (or other fruit in season)
1 glass of skim milk
Red clover tea (sugar or honey if desired)

Sunday

BREAKFAST:
1 cup of unsweetened applesauce (or other fruit in season)
Coffee, tea, or red clover tea (sugar or honey if desired)

LUNCH:
3 ounces of hard cheese
1 slice of rye toast
Large green salad with clear diet dressing*
2 tangerines (or other fruit in season)
1 glass of skim milk
Coffee (sugar or honey if desired)

DINNER:
Stir-Fried Fish Fillets* (or use your own fish recipe, prepared without breading or additional oil)
$^{1}/_{2}$ cup of bulgur wheat
2 fresh figs (or other fruit in season)
1 glass of skim milk
Red clover tea (sugar or honey if desired)

THE G-TYPE LAST
FIVE POUNDS DIET

Remember, do not begin this diet until you have followed the Basic G-Type Weight Loss Diet for *at least* a week. The sequence of diets (see page 82) is vital not only for losing weight, but for bringing your metabolism into balance so that you can stay at your ideal weight.

The G-Type Last Five Pounds Diet is a special diet. It is designed for breaking the "plateaus" that occur regularly in the course of losing weight, as well as for getting off the last five pounds that are particularly difficult to lose for everyone. It contains about 1,000 calories per day, 200 less than the G–Type Basic Weight Loss Diet. If you were to begin the Last Five Pounds Diet immediately, right at the start of your dieting program, you would undoubtedly feel quite hungry. However, since you have already followed the G–Type Basic Weight Loss Program for at least a week, your metabolism has been strengthened and brought into improved balance. A healthier and more balanced body is far less likely to experience excessive hunger while dieting.

Be aware that the interval between meals is longer on the Last Five Pounds Diet than on the Basic Weight Loss Diet. Again, the more balanced state of your metabolism will allow you to observe the longer interval comfortably.

The Last Five Pounds Diet is only to be followed for a week at a time. If, at the end of a week, you have not yet reached your ideal weight, change back to the G–Type Basic Weight Loss Diet for one, two, or three more weeks, as necessary, until you are within five pounds of your ideal weight. Use the Last Five Pounds Diet for these last, stubborn pounds. Then, when you are at your ideal weight, change to the G–Type Health and Weight Maintenance Program (see page 95 for the complete program).

The days you spend on the G–Type Last Five Pounds Diet are the most important days of your diet. These are the days when your body is most active in removing fat and, especially, cellulite. The loss of cellulite you will be experiencing indicates that your body is reaching a healthy state of equilibrium among the glands. Without this state of equilibrium, you always have the potential for becoming overweight again. The loss of cellulite tells you that your body is acquiring the ability to maintain itself at its ideal weight.

THE LAST FIVE POUNDS DIET: GENERAL GUIDELINES

Breakfast

One small piece of fruit—you may choose any available fruit, from apples, cherries, and peaches to mangos, kiwis, and star fruit. The

quantity of fruit is one piece, or a cup of fruit like grapes or
berries. To make the best fruit choice, look for fruits that are locally grown and in season. The more flavorful and fresh the fruit,
the better it is for you.

Coffee, tea, or red clover tea (with a small amount of sugar or honey
if desired)

WAIT FIVE HOURS

Lunch

3 ounces low-fat firm cheese (such as string cheese or low-fat mozzarella)

1 slice of whole-grain bread

1 teaspoon of vegetable oil or butter

1 piece of fruit (same choices as breakfast)

G-Type Vegetable Soup,* as much as you like

Red clover tea (with 1/2 teaspoon of sugar or honey, if desired)

WAIT SIX HOURS

Dinner

Your choice of 1 1/2 cups of plain yogurt OR 4 ounces of low-fat
cheese OR 2 eggs OR 1 egg and 2 ounces of low-fat cheese

G-Type Vegetable Soup,* as much as you like

1 teaspoon of vegetable oil or butter (you may cook your egg in this,
or use it on your bread or rice)

1/2 cup of brown or white rice or 1 slice of whole-grain bread

1 piece of fruit (same choices as breakfast)

Red clover tea (with 1/2 teaspoon of sugar or honey, if desired)

THE G-TYPE LAST FIVE POUNDS DIET: A WEEK OF SAMPLE MENUS

Monday

BREAKFAST:
Your choice of fruit—1 small piece
Coffee, tea, or red clover tea (sugar or honey if desired)

LUNCH:
G-Type Vegetable Soup★ (as much as you like)
1 slice of whole-grain bread
1 teaspoon of butter
3 ounces of mozzarella cheese
Your choice of fruit
Red clover tea (sugar or honey if desired)

DINNER:
1½ cups of yogurt
G-Type Vegetable Soup★ (as much as you like)
½ cup of brown rice
1 teaspoon of olive oil
Your choice of fruit
Red clover tea (sugar or honey if desired)

Tuesday

BREAKFAST:
Your choice of fruit
Coffee, tea, or red clover tea (sugar or honey if desired)

LUNCH:
G-Type Vegetable Soup★ (as much as you like)
1 slice of whole-grain bread
1 teaspoon of butter
3 ounces of string cheese
Your choice of fruit
Red clover tea (sugar or honey if desired)

DINNER:
Eggs Mornay★
G-Type Vegetable Soup★ (as much as you like)
1 slice of whole-grain bread
1 teaspoon of butter
Your choice of fruit
Red clover tea (sugar or honey if desired)

Wednesday

BREAKFAST:
Your choice of fruit
Coffee, tea, or red clover tea (sugar or honey if desired)

LUNCH:
G-Type Vegetable Soup★ (as much as you like)
1 slice of whole-grain bread
1 teaspoon of butter
3 ounces of string cheese
Your choice of fruit
Red clover tea (sugar or honey if desired)

DINNER:
Herb Omelette★
G-Type Vegetable Soup★ (as much as you like)
1/2 cup of polenta
1 teaspoon of olive oil
Your choice of fruit
Red clover tea (sugar or honey if desired)

Thursday

BREAKFAST:
Your choice of fruit
Coffee, tea, or red clover tea (sugar or honey if desired)

LUNCH:
G-Type Vegetable Soup★ (as much as you like)
1 slice of whole-grain bread
1 teaspoon of butter
1 cup of cottage cheese
Your choice of fruit
Red clover tea (sugar or honey if desired)

DINNER:
1¹/₂ cups of plain yogurt
G-Type Vegetable Soup★ (as much as you like)
1 slice of whole-grain bread
1 teaspoon of olive oil
Your choice of fruit
Red clover tea (sugar or honey if desired)

Friday

BREAKFAST:
Your choice of fruit
Coffee, tea, or red clover tea (sugar or honey if desired)

LUNCH:
G-Type Vegetable Soup★ (as much as you like)
1 slice of whole-grain bread
1 teaspoon of butter
3 ounces of low-fat string cheese
Your choice of fruit
Red clover tea (sugar or honey if desired)

DINNER:
2 poached eggs
G-Type Vegetable Soup★ (as much as you like)
¹/₂ cup of millet
1 teaspoon of butter
Your choice of fruit
Red clover tea (sugar or honey if desired)

Saturday

BREAKFAST:
Your choice of fruit
Coffee, tea, or red clover tea (sugar or honey if desired)

LUNCH:
G-Type Vegetable Soup★ (as much as you like)
1 slice of whole-grain bread
1 teaspoon of butter
3 ounces of mozzarella cheese
Your choice of fruit
Red clover tea (sugar or honey if desired)

DINNER:
Whole-wheat spaghetti topped with 2 ounces of Parmesan cheese★
G-Type Vegetable Soup★ (as much as you like)
Your choice of fruit
Red clover tea (sugar or honey if desired)

Sunday

BREAKFAST:
Your choice of fruit
Coffee, tea, or red clover tea (sugar or honey if desired)

LUNCH:
G-Type Vegetable Soup★ (as much as you like)
1 slice of whole-grain bread
1 teaspoon of butter
3 ounces of low-fat string cheese
Your choice of fruit
Red clover tea (sugar or honey if desired)

DINNER:
1¹/₂ cups of plain yogurt
G-Type Vegetable Soup★ (as much as you like)
¹/₂ cup of rice

1 teaspoon of butter
Your choice of fruit
Red clover tea (sugar or honey if desired)

THE G-TYPE HEALTH AND WEIGHT MAINTENANCE PROGRAM

The surest formula for keeping the ideal weight you've achieved through your Gonadal Type Weight Loss Program is to have a continuing awareness of your body type and its special needs. Your G-Type Diet has brought about a state of balance in your metabolism; the G-Type Health and Weight Maintenance Program is designed to make it easy for you to *maintain* that balance, and to keep your ideal weight.

"Plenty," "Moderation," and "Rarely" Foods and the G-Type Food Pyramid

To make it as easy as possible for you to keep your body type requirements in mind, your program includes a *short, simple set* of guidelines for you as a G-Type. You need only remember 1) your Plenty foods (foods you can always eat, which will always be good for you); 2) your Moderation foods (foods you can eat as long as you don't overdo them); and 3) your Rarely foods (ones you should save for special occasions only, because eating them will tend to revive your old cravings and make it harder for you to keep to your guidelines).

Continue to use your herbal tea and your vegetable soup. They will continue to strengthen your metabolism and are the best possible means for you to maintain the healthy balance you have achieved.

To help you internalize your Plenty, Moderation, and Rarely foods, I have arranged them into a Food Pyramid. The Plenty foods are on the bottom—they create a solid foundation for your continued balance. Moderation foods appear next; these are foods that are balancing for you in moderation but that have the *potential* to become overstimulating or unbalancing unless you keep half an eye on them. Finally, the Rarely foods are at the top of the pyramid. No food is absolutely forbidden; but if you eat these foods often they can certainly make your life harder for you by reviving your cravings.

Patients often ask me about the right quantities of the Plenty, Moderation, and Rarely foods. My advice to them, and to you, is that by the time you have become balanced through your Body Type Program, *you* are a much better judge of quantities than I am. Consult yourself, your feelings, your energy level, your emotional stability. Check your cravings (any food that revives your cravings should come under suspicion that you are eating too much of it). Finally, adjust your own quantities yourself. The ability to do this is very much a part of being balanced.

If You Forget the Guidelines and Gain Weight

If you stay with your guidelines you will not find yourself putting on weight. But if you let your guidelines go for a while (for instance, during a holiday season or on a vacation) and you find yourself three to five pounds above your ideal weight, then go back to your original G-Type Weight Loss Program. With five extra pounds, you will need only a week of the G-Type Basic Weight Loss Diet and a weekend of the G-Type Last Five Pounds Diet to be right back at your perfect weight. It'll be all but painless, since you'll have going for you the fundamentally balanced, healthy state that you achieved on the Body Type Program.

THE G-TYPE HEALTH AND WEIGHT MAINTENANCE PROGRAM: GENERAL GUIDELINES

1. YOUR PLENTY FOODS:

Fruit
Vegetables
Legumes

Whole grains
Yogurt
Cottage cheese
Skim milk
Red clover tea

2. YOUR MODERATION FOODS:

Poultry
Fish
Eggs
Light cheese
Vegetable oils
Light desserts
Coffee or tea

3. YOUR RARELY FOODS:

Red meat
Spices
Sour cream
Ice cream
Cream
Butter
Rich desserts

4. YOUR IDEAL EATING SCHEDULE:

A very light breakfast
A light lunch: salad and a sandwich
Your main meal at night
Watch out for evening and late-morning snacking!

Breakfast

A large piece of fruit and $^1/_2$ cup of plain yogurt OR 1 cup of whole-grain cereal with skim milk

Coffee, tea, or red clover tea (with a small amount of sugar if you wish)

Lunch

A large green salad with your favorite vegetables, and just a little olive oil dressing
A serving of low-fat cottage cheese or hard cheese
2 slices of whole-grain bread OR 1 cup of brown rice OR 1 cup of bulgur wheat OR 1 cup of millet
A glass of skim milk
A piece of fruit
Coffee, tea, or red clover tea (with a small amount of sugar if you wish)

Dinner

A serving of fish or poultry OR 2 eggs. Eat meat once a week or less. Avoid pork and "variety meats" (salami, cold cuts, organ meats, poultry "rolls")
A serving of grain. I recommend whole grain, but you can have refined grains up to 3 times a week if you wish
Vegetables, cooked or raw, as much as you like
A glass of skim milk
A piece of fruit or a small, light dessert—but in general, avoid creamy desserts and whipped cream
Coffee, tea, or red clover tea (with a small amount of sugar if you wish)

SPECIAL NOTE:
G-TYPES AND MENOPAUSE

Uniquely, your body type is not set for life, because your dominant glands, the ovaries, wind down at menopause and in time no longer dominate your metabolism. So, unlike Thyroid, Pituitary, and

Gonadal Type Pyramid

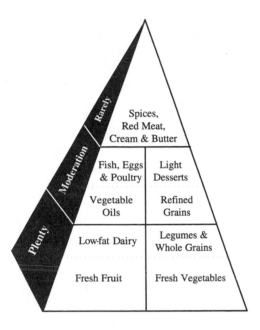

Adrenal Types, who have the same body type always, you will eventually no longer be a Gonadal Type. Your system will come to be dominated by your *next most active gland,* or secondary gland.

However, you won't be exactly like a person whose dominant gland has always been that one. If your secondary gland is your thyroid, and it begins to dominate your system at some point after menopause, you will nevertheless not look, feel, or function exactly like someone who has always been a Thyroid Type. Your body structure was formed under the dominant influence of your ovaries, and although your fat location will shift somewhat, it will never shift entirely away from the G-Type location (rear end and saddlebags). Your system will become more like a T-Type's (less steady, more subject to fatigue and sweets cravings) but it will not entirely lose its G-Type steadiness. You will acquire some features of your new dominant gland but will not entirely lose your G-Type characteristics.

So it is not really right to call you a Thyroid Type; more correctly you will be a "postmenopausal G, now T." Or, if your secondary gland was the pituitary or the adrenals, a "postmenopausal G, now P" or "now A."

In the 1983 edition, I stated categorically that as a G-Type woman, you would change to the body type of your secondary gland at menopause. I am now modifying that statement, based on the much larger number of women who are taking hormone replacement therapy (HRT) in various forms, from pills to creams.

The general effect of HRT is to keep your system functioning as a G-Type even after menopause. I have now been able to follow patients who have taken HRT for twenty years or more, and they have remained G-Types for much longer than they would have without it, sometimes even into their seventies. But even with hormones, your system will not remain G forever. Hormone replacement can't totally create the effect of fully functioning ovaries, and eventually, even with HRT, the secondary gland will become dominant.

Even without HRT, there are G-Type women who continue to be quite G even after menopause. The ovaries are not the only gland that produces estrogen. The adrenals also produce some estrogen, as do fat cells. A heavier G-Type woman whose secondary gland is the adrenals may well remain functionally G for some time after menopause.

The question, then, is *when*. When you reach menopause, how long will it take your system to change from G to your next dominant gland? How do you know when you've changed? This is a question that requires individual answers, not one I can answer categorically in a book. I wish I could; but it varies too much from woman to woman. A certified Body Type Counselor is your best resource if, after reading the next section carefully, you are not sure where in this process to find yourself.

The Postmenopausal G:
Implications for Diet

As you make the transition from G-Type to "postmenopausal G, now T, A, or P," you will also need to make the appropriate modifications to your diet. How exactly you modify depends, obviously, on your secondary gland. If your next most dominant gland is the thyroid or the pituitary, then your change in diet will be more drastic than if it is the adrenals. The A-Type and G-Type diets, especially the Health and Weight Maintenance Diets, are fairly close to one another, as these two types of metabolism are. But the T-Type and P-Type diets are quite different—the T program contains more protein, and the P program contains *much* more protein, than the G-Type.

Whichever your secondary gland, the change will be gradual. You will not wake up one morning and find yourself suddenly a T-Type; like menopause itself, the change of body type happens over a period of time. So should your change in diet. If you are changing to T-Type, do not suddenly start eating two eggs for breakfast. You may never need to go that far, in fact. Simply add a little more protein to each meal. Make the heavier protein choices rather than the lighter ones: Choose chicken or meat more often, rather than fish, legumes, or tofu. Have an egg for breakfast once or twice a week, and note how you feel.

As a general rule, let your cravings be your guide. If you are still mainly craving rich or spicy foods, then your system is still functioning in a Gonadal-Type manner. If you find yourself craving sweets more and more often, your system may be making a transition to a more thyroidal style of functioning, and your diet should follow the cravings.

THE ADRENAL BODY TYPE WEIGHT LOSS PROGRAM

The weight loss program you are about to learn is much more than a "diet." It's a whole new way of thinking about food, one that will ultimately put you in complete charge of your body—not just your weight but your energy level, your physical endurance, your mood, your health, and much more. It's called a "weight loss program" because reaching your best weight is the first step, and it's the one you're probably most interested in right now. But while you're working on that goal, the other benefits will be coming along, too, automatically, as part of the package.

As an A-Type, you have gained weight in the past by eating foods that stimulate your adrenal glands: fatty foods like meat and cheese, and salty foods like salted nuts and french fries. This is the origin of A-Type weight problems. The overstimulation of your adrenals has created a state of imbalance and given you an overactive appetite; the result is fat that has accumulated on your stomach and upper back.

The A-Type Diet uses a special strategy to reestablish balance in your system. What you will be doing is cutting back on adrenal-stimulating foods, and increasing foods that support and stimulate your pituitary and thyroid glands. You will accomplish this by cutting down on red meat, full-fat cheese, and salty foods—these are the adrenal-stimulating foods. Equally important, you must eat plenty of fresh vegetables, whole grains, fruit, light dairy products, and a small amount of caffeine and sugar—these are the foods that stimulate your pituitary and thyroid. You will meet your protein needs mainly from poultry and fish.

You'll enjoy, as a result, a lighter, more flexible metabolism; quicker weight loss than you've experienced in the past, once the energy-burning qualities of your thyroid gland kick in; and a greatly reduced appetite, since a large appetite is a result of overstimulated adrenals. Your fat and/or cellulite on your abdomen, back, and upper arms will come off, especially during the weeks on the Last Five Pounds Diet.

THE BASIC STRATEGY FOR A-TYPES

The strategy of reducing stimulation to your adrenal glands and increasing support and stimulation to your pituitary and thyroid glands is your special key to successful weight loss. Again, to rest the adrenals, you will need to cut back on red meat and on rich, salty foods like cheese. You'll be meeting your protein needs mainly with poultry and fish, along with legumes, light dairy products, or tofu. You have the option of eating a small portion of red meat two to three times a week, but you could eliminate it completely if you wish.

An A-Type patient once complained bitterly about the reduction in red meat. Apparently he didn't feel he'd eaten unless he'd had an enormous steak. But after just two weeks on the diet his opinion changed. He said that maybe he'd always like steak, but he didn't have to eat it every night. He felt so much better on his diet, and besides, he said, "chicken and fish are really good!" His tastes had changed as his balance increased—this is a common result and one you will appreciate.

Carbohydrates and Dairy Products Are Fine

While you are resting your adrenals, you will also be stimulating your thyroid with carbohydrates, and supporting your pituitary with an abundance of light dairy products—cottage cheese, yogurt, nonfat milk.

Your carbohydrates are divided between whole-grain and refined. You eat whole-grain carbohydrates at breakfast and most lunches, but at dinner and a few lunches you may eat a small amount of refined grains such as white flour and white rice. Unlike Thyroid and Pituitary Types, you don't usually have a problem with carbohydrate cravings, which is why you can eat refined grains occasionally. If you prefer whole grains the entire time, that's fine.

My A-Type patients are often surprised to find that I also allow a small, very light dessert twice a week. This is unusual on a diet but, in your case, beneficial. Your metabolism is helped by the thyroidal stimulation that desserts afford.

Caffeine—OK for You

Caffeine, which is practically a "street drug" to the Thyroid Type, for you is beneficial in moderation. By stimulating your thyroid it adds "swirls and eddies" to the steady flow of the A-Type metabolism. There is not much danger of your drinking too much caffeine, since it doesn't correspond to your innate cravings structure.

Eat Plenty of Vegetables

Your eating plan includes an abundance of vegetables, both cooked and raw. This may be a bit of a change for you—some A-Types are strictly "meat and potatoes" types, especially A-Type men. A-Type women may also be meat-and-potatoes eaters, or they may be constant cheese-munchers—the effect on the adrenals is not so different, as both meat and cheese are adrenal stimulators. If this is you, you'll need to make a real plan not just to eat but to learn to *enjoy* vegetables. Use your gourmet instincts to find the tastiest, freshest tomatoes, squash, baby carrots, sugar snap peas, or whatever, until you realize how really delicious vegetables are.

As a matter of fact, a vegetarian diet is very suitable for your type of metabolism, although it is not *necessary* for you to be a vegetarian if you don't wish to be. You must be careful to get enough protein from milk and low-fat cheese, but as long as you do this you can prosper on a vegetarian diet indefinitely.

The Total Strategy

To summarize your diet strategy: much less red meat and full-fat cheese; plenty of fresh vegetables, whole grains, and fruit; protein mainly from poultry and fish; lots of light dairy products; a small amount of caffeine and sugar.

In addition to the reduced appetite, the lighter metabolism, the increased energy, and the smooth, fast weight loss, you'll find that you'll feel more creative and thoughtful—an interesting side effect of the thyroid and pituitary stimulation of the A-Type Diet.

THE A-TYPE MEAL SCHEDULE

Eat a Light Breakfast

The key to your food timing is to eat a light breakfast. A-Types are usually of the eggs-bacon-and-buttered-toast school, but this is the wrong way for someone with your type of metabolism to start the day. Cereal or dairy products start your day with mild thyroidal or pituitary stimulation, a much better strategy for you.

The adrenal glands become more and more active as the day progresses, with the afternoon and evening being their most active time. As they become more active, your appetite increases. It's extremely important that you avoid stimulating them first thing in the morning, or you will be ravenously hungry all day.

Keep It Light at Lunchtime

Lunch should also be light: salad or cooked vegetables, dairy products or fish, and fruit. This will help keep your appetite under control later on; the longer you can wait for your main meal, the easier dieting will be.

Dinner Is Your Main Meal

Your main meal comes at night, when your adrenals can handle it, though even dinner is not very heavy: poultry, fish, or legumes; vegetables and fruit.

Observe the Interval Between Meals

You must be sure to keep to the full interval between meals: four hours between breakfast and lunch and six hours between lunch and dinner on the Weight Loss Diet; five hours between breakfast and lunch and six hours between lunch and dinner on the Last Five Pounds Diet. It is during these hours that your body burns fat and rebalances itself metabolically. If you eat again too soon after a meal, you waste most of your dieting effort.

Losing weight, we now know, is not a simple matter of reducing calories, although that is obviously one basic ingredient. Losing weight means metabolizing fat, and you must give your body a chance to do it!

Your Danger Periods

Your danger period for snacking is late afternoon, because this is a period of tiredness after the workday that happens to correspond with the beginning of the adrenal glands' more active period. The combination of tiredness (which makes you want to increase your energy by stimulating your dominant gland) and increased appetite means that you experience a double danger period.

One A-Type patient who was just starting on the A-Type Diet told me that he can go without breakfast and lunch without difficulty, but that when five o'clock comes around he finds himself snacking on all kinds of adrenal-stimulators—his favorites being peanuts, salami, and Roquefort cheese—throughout the "cocktail hour." This is not uncommon. A-Types are also inclined to drink then; with their great energy, they seem to be particularly attracted to the relaxation provided by alcohol. Combine the two habits and you have a downfall period indeed.

Your Best Snack Is No Snack at All

The fact that your adrenals are actually increasing in activity as the day progresses means that you should not, technically, have to snack at all. Your adrenals don't have a "lag" period the way the thyroid does, so your energy remains strong and steady throughout the day. All you really have to do if you have the desire for a snack is to wait, and drink mineral water or parsley tea. Or you can have a serving of your A-Type Vegetable Soup.

If you absolutely must have a snack other than your soup, the best thing to do is to have half a carton of yogurt or half a glass of skim milk. By giving this stimulation to your pituitary and skipping a salty snack, you can also avoid another temptation for your body type, the desire to have an alcoholic drink.

The A-Type Herbal Help: Parsley Tea

The herbal tea that does the most for you is parsley tea. It has a refreshing, astringent quality that will satisfy your desire for a savory taste; this is in addition to its purifying effect on the adrenal glands. It is also mildly diuretic.

It is paradoxical that you A-Types, who are known for your hearty appetites, are very good dieters once you get started. The reason is the basic strength of the Adrenal-Type metabolism. It is quite rare for you to be overwhelmed by cravings, because your adrenals give you so much energy. But, of course, no one is completely immune from cravings, so if it should happen that you do get a strong desire to eat something salty and fattening, a cup of parsley tea will get you over it in no time.

Parsley tea is made by adding a teaspoon of dried (not fresh) parsley leaves to boiling water for each cup of tea you want. Allow to steep for five minutes but do not boil the leaves. Strain and serve. You may add a half-teaspoon of sugar or honey to this tea if you wish.

Rules for A-Type Dieting

In the following pages are general guidelines for A-Types (a complete list of exactly what you are to eat for each meal on the A-Type

Weight Loss Diet and the A–Type Last Five Pounds Diet), along with a week of sample menus for each of these diets. You may use these menus or substitute your own, as long as you use the same foods and follow the guidelines closely.

You may substitute freely *within the boundaries allowed for each meal,* but do not rearrange the food among the meals, as the order and distribution are important. Meat, poultry, and fish should be boiled, grilled or barbecued, or baked, with all visible fat removed (see the guidelines for each meal). Vegetables may be steamed, boiled in a small amount of water, broiled with a small amount of oil, or sautéed in the permitted vegetable oil only. Poultry is to be eaten without skin. Seasonal fruit may be substituted for the suggested fruit at any meal. *Do not omit anything; every food is there for a reason.*

THE COMPLETE ADRENAL-TYPE WEIGHT LOSS PROGRAM

Begin with the A–Type Weight Loss Diet. What happens after that depends on how much weight you want and need to lose.

TO LOSE MORE THAN FIFTEEN POUNDS:
Follow the A–Type Weight Loss Diet for three weeks, then change to the A–Type Last Five Pounds Diet for a week. Then go back to the Basic A–Type Weight Loss Diet, continuing to change to the Last Five Pounds Diet every fourth week. Once you are within five pounds of your ideal weight, use the Last Five Pounds Diet to lose these last stubborn pounds.

TO LOSE FIVE TO FIFTEEN POUNDS:
Follow the Basic A–Type Weight Loss Diet for two weeks, then change to the A–Type Last Five Pounds Diet for a week (or less, if you reach your ideal weight before the week is done).

TO LOSE FIVE POUNDS OR LESS:
Follow the Basic A–Type Weight Loss Diet for one week and go to the A–Type Last Five Pounds Diet for a week (or less).

WHEN YOU REACH YOUR IDEAL WEIGHT:
Change to the A–Type Health and Weight Maintenance Diet.

Dishes that are marked with a star are those for which a recipe is provided in Appendix 2.

THE A-TYPE WEIGHT LOSS DIET: GENERAL GUIDELINES

Breakfast

Your choice of 1 cup of yogurt OR ¹/₂ cup of low-fat cottage cheese OR 1 cup of whole-grain cereal with ¹/₂ cup of skim milk

Coffee, tea, or parsley tea (with a small amount of sugar or honey if desired)

WAIT FOUR HOURS

Lunch

A large green salad made with any combination you like of lettuce or other fresh greens (the darker the better), cucumber, mushrooms, celery, sprouts, radishes, bell pepper, tomato, or onion

1 tablespoon of any *clear* diet dressing (Note: not a creamy dressing—even a "reduced fat" blue cheese or ranch will be too stimulating to your adrenals) or 1 teaspoon of olive or canola oil

¹/₂ cup of a cooked sweet vegetable such as beets, carrots, pumpkin, squash, or turnip

Your choice of 1¹/₂ cups of plain yogurt OR 1 cup of low-fat cottage cheese OR 3 ounces of low-fat firm cheese (such as mozzarella or string cheese) OR 3 ounces of fish (but not shellfish)

1 small piece of fruit—you may choose any available fruit, from apples, cherries, and peaches to mangos, kiwis, and star fruit. The quantity of fruit is 1 piece, or 1 cup of fruit like grapes or berries. To make the best fruit choice, look for fruits that are locally grown and in season. The more flavorful and fresh the fruit, the better it is for you.

1 serving of grain—your choice of a slice of whole-grain bread (rye bread is particularly recommended) OR ¹/₂ cup of cooked grain such as brown rice or bulgur wheat OR ¹/₂ cup of pasta.

Coffee, tea, or parsley tea (with a small amount of sugar or honey if
    desired)
WAIT SIX HOURS

Dinner

Your choice of 4 ounces of white meat poultry, fish, meat OR 2
    eggs OR ³/₄ cup of legumes (have the eggs no more than twice
    a week and the meat no more than three times a week)
A serving of grain, your choice, whole or refined (but give prefer-
    ence to whole grains such as brown rice, whole wheat, or
    whole-grain pasta). As at lunch, a serving is ¹/₂ cup.
Steamed vegetables, your choice, as much as you like
2 teaspoons of vegetable oil (you may use it in preparation of the
    poultry, fish, or eggs, or on the vegetables)
1 glass of skim milk
Choice of the same fruits as for lunch OR 2 Chocolate Cookies★
    OR Fruit Ice★
Parsley tea (with a small amount of sugar or honey if desired)

THE A-TYPE WEIGHT LOSS DIET: A WEEK OF SAMPLE MENUS

Monday

BREAKFAST:
1 cup of plain yogurt
Coffee or tea (with 1 teaspoon of sugar if desired)

LUNCH:
A large green salad with clear diet dressing★
3 ounces of broiled fresh salmon, or 3 ounces water-packed canned
    salmon (salt rinsed out)
Steamed spinach
1 piece of rye Krispbread
1 peach
Coffee, tea, or parsley tea (with 1 teaspoon of sugar if desired)

DINNER:
Stir-Fried Flank Steak★ (or substitute your own recipe, using only 4 ounces of meat and any vegetables)
$^{1}/_{2}$ cup of white rice
1 piece of fruit
1 glass of skim milk
Parsley tea (with a teaspoon of sugar if desired)

Tuesday

BREAKFAST:
$^{1}/_{2}$ cup of low-fat cottage cheese
Coffee or tea (with a small amount of sugar or honey if desired)

LUNCH:
A large green salad with clear diet dressing★
$1^{1}/_{2}$ cups of plain yogurt with 1 cup of sliced strawberries
Steamed green beans
1 slice of whole-wheat bread
Coffee, tea, or parsley tea (with a small amount of sugar or honey if desired)

DINNER:
Red Snapper "Scallops"★ (or use your own fish recipe, as long as the fish isn't breaded and you use the permitted oil only)
Steamed fresh spinach
1 slice of French bread
$^{1}/_{2}$ cup of Fruit Ice★
1 glass of skim milk
Parsley tea (with 1 teaspoon of sugar if desired)

Wednesday

BREAKFAST:
1 cup of whole-grain cereal with $^{1}/_{2}$ cup of skim milk
Coffee or tea (with 1 teaspoon of sugar if desired)

LUNCH:

A large green salad with clear diet dressing★
3 ounces of water-packed tuna with celery and a tablespoon of low-
    fat mayonnaise
$1/2$ cup cooked sweet peas
1 slice of whole-grain bread
1 bunch of grapes (about a cup)
Coffee, tea, or parsley tea (with a small amount of sugar or honey if
    desired)

DINNER:

Chicken Burgers★ (or your own chicken recipe, as long as you use
    the permitted oil only, and remove the skin)
Steamed zucchini and string beans
$1/2$ cup of bulgur wheat★
1 glass of skim milk
1 piece of fruit
Parsley tea (with a small amount of sugar or honey if desired)

Thursday

BREAKFAST:

1 cup of plain yogurt
Coffee or tea (with a teaspoon of sugar if desired)

LUNCH:

A large green salad with clear diet dressing★
3 ounces of poached fish (or use your own fish recipe, preparing the
    fish without breading or added oil)
1 small baked or boiled potato
1 apple
Coffee, tea, or parsley tea (with a small amount of sugar or honey if
    desired)

DINNER:

Turkey Kabobs★ (or substitute your own turkey recipe, and do not
    eat the skin)
Coleslaw made with cabbage and a tablespoon of diet mayonnaise
    only

1 glass of skim milk
1 piece of rye Krispbread
Chocolate Cookies*
Parsley tea (with a teaspoon of sugar if desired)

Friday

BREAKFAST:
1/2 cup of low-fat cottage cheese
Coffee or tea (with a teaspoon of sugar if desired)

LUNCH:
A large green salad with clear diet dressing*
3 ounces of mozzarella cheese toasted on 1 slice of whole-grain
    bread
Steamed spinach
1 cup of fresh cherries
Iced tea or parsley tea (with a teaspoon of sugar if desired)

DINNER:
Chicken Vegetable Soup* (or use your own chicken recipe, using
    permitted oil only and omitting the skin)
A small matzoh ball or dumpling
1 piece of fruit
1 glass of skim milk
Parsley tea (with a teaspoon of sugar if desired)

Saturday

BREAKFAST:
1 cup of hot whole-grain cereal with 1/2 cup of skim milk
Coffee or tea (with a teaspoon of sugar if desired)

LUNCH:
A large green salad with clear diet dressing*
3 ounces of water-packed tuna
Steamed green beans

1 slice of French bread
$^1/_2$ cantaloupe
Coffee, tea, or parsley tea (with a small amount of sugar or honey if
    desired)

DINNER:
4 ounces broiled steak (or you may substitute poultry, fish, or
    legumes)
$^1/_2$ cup of bulgur wheat★
Steamed zucchini
1 glass of skim milk
1 piece of fruit
Parsley tea (with a teaspoon of sugar if desired)

Sunday

BREAKFAST:
1 cup of whole-grain cereal with $^1/_2$ cup of skim milk
Coffee or tea (with a teaspoon of sugar if desired)

LUNCH:
A large green salad with clear diet dressing★
3 ounces of Ceviche with Melon★ (or substitute your own fish
    recipe according to A-Type guidelines)
Steamed celery hearts
2 sesame crackers
Coffee, tea, or parsley tea (with a small amount of sugar or honey if
    desired)

DINNER:
Eggs Mornay★ (or substitute your own egg recipe or make a 2-egg
    omelette)
Spinach and mushroom salad
$^1/_2$ cup of Fruit Ice★
1 glass of skim milk
Parsley tea (with a teaspoon of sugar if desired)

THE A-TYPE LAST FIVE
POUNDS DIET

Remember, even if you have only five pounds of extra weight to lose, you should not begin the A-Type Last Five Pounds Diet until you have followed the A-Type Weight Loss Diet for *at least* a week. The sequence of diets (see page 108) is vital, not only for losing weight but in bringing about a balance in your metabolism.

The A-Type Last Five Pounds Diet is a very special diet. It is a rapid weight-loss diet, containing only about 1,000 calories per day, 200 calories less than the Weight Loss Diet. If you were to begin this diet immediately at the start of your dieting program, you would probably feel quite hungry. However, since you have followed the A-Type Basic Weight Loss Diet for at least a week, your metabolism has been strengthened and your balance improved. This means that you will not feel as hungry on your Last Five Pounds Diet as you otherwise would.

The Last Five Pounds Diet is only to be followed for a week at a time. If at the end of a week you are not at your ideal weight, change back to the A-Type Weight Loss Diet for one, two, or three weeks, depending on your remaining extra weight. You change to the A-Type Last Five Pounds Diet every fourth week, or whenever you are within five pounds of your ideal weight. Once you have reached your ideal weight, you are ready for the A-Type Health and Weight Maintenance Program (see page 120 for the complete program).

The days you spend on the Last Five Pounds Diet are the most important of your diet. These are the days when your body is most active in burning fat and in ridding itself of cellulite, the wrinkly fat that is the most difficult of all to lose. The loss of cellulite you will experience at this time indicates that your body is reaching a positive state of balance among the glands. Without this equilibrium, you always have the potential for becoming overweight again; but once you have it, you will be able to maintain your ideal weight with ease.

Note that the interval between meals is longer than on the Weight Loss Diet. Be sure to observe these intervals; they are a vital part of your success.

THE A-TYPE LAST FIVE POUNDS DIET: GENERAL GUIDELINES

Breakfast

1 cup of plain yogurt OR ½ cup of low-fat cottage cheese OR 1 cup of whole-grain cereal with ½ cup skim milk
Coffee, tea, or parsley tea (with a small amount of sugar or honey if desired)
WAIT FIVE HOURS

Lunch

A-Type Vegetable Soup,★ as much as you like
1 slice of whole-grain bread (without butter)
1 piece of your choice of fruit
Parsley tea (with a small amount of sugar or honey if desired)
WAIT SIX HOURS

Dinner

4 ounces of chicken, turkey, or fish OR 2 eggs (eggs twice a week only)
1 teaspoon of olive or canola oil
½ cup of whole grain (brown rice, whole wheat, whole-grain pasta) OR 1 slice of whole-grain bread
A-Type Vegetable Soup,★ as much as you like
Parsley tea (with a small amount of sugar or honey if desired)

THE A-TYPE LAST FIVE POUNDS DIET: A WEEK OF SAMPLE MENUS

Monday

BREAKFAST:
1 cup of plain yogurt

Coffee, tea, or parsley tea (with a small amount of sugar or honey if desired)

LUNCH:
A-Type Vegetable Soup★ (as much as you like)
1 slice of whole-grain bread
1 piece of fruit, your choice
Coffee, tea, or parsley tea (with a small amount of sugar or honey if desired)

DINNER:
Chicken Breast Piquant★
$^1/_2$ cup of rice
A-Type Vegetable Soup★
Parsley tea (with a small amount of sugar or honey if desired)

Tuesday

BREAKFAST:
$^1/_2$ cup of low-fat cottage cheese
Coffee, tea, or parsley tea (with a small amount of sugar or honey if desired)

LUNCH:
A-Type Vegetable Soup★ (as much as you like)
1 slice of whole-grain bread
1 piece of fruit, your choice
Coffee, tea, or parsley tea (with a small amount of sugar or honey if desired)

DINNER:
Turkey Kabobs★
$^1/_2$ cup of bulgur wheat★
A-Type Vegetable Soup★
Parsley tea (with a small amount of sugar or honey if desired)

Wednesday

BREAKFAST:
1 cup of whole-grain cereal with ½ cup of skim milk
Coffee, tea, or parsley tea (with a small amount of sugar or honey if
    desired)

LUNCH:
A-Type Vegetable Soup★ (as much as you like)
1 slice of whole-grain bread
1 piece of fruit, your choice
Coffee, tea, or parsley tea (with a small amount of sugar or honey if
    desired)

DINNER:
Seafood Veronique A-Type★
½ cup of millet★
A-Type Vegetable Soup★ (as much as you like)
Parsley tea (with a small amount of sugar or honey if desired)

Thursday

BREAKFAST:
1 cup of plain yogurt
Coffee, tea, or parsley tea (with a small amount of sugar or honey if
    desired)

LUNCH:
A-Type Vegetable Soup★ (as much as you like)
1 slice of whole-grain bread
1 piece of fruit, your choice
Coffee, tea, or parsley tea (with a small amount of sugar or honey if
    desired)

DINNER:
Chicken Burgers★
½ whole-wheat burger bun

A-Type Vegetable Soup★ (as much as you like)
Parsley tea (with a small amount of sugar or honey if desired)

Friday

BREAKFAST:
1 cup of low-fat cottage cheese
Coffee, tea, or parsley tea (with a small amount of sugar or honey if
   desired)

LUNCH:
A-Type Vegetable Soup★ (as much as you like)
1 slice of whole-grain bread
1 piece of fruit, your choice
Coffee, tea, or parsley tea (with a small amount of sugar or honey if
   desired)

DINNER:
Herb Omelette★ (see Appendix 1)
1/2 cup of rice
A-Type Vegetable Soup★ (as much as you like)
Parsley tea (with a small amount of sugar or honey if desired)

Saturday

BREAKFAST:
1 cup of whole-grain cereal with 1/2 cup of skim milk
Coffee, tea, or parsley tea (with a small amount of sugar or honey if
   desired)

LUNCH:
A-Type Vegetable Soup★ (as much as you like)
1 slice of whole-grain bread
1 piece of fruit, your choice
Coffee, tea, or parsley tea (with a small amount of sugar or honey if
   desired)

DINNER:
Sole Provençal★
¹/₂ cup of bulgur wheat★
A-Type Vegetable Soup★ (as much as you like)
Parsley tea (with a small amount of sugar or honey if desired)

Sunday

BREAKFAST:
1 cup of plain yogurt
Coffee, tea, or parsley tea (with a small amount of sugar or honey if
    desired)

LUNCH:
A-Type Vegetable Soup★ (as much as you like)
1 slice of whole-grain bread
1 piece of fruit, your choice
Coffee, tea, or parsley tea (with a small amount of sugar or honey if
    desired)

DINNER:
Lemon Chicken Kabobs★
¹/₂ cup of millet★
A-Type Vegetable Soup★ (as much as you like)
Coffee, tea, or parsley tea (with a small amount of sugar or honey if
    desired)

THE A-TYPE HEALTH AND WEIGHT MAINTENANCE PROGRAM

The surest formula for keeping the ideal weight you've achieved
through your Adrenal Type Weight Loss Program is to have a continuing awareness of your body type and its special needs. The
A-Type Diet has brought about a state of balance in your metabolism; the A-Type Health and Weight Maintenance Program is designed to make it easy for you to *maintain* that balance, and to keep
your ideal weight.

"Plenty," "Moderation," and "Rarely" Foods and the A-Type Food Pyramid

To make it as easy as possible for you to keep your body type requirements in mind, your program includes a *short, simple set* of guidelines for you as an A-Type. You need only remember 1) your Plenty foods (foods you can always eat, that will always be good for you); 2) your Moderation foods (foods you can eat as long as you don't overdo them); and 3) your Rarely foods (ones you should save for special occasions only, because eating them will tend to revive your old cravings and make it harder for you to keep to your guidelines).

Continue to use your herbal tea and your vegetable soup. They will continue to strengthen your metabolism, and are the best possible means for you to maintain the healthy balance you have achieved.

To help you internalize your Plenty, Moderation, and Rarely foods, I have arranged them into a Food Pyramid. The Plenty foods are on the bottom—they create a solid foundation for your continued balance. Moderation foods appear next; these are foods that are balancing for you in moderation but that have the *potential* to become overstimulating or unbalancing unless you keep half an eye on them. Finally, the Rarely foods are at the top of the pyramid. No food is absolutely forbidden; but if you eat these foods often they can certainly make your life harder for you by reviving your cravings.

Patients often ask me about the right quantities of the Plenty, Moderation, and Rarely foods. My advice to them, and to you, is that by the time you have become balanced through your Body Type Program, *you* are a much better judge of quantities than I am. Consult yourself, your feelings, your energy level, your emotional stability. Check your cravings (any food that revives your cravings should come under suspicion that you are eating too much of it). Finally, adjust your own quantities yourself. The ability to do this is very much a part of being balanced.

If You Forget the Guidelines and Gain Weight

If you stay with your guidelines you will not find yourself putting on weight. But if you let your guidelines go for a while (for example, on vacation) and find yourself three to five pounds above your ideal weight, then go back to the A-Type Weight Loss Program. With five extra pounds, you will need only a week of your A-Type Weight Loss Diet and a weekend of the A-Type Last Five Pounds Diet to be right back at your perfect weight.

THE A-TYPE HEALTH AND WEIGHT MAINTENANCE PROGRAM: GENERAL GUIDELINES

1. YOUR PLENTY FOODS:

Low- or nonfat dairy foods (yogurt, cottage cheese, part-skim moz-
zarella, string cheese)
Skim milk
Fruit
Vegetables
Whole grains
Legumes
Parsley tea

2. YOUR MODERATION FOODS:

Fish
Poultry
Eggs
Coffee or tea
Light desserts
Vegetable oils, especially olive and canola oils

3. YOUR RARELY FOODS:

Salty foods
Yellow or aged cheese
Red meat
Butter
Shellfish
Alcohol

4. YOUR IDEAL EATING SCHEDULE:

A light breakfast of dairy products and whole grains
A fairly light lunch, with only a small amount of protein
Your main meal at night

Breakfast

A serving of yogurt or cottage cheese OR a bowl of whole-grain
cereal with skim milk
Coffee, tea, or parsley tea (with a small amount of sugar or honey if
desired)

Lunch

A large green salad with all your favorite vegetables, and clear diet
dressing or olive oil and vinegar
A small serving of chicken, fish, or legumes. Lamb or shellfish may
be substituted once a week if you like
2 slices of whole-grain bread OR an equivalent serving of other
whole grain
A glass of skim milk
A piece of fruit
Coffee, tea, or parsley tea (with a small amount of sugar or honey if
desired)

Dinner

A serving of meat, fish, poultry, or legumes. Eat meat once or twice
weekly at the most. Ideally, have two or more meatless dinners
per week, using whole grains, eggs, legumes, or light dairy products
Vegetables, cooked or raw, as much as you like
A serving of grain, which should be whole-grain 4 times a week at
least
A piece of fruit or a light dessert such as Chocolate Cookies* or
Fruit Ice*

Coffee, tea, or parsley tea (with a small amount of sugar or honey if desired)

ADDITIONAL NOTES ON THE A-TYPE DIET

One of the most interesting developments since the first edition has been the continuing interest in the relationship among abdominal fat, the risk of heart disease, and diet. The research very much confirms the body type predictions that people with more abdominal fat are at higher risk for heart disease. Even more confirming are the studies that show that a diet which corresponds almost exactly to my Adrenal Type recommendations is the right one for reducing abdominal fat *and* for lowering the risk of heart disease.

Adrenal Type Pyramid

In October 1997, the Tufts University *Health & Nutrition Letter* stated:

> *"Fat around the waist, more than fat deposits elsewhere on the body, is associated with an increased risk for heart disease and diabetes and perhaps certain cancers as well. . . .*
>
> *The good news is that scientists are finding some clues about how to keep fat from creeping over the middle as decades pass. One piece of research suggests that tummies stay trimmer with* a diet high in vegetables rather than in meat.
>
> *Scientists with the American Cancer Society who followed almost 80,000 middle-aged people for 10 years found that those who ate at least 19 servings of vegetables a week were significantly less likely to gain weight at the waist than people who ate relatively little in the way of vegetables. Conversely, those who ate more than 3 servings of red meat each week appeared to be more likely to gain weight around the belt line.*
>
> *It's not clear why vegetables were linked to staving off fat accumulation around the belly. They may simply have been markers for healthful lifestyles overall,* or there may be some as yet unexplained mechanism for how they might influence body fat distribution."

A-Types, are you listening? This advice is completely right for you (you can take it just by following the A-Type Program). And the "unexplained mechanism" the scientists at the American Cancer Society are looking for is a clear understanding of how to create balance in each body type.

Another confirmation of body type ideas comes with the DASH Diet—a diet devised in a study that took place at six major medical centers around the country. DASH stands for Dietary Approaches to Stop Hypertension, and again, hypertension is much more common among A-Types than the other body types. By far, the best results in lowering hypertension were found when research subjects ate a low-fat, high-produce plan. Those subjects who started out with hypertension generally ended up with reductions in their blood pressure similar to those achieved with drug therapy. The DASH Diet corresponds very closely to the A-Type Diet, with a strong emphasis on grains, vegetables, fruits, and low-fat or nonfat dairy.

It is particularly gratifying that these diets are designed particularly for people with a particular risk factor, and that a marker that closely corresponds to body type (i.e., body shape/fat location) is being used to pinpoint the people who can most benefit from them. Ideally, I would like to see the complete body type concept used; it can provide even more insights to the right eating plan for all body types.

THE THYROID BODY TYPE
WEIGHT LOSS PROGRAM

The weight loss program you are about to learn is much more than a "diet." It's a whole new way of thinking about food, one that will ultimately put you completely in charge of your body—not just your weight but your energy level, your physical endurance, your mood, your health, and much more. It's called a "weight loss program" because reaching your best weight is the first step, and it's the one you're probably most interested in right now. But while you're working on that goal, the other benefits will be coming along, too, automatically, as part of the package.

As a T-Type, you have gained weight in the past by eating foods that overstimulate your thyroid: sweets such as candy and soft drinks, starches such as bread and pasta, and caffeine drinks, including coffee, tea, and cola. The overstimulation of your thyroid has led to a state of exhaustion and imbalance, and this in turn has led to the accumulation of fat and/or cellulite on your hips, thighs, and lower abdomen.

The T-Type Diet uses a special strategy to reestablish balance in your system. The technique is to cut back on thyroid-stimulating foods, and to increase foods that are supportive and stimulating to your adrenals and gonads. You accomplish this by cutting back on caffeine and on all refined carbohydrates (sugar, white flour, white rice, or other refined grains) and on fruit—these are the thyroid-stimulating foods. Equally important, you must eat eggs every day, get lots of protein from chicken, fish, and a moderate amount of red meat, have plenty of fresh vegetables, and eat just a small amount of carbohydrates from whole-grain sources.

As a result, you'll have steadier energy throughout the day. You'll be less nervous and irritable. Your fat will come off more quickly than you've ever imagined it could, and you'll enjoy a dramatic loss of your cellulite, especially during the Last Five Pounds phase of your diet.

THE BASIC STRATEGY
FOR T-TYPES

The key to weight loss for you as a Thyroid Type is to reverse your habit of overstimulating your thyroid gland. As long as your thyroid is in its present, overstimulated state, you will never lose weight and keep it off.

Thyroid Types have been the main victims of what I can only call the failure of the one-size-fits-all low-fat dieting prescription. The idea was good, the intentions were the finest; perhaps it was simply explained wrong. The fact is, the longer you T-Types have been told to watch fats and nothing else, the more you have lost energy, gained weight in your hips and thighs, and generally suffered the results of eating a diet that's wrong for your body type. All the "healthy" foods like pasta, cereal, and bagels, which you were told to fill up on freely, are so stimulating to your thyroid that the *real* goal—of creating balance in your system—has receded farther and farther while your weight has risen.

What is essential to reverse this process is that you cut out all *refined* carbohydrates: white flour, white sugar, white rice, pasta made with white flour, and indeed anything made with these ingredients. You cannot eliminate carbohydrates completely, for carbohydrates are an essential part of a healthy diet. But those you eat should be whole grains only: brown rice, whole wheat, rye, or millet. In this way you supply your body with the carbohydrates you need, while avoiding the overstimulation of refined carbohydrate products.

No Fruit for Now

You also do not eat fruit while dieting. Fruit is a "natural" or whole food, unlike refined sugar and flour, but it contains too much thyroid-stimulating simple sugar while you are resting your thyroid. Later, when you have lost your excess weight and restored your metabolic balance, you can put back into your diet a moderate amount of fruit (three or four pieces per week). But you never can go back to eating sugary sweets; for you they are truly a drug, not a food.

Eliminate Caffeine

The elimination of caffeine for the duration of your weight loss period is also very important. This means no coffee, tea, or cola—not even diet cola. Surprisingly, many soft drinks besides cola contain caffeine. Diet Mr. Pibb and Diet Dr Pepper are two sugar-free drinks that are very high in caffeine (check *Consumer Reports* for the breakdown). I am not in favor of diet soft drinks in general (artificial sweeteners, whatever else they may be, are certainly not food) but if you must drink them, Diet 7Up and Diet Sunkist Orange at least have the advantage of being caffeine-free. I would much prefer you drink uncarbonated mineral water or, best of all, water. These drinks are refreshing, natural, good for you, have no calories, and are much kinder to the thyroid gland.

A cup of decaffeinated coffee or tea is permitted with your breakfast. Do without it if you can. Even "decaffeinated" drinks contain some caffeine. If you have been drinking a great deal of caffeine for years, you may find that cutting it out suddenly gives you a headache. Caffeine is addictive and the headache is a withdrawal symptom. You will also feel the effects of withdrawing from thyroidal stimulation. If this happens, cut down gradually on your consumption, reducing it by a cup a day, until you are off caffeine entirely.

Eat Eggs Every Day

The second aspect of your strategy, after reducing overstimulation of the thyroid gland, is to create balance by building up your adrenals. The best way for you to do this is by eating eggs every day. Eggs supply a highly useful form of cholesterol that is used in the manufacture of adrenal hormones.

Start every day with two eggs for breakfast. My T–Type patients sometimes protest that they can't look at anything but coffee and toast in the morning. But the eggs are a vital part of your strategy, and after a week or two on eggs for breakfast I see the most striking transformations of my patients. The support given to the adrenals does absolute wonders.

T–Type men may be concerned about their cholesterol levels if they eat eggs every day. This is a controversial question on which all the evidence is not yet in, but the latest findings indicate that cholesterol in the diet has very little effect on blood cholesterol levels, particularly in people with the T–Type metabolism. You are much more likely to have high triglycerides due to your overconsumption of refined carbohydrates—this is the common T–Type pattern, and it responds very well to the T–Type Diet.

However, you should consult your physician and follow his or her advice. If you are advised to restrict your egg intake, then substitute four ounces of white poultry meat for each two-egg serving in your diet. But if you can, you should eat the eggs.

By the way, don't think you are eating eggs if you are eating egg whites. It's the yolk that contains the adrenal-supporting cholesterol, and that is what you need.

Eat Plenty of Poultry and Fish, Some Red Meat, Lots of Vegetables

Besides eggs, the best adrenal-strengthening foods for you are chicken and other poultry, and fish. These light animal proteins are nourishing to your adrenals, but do not stimulate them too much, as eating a great deal of red meat would do. If you eat small portions of red meat two or three times a week, that is plenty.

You need to eat an abundance of vegetables, both raw in salads and lightly cooked. The vegetables supply vitamins, vital trace minerals, and a feeling of fullness, so that you never feel deprived or "empty." When choosing between raw and cooked vegetables, you needn't feel that unless you have them raw in salads, you will not get the vitamins from them. Many vegetables actually give you their nutrients more readily when cooked than raw, because cooking breaks down the insoluble fiber and makes the nutrients more available.

Since many T-Types tend to be cold and to feel the cold more than other body types, they have told me they prefer cooked vegetables over salad. This is fine. If you wish, you may have all your vegetables cooked—just be sure to eat a lot of them! Especially since you don't eat fruit at the beginning, it's especially important that you eat an abundance of vegetables every day.

The Total Strategy

Your total dieting strategy, in summary, is: eggs every day, lots of protein from chicken and fish, a moderate amount of red meat, a small amount of carbohydrates from whole-grain sources, lots of fresh vegetables and salads, and no fruit.

In addition to feeling much steadier throughout the day, being less nervous and irritable, and enjoying the weight loss from your hips, thighs, and tummy, you should also experience a reduction in many small health problems—for example, you may find you get colds less frequently. This is a direct result of increased balance in your system, especially the increased strength and activity of your adrenal glands.

THE T-TYPE MEAL SCHEDULE

Eat Three Equal Meals a Day

The most important factor in T-Type timing is the necessity to steady your energy and reduce its up-and-down quality. This is done by distributing your caloric intake evenly among the three meals.

You may have been in the habit of skipping breakfast, or having only coffee and toast or a pastry, but this is a mistake. If you eat a thyroid–stimulating breakfast like this you'll be nervous and hungry by midmorning, will "need" another cup of coffee, a cola, or a sweet, and will be eating thyroid–stimulating foods all day. You need protein at every meal in order to avoid thyroid "lows," weakening of your energy, and sweet cravings.

Observe the Intervals Between Meals

You must be careful to observe the intervals I specify between meals. These are four hours between breakfast and lunch and six hours between lunch and dinner on the Basic T–Type Weight Loss Diet, and five hours between breakfast and lunch and six hours between lunch and dinner on the Last Five Pounds Diet. These are the intervals in which fat is burned. If you start eating too soon after eating the last meal, you will not get the full benefit of your Body Type Diet.

Your Danger Periods

The danger period for T–Type cravings is whenever the thyroid gland is low. Unfortunately, this can happen at any time. The key to knowing when it will be low is to realize that it will happen at definite intervals following stimulation of the gland with starches or caffeine.

Thyroid fatigue occurs in two waves. First there is a wave of tiredness (accompanied by the urge to snack) about an hour and a half after stimulation; then there is a second wave of fatigue three to four hours later.

Your Best Snack

Even though you are eating eggs for breakfast, having protein at lunch, and eliminating caffeine, all of which do a great deal to mitigate thyroidal fatigue, you may still find you have an urge to snack in the late afternoon, when the thyroid is naturally least active. This is the time to have, not a thyroid–stimulator, but half a hard–boiled egg or other protein snack. An ounce or two of chicken left over from dinner, or a piece of turkey jerky if you can find a healthy one, also works.

I always tell my T-Type patients to keep a protein snack handy all the time, so it's easier to have one than to take a cookie. Do this. It works. One of the most exhausted T-Types I ever met was a young woman who ate half a cookie whenever she wanted because "it was only a half and didn't really count." Actually, I'm a Thyroid Type myself and I do understand this. When I'm tired, I want something easy and I want it *now*. If the half an egg or the turkey jerky is handy and I have it, I feel so much better—you'll be amazed at the difference.

The T-Type Herbal Help: Raspberry Leaf Tea

Raspberry leaf tea will help you immeasurably on your Weight Loss Program. Drink as much of it as you like, but be sure to drink at least the amounts called for in your diet. If you have a cup at moments when you are experiencing cravings, you will find that your craving often vanishes, since the tea both soothes and strengthens your metabolism.

Make raspberry leaf tea like this: Bring water to a boil. Add the boiling water to a teaspoon of raspberry leaves for each cup of water. Allow to steep for five minutes, strain, and serve. Don't add any sugar or honey—they're thyroid-stimulators. In any case, the taste is pleasant. Raspberry leaves are available in most health food stores.

Rules for T-Type Dieting

In the following pages are both general guidelines for T-Type dieting (a complete list of exactly what you can eat for each meal, both for the Weight Loss Diet and the Last Five Pounds Diet) and a week of sample menus for each of the diets. You may use these menus or substitute your own, as long as you use the same foods and follow the guidelines closely.

You may substitute freely *within the boundaries allowed for each meal,* but do not rearrange the food among the meals, as the order and distribution are important. Meat, poultry, and fish should be boiled, grilled or barbecued, or baked, with all visible fat removed (see the guidelines for each meal). Vegetables may be steamed, boiled in a small amount of water, broiled with a small amount of oil, or sautéed in the permitted vegetable oil only. Poultry is to be eaten without skin. *Do not omit anything; every food is there for a reason.*

THE COMPLETE THYROID-TYPE WEIGHT LOSS PROGRAM

Your program begins with one week of the T-Type Weight Loss Diet. How long you follow it depends on how much weight you want to lose.

TO LOSE MORE THAN FIFTEEN POUNDS:
Follow the T-Type Weight Loss Diet for three weeks, then change to the T-Type Last Five Pounds Diet for a week. Then go back to the T-Type Weight Loss Diet, changing to the T-Type Last Five Pounds Diet every fourth week for as long as needed. Once you are within five pounds of your ideal weight, use the Last Five Pounds Diet and finish your weight loss program with it.

TO LOSE FIVE TO FIFTEEN POUNDS:
Follow the T-Type Weight Loss Diet for two weeks, then the T-Type Last Five Pounds Diet for a week (or less, if you reach your ideal weight before the end of the week).

TO LOSE FIVE POUNDS OR LESS:
Follow the T-Type Weight Loss Diet for one week and then the T-Type Last Five Pounds Diet for a week (or less).

WHEN YOU REACH YOUR IDEAL WEIGHT:
Begin the T-Type Health and Weight Maintenance Program.

Dishes marked with a star are those for which a recipe is provided in Appendix 3.

THE T-TYPE WEIGHT LOSS
DIET: GENERAL GUIDELINES

Breakfast

2 eggs, any style
1 teaspoon of butter, ghee, or vegetable oil (use either to cook the
    eggs, or on the toast)
1/2 slice of whole-grain bread or toast
1 cup only of decaffeinated coffee or tea, or raspberry leaf tea
WAIT FOUR HOURS

Lunch

Any combination of vegetables, cooked or raw—at least 1 cup total.
    You may make a salad of lettuce, cucumber, mushrooms, celery,
    sprouts, radishes, bell pepper, tomato, and onion, or have cooked
    vegetables such as green beans or zucchini, or a combination of
    salad and cooked vegetables.
1 teaspoon of any clear diet dressing (not creamy or spicy)
1 teaspoon of butter or 1 tablespoon of diet mayonnaise
Your choice of 4 ounces of poultry or fish
One serving of whole grain (one slice of whole-grain bread OR 1/2
    cup of cooked whole wheat, brown rice, kamut, amaranth, or
    quinoa)★
1 cup of skim milk
Raspberry leaf tea
WAIT SIX HOURS

Dinner

Your choice of 4 ounces of chicken, turkey, fish, lamb, beef, or or-
    gan meat (liver, kidneys, or heart)★ (Note: Have beef 2 or 3
    times a week only)
Raw or steamed vegetables, your choice, as much as you wish
One serving of whole grain (see lunchtime choices)

1 cup of skim milk
Raspberry leaf tea

THE T-TYPE WEIGHT LOSS DIET:
A WEEK OF SAMPLE MENUS

Monday

BREAKFAST:
2 scrambled eggs cooked in a teaspoon of vegetable oil
$^1/_2$ slice of whole-wheat toast
Decaffeinated coffee, 1 cup only, or raspberry leaf tea

LUNCH:
Any combination of vegetables, cooked or raw
Open-faced tuna salad sandwich made with 4 ounces of water-
    packed tuna and 1 tablespoon of diet mayonnaise, on 1 slice of
    whole-grain bread
1 glass of skim milk
Raspberry leaf tea

DINNER:
Mexican Stuffed Chicken* (or use your own chicken recipe, prepar-
    ing the chicken without skin and with 1 teaspoon of vegetable
    oil only)
$^1/_2$ cup of brown rice*
Cucumber salad dressed with 1 tablespoon of yogurt
1 glass of skim milk
Raspberry leaf tea

Tuesday

BREAKFAST:
2 poached eggs
$^1/_2$ slice of whole-grain toast with 1 teaspoon of butter
Decaffeinated tea, 1 cup only, or raspberry leaf tea

LUNCH:

Any combination of vegetables, cooked or raw
4 ounces of cooked chicken
1 teaspoon of butter or mayonnaise
$^1/_2$ of a whole-grain English muffin
1 glass of skim milk
Raspberry leaf tea

DINNER:

Baked Halibut Steak★ (or use your own fish recipe, prepared with-
    out breading or added oil)
Steamed spinach, as much as you like
$^1/_2$ cup of Kamut★
1 glass of skim milk
Raspberry leaf tea

Wednesday

BREAKFAST:

2 fried eggs, cooked in 1 teaspoon of vegetable oil
$^1/_2$ slice of seven-grain toast
Raspberry leaf tea

LUNCH:

4 ounces of salmon (fresh if available, canned if not)
1 slice of whole-grain bread with 1 teaspoon of butter or 1 table-
    spoon of diet mayonnaise
Any combination of vegetables, cooked or raw
1 glass of skim milk
Raspberry leaf tea

DINNER:

4 ounces of lean steak, broiled
Steamed zucchini and string beans
1 teaspoon of butter on the vegetables
1 small baked potato
1 glass of skim milk
Raspberry leaf tea

Thursday

BREAKFAST:
2 eggs, scrambled, cooked in 1 teaspoon of vegetable oil
1/2 slice of whole-wheat toast
Decaffeinated coffee, 1 cup only, or raspberry leaf tea

LUNCH:
4 ounces of sliced turkey
1 tablespoon of diet mayonnaise
Any combination of vegetables, cooked or raw
2 pieces of rye Krispbread
1 glass of skim milk
Raspberry leaf tea

DINNER:
Barbecued Tuna* (or use your own fish recipe, using no breading
    and 1 teaspoon of vegetable oil only)
Steamed carrots with parsley
1/2 cup of bulgur wheat*
1 glass of skim milk
Raspberry leaf tea

Friday

BREAKFAST:
2 hard-boiled eggs
1/2 slice of rye toast with 1 teaspoon of butter
Decaffeinated coffee or tea, 1 cup only, or raspberry leaf tea

LUNCH:
4 ounces of water-packed tuna
1 tablespoon of diet mayonnaise
Any combination of vegetables, cooked or raw
1 glass of skim milk
1 slice of rye toast
Raspberry leaf tea

DINNER:

Chicken Stew★ (or use your own chicken recipe, prepared without
skin or added oil)
1 whole-wheat roll
1 glass of skim milk
Raspberry leaf tea

Saturday

BREAKFAST:

2 poached eggs
$^{1}/_{2}$ whole-grain English muffin with 1 teaspoon of butter
Decaffeinated coffee, 1 cup only, or raspberry leaf tea

LUNCH:

Chef's Salad★
2 pieces of rye Krispbread
Any combination of vegetables, cooked or raw
1 glass of skim milk
Raspberry leaf tea

DINNER:

Sesame Shrimp with Asparagus★ (or use your own shrimp recipe,
using no breading and 1 teaspoon of vegetable oil only)
$^{1}/_{2}$ cup of brown rice★
Steamed green beans
1 glass of skim milk
Raspberry leaf tea

Sunday

BREAKFAST:

Herb Omelette★
$^{1}/_{2}$ slice of whole-grain bread
Decaffeinated coffee, 1 cup only, or raspberry leaf tea

LUNCH:
4 ounces of broiled chicken breast
1 slice of whole-grain bread with 1 teaspoon of butter
Any combination of vegetables, cooked or raw
1 glass of skim milk
Raspberry leaf tea

DINNER:
4 ounces of roast lamb
1 teaspoon of mint sauce (not mint jelly)
1 small baked potato with 1 teaspoon of butter
1 glass of skim milk
Raspberry leaf tea

THE T-TYPE LAST
FIVE POUNDS DIET

Remember, even if you have only five pounds of extra weight, you should not begin your T-Type Last Five Pounds Diet until you have followed the Basic T-Type Weight Loss Diet for a week. The sequence of diets (see page 135) is vital for balancing your metabolism, as well as producing fast, efficient loss of weight.

The T-Type Last Five Pounds Diet is a very special diet. It has just over 900 calories per day, about 300 calories per day less than the T-Type Weight Loss Diet; and the food you eat is especially programmed to get you off the periodic plateaus of dieting, as well as to assist you in losing the stubborn last five pounds of excess weight. If you were to begin this diet at the start of your program you would probably find it difficult. But since you have been on the T-Type Weight Loss Diet for at least a week, your metabolism is strengthened and in better balance, and you will be able to handle the Last Five Pounds Diet comfortably.

The Last Five Pounds Diet is only to be followed for a week at a time. If, at the end of a week, you have not reached your ideal weight, return to the T-Type Weight Loss Diet for one, two, or three weeks, depending on your situation; you may use the Last Five Pounds Diet every fourth week until you reach your weight goal.

And as you come within five pounds of your ideal weight, change to the Last Five Pounds Diet to lose that last bit of weight. Once you have reached your ideal weight, you are ready for the T-Type Health and Weight Maintenance Program (see page 145 for the complete program).

Note that the interval of time between meals has been increased on the Last Five Pounds Diet. Be sure to observe the full interval, as the hours between meals are the periods when your body is most active in burning fat.

THE T-TYPE LAST FIVE POUNDS DIET: GENERAL GUIDELINES

Breakfast

2 eggs, any style
1 teaspoon of vegetable oil
T-Type Vegetable Soup,★ as much as you like
Raspberry leaf tea
WAIT FIVE HOURS

Lunch

4 ounces of fish or shellfish
T-Type Vegetable Soup,★ as much as you like
Raspberry leaf tea
WAIT SIX HOURS

Dinner

Your choice of 4 ounces of poultry, fish, or shellfish
T-Type Vegetable Soup,★ as much as you like
Your choice of ½ cup of millet, brown rice, whole wheat, amaranth, kamut, or quinoa OR 1 slice of whole-grain bread
Raspberry leaf tea

THE T-TYPE LAST FIVE POUNDS DIET: A WEEK OF SAMPLE MENUS

Monday

BREAKFAST:
2 eggs, any style, cooked in 1 teaspoon of vegetable oil
T-Type Vegetable Soup★
Raspberry leaf tea

LUNCH:
T-Type Vegetable Soup★ (as much as you like)
4 ounces of water-packed tuna
Raspberry leaf tea

DINNER:
Chicken Breast Piquant★ (or use your own chicken recipe, preparing chicken without skin and with 1 teaspoon of vegetable oil)
T-Type Vegetable Soup★ (as much as you like)
¹/₂ cup of brown rice★
Raspberry leaf tea

Tuesday

BREAKFAST:
2 eggs, any style, cooked in 1 teaspoon of vegetable oil
T-Type Vegetable Soup★
Raspberry leaf tea

LUNCH:
T-Type Vegetable Soup★ (as much as you like)
4 ounces of fresh or canned salmon
Raspberry leaf tea

DINNER:
Turkey Kabobs★ (or use your own turkey recipe, preparing turkey without skin)
T-Type Vegetable Soup★ (as much as you like)

1 slice of whole-grain bread
Raspberry leaf tea

Wednesday

BREAKFAST:
2 eggs, any style, cooked in 1 teaspoon of vegetable oil
T-Type Vegetable Soup★
Raspberry leaf tea

LUNCH:
T-Type Vegetable Soup★ (as much as you like)
4 ounces of Broiled Shrimp with Lemon★ (see Appendix 4)
Raspberry leaf tea

DINNER:
Baked Halibut Steak★ (or use your own fish recipe, prepared with-
    out breading and with 1 teaspoon of vegetable oil)
T-Type Vegetable Soup★ (as much as you like)
1/2 cup of amaranth★
Raspberry leaf tea

Thursday

BREAKFAST:
2 eggs, any style, cooked in 1 teaspoon of vegetable oil
T-Type Vegetable Soup★
Raspberry leaf tea

LUNCH:
T-Type Vegetable Soup★ (as much as you like)
4 ounces of water-packed tuna
Raspberry leaf tea

DINNER:
Stir-Fried Chicken★ (or use your own chicken recipe)
T-Type Vegetable Soup★ (as much as you like)

$^{1}/_{2}$ cup of millet★
Raspberry leaf tea

Friday

BREAKFAST:
2 eggs, any style, cooked in 1 teaspoon of vegetable oil
T-Type Vegetable Soup★
Raspberry leaf tea

LUNCH:
T-Type Vegetable Soup★ (as much as you like)
4 ounces of broiled scallops
Raspberry leaf tea

DINNER:
Stir-Fried Flank Steak★ (see Appendix 2 or use your own beef
      recipe, using 4 ounces of beef and 1 teaspoon of vegetable oil)
T-Type Vegetable Soup★ (as much as you like)
$^{1}/_{2}$ cup of brown rice★
Raspberry leaf tea

Saturday

BREAKFAST:
2 eggs, any style, cooked in 1 teaspoon of vegetable oil
T-Type Vegetable Soup★
Raspberry leaf tea

LUNCH:
T-Type Vegetable Soup★ (as much as you like)
4 ounces water-packed canned shrimp
Raspberry leaf tea

DINNER:
Chicken Stew★ (or use your own chicken recipe, cooking chicken
      without skin)

T-Type Vegetable Soup★ (as much as you like)
½ cup of bulgur wheat★
Raspberry leaf tea

Sunday

BREAKFAST:
2 eggs, any style, cooked in 1 teaspoon of vegetable oil
T-Type Vegetable Soup★
Raspberry leaf tea

LUNCH:
T-Type Vegetable Soup★ (as much as you like)
Turkey patty made with 4 ounces of ground turkey
Raspberry leaf tea

DINNER:
Salmon Steak Florentine★ (or use your own fish recipe, using no
    breading and 1 teaspoon of vegetable oil only)
T-Type Vegetable Soup★ (as much as you like)
½ cup of millet★
Raspberry leaf tea

THE T-TYPE HEALTH AND WEIGHT MAINTENANCE PROGRAM

The formula for keeping the ideal weight you've achieved through your Body Type Diet is to have a continuing awareness of your body type and its special needs. Your T-Type Diet has brought about a state of balance in your metabolism; the T-Type Health and Weight Maintenance Program is designed to make it easy for you to maintain that balance, and to keep your ideal weight.

"Plenty," "Moderation," and "Rarely" Foods and the T-Type Food Pyramid

To make it as easy as possible for you to keep your body type requirements in mind, your program includes a *short, simple set* of guidelines for you as a T-Type. You need only remember 1) your Plenty foods (foods you can always eat, that will always be good for you); 2) your Moderation foods (foods you can eat as long as you don't overdo them), and 3) your Rarely foods (ones you should save for special occasions only, because eating them will tend to revive your old cravings and make it harder for you to keep to your guidelines).

Continue to use your herbal tea and your vegetable soup. They will continue to strengthen your metabolism and are the best possible means for you to maintain the healthy balance you have achieved.

To help you internalize your Plenty, Moderation, and Rarely foods, I have arranged them into a Food Pyramid. The Plenty foods are on the bottom—they create a solid foundation for your continued balance. Moderation foods appear next; these are foods that are balancing for you in moderation but that have the *potential* to become overstimulating or unbalancing unless you keep half an eye on them. Finally, the Rarely foods are at the top of the pyramid. No food is absolutely forbidden; but if you eat these foods often they can certainly make your life harder for you by reviving your cravings.

Patients often ask me about the right quantities of the Plenty, Moderation, and Rarely foods. My advice to them, and to you, is that by the time you have become balanced through your Body Type Program, *you* are a much better judge of quantities than I am. Consult yourself, your feelings, your energy level, your emotional stability. Check your cravings (any food that revives your cravings should come under suspicion that you are eating too much of it). Finally, adjust your own quantities yourself. The ability to do this is very much a part of being balanced.

If You Forget the Guidelines and Gain Weight

If you stay with your guidelines you will not find yourself overweight. But if you should let your guidelines go for any reason and you find yourself three to five pounds above your ideal weight, then go back to your original T-Type Weight Loss Program. With five extra pounds, you will need only a week of your T-Type Weight Loss Diet and a weekend of the T-Type Last Five Pounds Diet to be right back at your perfect weight.

THE T-TYPE HEALTH AND WEIGHT MAINTENANCE PROGRAM: GENERAL GUIDELINES

1. YOUR PLENTY FOODS:

Eggs
Low-fat dairy
Poultry: chicken, turkey, game hen
Fish and shellfish
Fresh vegetables
Raspberry leaf tea

2. YOUR MODERATION FOODS:

Red meat
Organ meats: liver, kidneys, heart
Legumes and whole grains
Fruit
Butter and vegetable oils

3. YOUR RARELY FOODS:

Refined grains
Caffeine
Sugar

4. YOUR IDEAL EATING SCHEDULE:

Eggs for breakfast (a good lifetime habit for T-Types)
Your total food intake divided more or less evenly among your meals
Protein at each meal

A protein snack (e.g., half a hard-boiled egg) in the late afternoon if
you feel tired

Breakfast

2 eggs, any style
1 slice of whole-grain toast with butter
Decaffeinated coffee, tea, or raspberry leaf tea

Lunch

Vegetables, cooked or raw, as much as you like
A serving of hard cheese, yogurt, or cottage cheese OR serving of
meat or fish
2 slices of whole-grain bread, or an equivalent serving of other
whole grains*
A glass of milk
A piece of fruit
Decaffeinated coffee, tea, or raspberry leaf tea

Dinner

A serving of meat, poultry, or fish. Plan to eat meat about twice a
week, fish or poultry on the remaining nights
Vegetables, cooked or raw, as much as you like
A serving of whole grain*
A glass of milk
A piece of fruit or a small dessert (but not more than twice a week!)
Raspberry leaf tea

ADDITIONAL NOTES ON THE T-TYPE DIET

I suggested earlier in this chapter that Thyroid Types have suffered
from today's emphasis on low-fat eating. Of course, I don't mean to

Thyroidal Type Pyramid

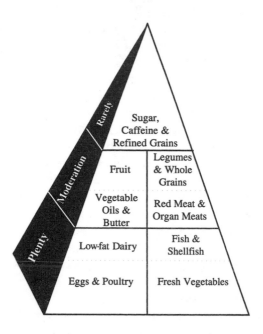

advise that you eat a *high*-fat diet. On the contrary, my concern is with the interpretation of the words "low-fat" as meaning "all the cookies you want, as long as they're low-fat." And to be honest, I find that this is a plausible interpretation of some experts' advice. We hear that getting the fat out of your diet is all that matters, and that doing so will lower your risk of heart disease, breast cancer, colon cancer, and much more. The labeling laws require that food manufacturers prominently lay out how much fat is in each item—again, as if this were all that mattered.

Yet fat does have its uses in the diet. It's a concentrated source of calories, and has been valued as such from times when the deficiency most people had to worry about was not getting enough to eat, period. It's the source of fat-soluble nutrients, like vitamins A, K, and E. It supports and stimulates your adrenals and your sex glands.

It also has brain effects. Eating fat makes you feel strong, powerful, and satisfied. And of course, it's delicious. It's invaluable in any cuisine; it carries and intensifies flavors, and gives food richness, smoothness, crunchiness, and texture. Where would French cooking be without butter and cream, Italian food without olive oil, or Chinese food without sesame and peanut oil? In short, it's fat—as in the fat of the land—and we all like living off it. You don't need to give it up completely and you probably wouldn't be able to. The key is getting the right balance of fat into your diet—balancing taste, emotional effects, and health benefits, none of which needs to be mutually exclusive.

In the 1983 edition, fat-gram counting wasn't widespread, and I didn't present the diets in those terms. But that doesn't mean I didn't consider the subject. I devised your T-Type Diet with the amount of fat in mind that would balance your particular metabolism.

The T-Type Weight Loss Diet has about 36–50 fat grams per day, on a 1,200-calorie-per-day diet. That translates to between 27 and 37 percent of your calories from fat. The difference comes in which meat you choose for dinner. When you choose beef, you come out at the higher end, and when you choose fish or chicken you are at the lower end. So you can stay within the government's recommendation of no more than 30 percent of your calories from fat by choosing chicken and fish.

Yours is actually the highest-fat of the Body Type Diets, because you are in the most need of the adrenal stimulation provided by fat. This amount of fat is balancing to your metabolism. Yet you cannot call it a high-fat diet. It's low-fat by most standards. Certainly, it is much lower in fat than the average American's diet, which gets 40 percent of its calories from fat. A Big Mac all by itself contains 26 grams of fat. Fries with that? Another 17 grams. Finish with a candy bar (average: 14 grams of fat) and you've had 57 grams—and that was only lunch!

Later on, when you have balanced your system and lost the weight you want, your T-Type program is even lower in fat. You will be eating more calories, but you won't be adding fat, or not much fat. Most of what you will add is whole grains, vegetables, and fruit. Under the T-Type Health and Weight Maintenance guidelines, your level of fat consumption will settle into a healthy level of between 25 and 30 percent of your calories from fat. This is low-fat eating that is truly right for *you*!

THE PITUITARY BODY TYPE
WEIGHT LOSS PROGRAM

The weight loss program you are about to learn is much more than a "diet." It's a whole new way of thinking about food, one that will ultimately put you in complete charge of your body—not just your weight but your energy level, your physical endurance, your mood, your health, and much more. It's called a "weight loss program" because reaching your best weight is the first step, and it's the one you're probably most interested in right now. But while you're working on that goal, the other benefits will be coming along, too, automatically, as part of the package.

As a P-Type, you have gained weight in the past by eating foods that stimulate your pituitary gland—mainly dairy products such as milk, yogurt, and ice cream. The overstimulation of your pituitary has created a state of exhaustion and imbalance that has allowed fat to accumulate all over your body, in the typical P-Type "baby fat" distribution.

The P-Type Diet uses a special strategy to reestablish balance in your system. The technique is to eliminate pituitary-stimulating foods, and thyroid-stimulating sweets and starches as well. This means that you will be cutting out dairy products from your diet, and also cutting back on sugar, white flour, and all refined grains such as white rice. Equally important, you will be increasing your intake of protein from animal sources, emphasizing beef and organ meats, with chicken and fish for variety. You will eat carbohydrates in moderation but from whole-grain sources only; fruit in moderation; and lots of fresh vegetables.

As a result, your digestion will improve. Your metabolism will become more active, so you'll lose weight quicker. You'll feel more in touch with your body, and learn only to eat when you are actually hungry, and to stop when you are full. You'll lose stubborn fat and even your cellulite, especially during the Last Five Pounds phase of your diet. And, interestingly, you'll find your sexuality blossoming in a very natural way.

The Basic Strategy for P-Types

To create balance in your system, you need to decrease stimulation of your overworked pituitary gland, and give more support and stimulation to your lower glands—your gonads and, especially, your adrenals. Stimulating your adrenals is the single most important factor for P-Types. It corrects two problems at once: It improves your digestion, which allows you to burn fat more efficiently, and it gives you steadier strength throughout the day, so that you are less inclined to snack on dairy products and sweets.

The most effective adrenal-stimulating food is meat, especially beef. Organ meats—liver, kidneys, and heart—also work well. Poultry and fish have some adrenal-stimulating qualities, and can be used to vary the diet. Organ meats have an additional advantage of stimulating the gonads as well.

Eliminate Dairy Products

To decrease stimulation of the pituitary, you need to drastically reduce the pituitary-stimulating dairy products you are so fond of. In fact, your P-Type metabolism works best when you eat no dairy products at all. After you have lost all your excess weight and created better balance in your system, your adrenals and digestion will both be stronger. This will make you better able to digest dairy foods, and also less dependent on the pituitary stimulation they provide. At that time you will be able to go back to eating low-fat or non-fat dairy such as skim milk and yogurt. But for now, the more faithfully you stay away from dairy products, the better you are going to feel.

Avoid Refined Carbohydrates and Caffeine (Whole Grains Are OK)

Your carbohydrate intake is from whole grains. The P-Type metabolism does not need or benefit from thyroidal stimulation, so you should avoid refined carbohydrates, by which I mean white sugar, honey, white flour, white bread, and pasta made from refined flour.

You may have up to two pieces of fruit per day. Caffeine is to be avoided as it gives you too much thyroid stimulation. You may drink decaffeinated coffee or tea if you wish, or you can stick with your P-Type herbal tea, fenugreek seed.

Eat Plenty of Fresh Vegetables

You'll eat an abundance of vegetables, both raw in salads and lightly cooked. The vegetables supply vitamins, vital trace minerals, and a feeling of fullness, so that you never feel deprived or "empty." When choosing between raw and cooked vegetables, you needn't feel that unless you have them raw in salads, you will not get the vitamins from them. Many vegetables actually give you their nutrients more readily when cooked than raw, because cooking breaks down the insoluble fiber and makes the nutrients more available.

Like T-Types, P-Types tend to be cold and to feel the cold when temperatures are low outside. If you are this way, you may prefer to eat cooked vegetables rather than salad. This is fine. If you wish, you may have all your vegetables cooked—just be sure to eat a lot of them! Your system benefits from an abundance of the protective phytochemicals found in vegetables.

The Total Strategy

To summarize your total dieting strategy: no dairy products, plenty of protein from animal sources, emphasizing beef and organ meats, with chicken and fish for variety; carbohydrates in moderation but from whole-grain sources only; fruit in moderation; no sugar or white flour; no caffeine; and plenty of fresh vegetables, both cooked and raw.

In addition to your improved digestion, more focused energy, and the smooth, fast weight loss, you will also be delighted with the more solid, "in touch" feeling you have inside—a direct result of creating more balance and harmony among your glands by enlivening your underactive adrenals and gonads.

THE P-TYPE MEAL SCHEDULE: REVERSE THE "USUAL" ORDER OF MEALS

The pituitary gland is active during the day, especially early in the day, and relatively inactive at night. This makes you a "morning person." Your ideal schedule is early to bed, early to rise, for you have your best energy early in the day.

To fit in with this natural rhythm and to help you lose weight most effectively, P-Types must reverse the usual order of meals. Instead of a light breakfast, moderate lunch, and substantial dinner, you do much better if you eat a substantial breakfast with meat, a moderate lunch, and a very light dinner.

Eat a Substantial Breakfast with Meat

Eating meat at breakfast accomplishes several purposes. It starts your day with the adrenal stimulation you need. It pulls your energies down into your body (by stimulating the adrenals and the sex glands, rather than the pituitary), which will help you focus during the day. It stays with you longer than your usual lighter breakfast (of yogurt or fruit) and will help you avoid snacking. Finally, it keeps you more in touch with your body, which will help you know when you actually are hungry and so can avoid eating from nervousness or tension.

Lunch should also contain some protein, to help you eliminate snacking throughout the afternoon. You don't need to have meat again unless you want to, but you will do much better if you have fish or chicken at lunchtime.

Eat Lightly at Night

Because your metabolism is so inactive late in the day, going to bed with a heavy meal on your stomach is to be avoided. You'll only suffer from indigestion and disturbed sleep. Leave the more substantial evening meals to the G's and A's. Besides, they had fruit or cereal and milk for breakfast, while you had your "main meal" at that time.

Observe the Interval Between Meals

Wait four hours between breakfast and lunch and six hours between lunch and dinner on the P-Type Weight Loss Diet. Wait five hours between breakfast and lunch and six between lunch and dinner on the P-Type Last Five Pounds Diet. It is vital that you keep to these intervals, which enable your body to complete the digestive process and to have some time, free of digestion, to rebalance itself. Eating too soon after a previous meal distracts your body from this vital process of rebalancing, which is also when the work of burning fat takes place.

Your Danger Period

Your danger period for snacking is late afternoon, as the pituitary gland becomes less and less active. At this time, many P-Types experience a desire for pituitary stimulation from dairy products such as ice cream, yogurt, or cheese. Occasionally you may also crave a thyroid-stimulator such as a sweet or a starch. These must be avoided at all costs as they will be extremely unbalancing.

Your Best Snack

Keep available in your refrigerator a small amount of already cooked meat—for example, a few ounces of cooked hamburger well-drained of fat. If you are overcome with the desire to snack, take a few bites of the meat. It will stimulate your adrenals and you'll feel more energetic, and you'll avoid creating imbalance in your system with a pituitary- or thyroid-stimulating food.

The P-Type Herbal Help: Fenugreek Tea

Fenugreek tea is an important feature of the Pituitary Type Diet. Drink as much of it as you wish, but be sure to drink at *least* the amounts specified in your diet. And drink it anytime you have a strong craving for ice cream or other dairy foods.

It is made as follows: Bring water to a boil and add a teaspoon of fenugreek seeds (available in most health food stores) for each two cups of water. Allow the seeds to boil in the water for five minutes. Unlike most herbal teas, fenugreek tea must be boiled to release the full value of the seeds. Strain and serve. You may use as much lemon as you wish, but no honey or sugar.

Rules for P-Type Dieting

In the following pages are both general guidelines for P-Type dieting (a complete list of what you are to eat for each meal, both for the P-Type Weight Loss Diet and the P-Type Last Five Pounds Diet) and a week of sample menus for each of the diets. You may use these menus or substitute your own, as long as you use the same foods and follow the guidelines closely.

You may substitute freely *within the boundaries allowed for each meal,* but do not rearrange the food among the meals, as the order and distribution are important. Meat, poultry, and fish should be boiled, grilled or barbecued, or baked, with all visible fat removed (see the guidelines for each meal). Vegetables may be steamed, boiled in a small amount of water, broiled with a small amount of oil, or sautéed in the permitted vegetable oil only. Poultry is to be eaten without skin. *Do not omit anything; every food is there for a reason.*

THE COMPLETE PITUITARY-
TYPE WEIGHT LOSS PROGRAM

Your program begins with the P-Type Weight Loss Diet. How long you follow it depends on how much weight you want to lose.

TO LOSE MORE THAN FIFTEEN POUNDS:
Follow the Weight Loss Diet for three weeks, then change to the Last Five Pounds Diet for a week, then go back to the P-Type Weight Loss Diet. Continue to change to the Last Five Pounds Diet every fourth week. Once you are within five pounds of your ideal weight, use the Last Five Pounds Diet to complete your weight loss program.

TO LOSE FIVE TO FIFTEEN POUNDS:
Follow the Weight Loss Diet for two weeks, then change to the P-Type Last Five Pounds Diet for a week (or less, if you reach your ideal weight before the completion of a week).

TO LOSE FIVE POUNDS OR LESS:
Follow the P-Type Weight Loss Diet for one week and then change to the Last Five Pounds Diet for a week (or less).

WHEN YOU REACH YOUR IDEAL WEIGHT:
Change to the P-Type Health and Weight Maintenance Program.

Dishes marked with a star are those for which a recipe is provided in Appendix 4.

THE P-TYPE WEIGHT LOSS
DIET: GENERAL GUIDELINES

Breakfast

Your choice of 4 ounces of lean beef, lean pork, dark poultry meat, lamb, liver★; kidney★; or heart★

One serving of whole grain—your choice: 1 slice of whole-grain bread or ¹/₂ cup of a whole grain such as brown rice, whole wheat, millet, amaranth, Kamut, or quinoa

1 cup of decaffeinated coffee, decaffeinated tea, or fenugreek tea

WAIT FOUR HOURS

Lunch

Any combination of vegetables, cooked or raw—at least 1 cup total. You may make a salad of lettuce, cucumber, mushrooms, celery, sprouts, radishes, bell pepper, tomato, and onion, or have cooked vegetables such as green beans or zucchini, or a combination of salad and cooked vegetables.

1 teaspoon of clear diet dressing★

4 ounces of fish, chicken, or shellfish

One serving of whole grain (see choices at breakfast)

1 small piece of fruit—you may choose any available fruit, from apples, cherries, and peaches to mangos, kiwis, and star fruit. The quantity of fruit is one piece, or 1 cup of fruit like grapes or berries. To make the best fruit choice, look for fruits that are locally grown and in season. The more flavorful and fresh the fruit, the better it is for you.

Fenugreek tea

WAIT SIX HOURS

Dinner

Your choice of 4 ounces of white poultry meat, fish, or shellfish OR two eggs

Fresh vegetables, steamed or raw, as much as you wish

1 piece of fruit, same choices as lunch
Fenugreek tea

THE P-TYPE WEIGHT LOSS DIET: A WEEK OF SAMPLE MENUS

Monday

BREAKFAST:
4 ounces of grilled calves' liver★
1 slice whole-wheat toast
Decaffeinated coffee

LUNCH:
Any combination of vegetables, cooked or raw—at least 1 cup total
4 ounces Broiled Shrimp with Lemon★
$^1/_2$ cup brown rice★
1 piece of fruit
Fenugreek tea

DINNER:
Stir-Fried Chicken★ (or use a chicken recipe of your own, as long
    as you cook the chicken without the skin)
Baked apple (or other fruit in season)
Fenugreek tea

Tuesday

BREAKFAST:
4 ounces grilled lean minute steak
$^1/_2$ cup brown rice★
Decaffeinated tea

LUNCH:
Any combination of vegetables, cooked or raw—at least 1 cup total
4 ounces broiled scallops
2 pieces of rye Krispbread

1 piece of fruit
Fenugreek tea

DINNER:
Celery-Onion Omelette★ (or use your own egg recipe, using no
    more than 1 teaspoon of vegetable oil in cooking)
Steamed zucchini and string beans
Nectarine (or other fruit in season)
Fenugreek tea

Wednesday

BREAKFAST:
4 ounces broiled calves' liver★
¹/₂ cup kamut★
Decaffeinated coffee

LUNCH:
Any combination of vegetables, cooked or raw—at least 1 cup total
4 ounces water-packed tuna salad made with 1 tablespoon diet may-
    onnaise
1 slice of whole-grain bread
1 piece of fruit
Fenugreek tea

DINNER:
Chicken Breast Piquant★ (or use a chicken recipe of your own,
    preparing the chicken without skin, see Appendix 2)
Steamed celery hearts
1 cup of grapes (or other fruit in season)
Fenugreek tea

Thursday

BREAKFAST:
Roasted chicken thigh (cooked in the oven the night before with
    your Chicken Breast Piquant★)

1 slice of whole-grain toast
Decaffeinated coffee

LUNCH:
Any combination of vegetables, cooked or raw—at least 1 cup total
4 ounces broiled shrimp
$1/2$ cup brown rice*
1 piece of fruit
Fenugreek tea

DINNER:
Sole Provençal* (or use your own fish recipe, as long as fish is not
    breaded and you use only 1 teaspoon of vegetable oil)
Poached Pear* (or other fruit in season)
Fenugreek tea

Friday

BREAKFAST:
4 ounces lean broiled pork chop
$1/2$ cup bulgur wheat*
Decaffeinated tea

LUNCH:
Any combination of vegetables, cooked or raw—at least 1 cup total
4 ounces of broiled scallops
1 slice of rye bread
1 piece of fruit
Fenugreek tea

DINNER:
Lemon Chicken Kabobs with Mushrooms and Zucchini* (or use
    your own chicken recipe, using chicken without skin)
$1/4$ cantaloupe (or other fruit in season)
Fenugreek tea

Saturday

BREAKFAST:
4 ounces of broiled veal kidney*
1/2 cup millet*
Decaffeinated coffee

LUNCH:
Any combination of vegetables, cooked or raw—at least 1 cup total
4 ounces of water-packed tuna with 1 tablespoon of diet mayonnaise
1 slice of whole-wheat toast
1 piece of fruit
Fenugreek tea

DINNER:
Stir-Fried Fish Fillets* (or use your own fish recipe, as long as fish is not breaded and you use only 1 teaspoon of vegetable oil)
1 cup of cherries (or other fruit in season)
Fenugreek tea

Sunday

BREAKFAST:
4 ounces grilled lean minute steak
1/2 cup brown rice*
Decaffeinated tea

LUNCH:
Any combination of vegetables, cooked or raw—at least 1 cup total
4 ounces of water-packed crabmeat
2 pieces of rye Krispbread
1 piece of fruit
Fenugreek tea

DINNER:
Scrambled eggs with mushrooms
Stir-Fried Green Beans*

1 cup sliced fresh pineapple (or other fruit in season)
Fenugreek tea

THE P-TYPE LAST FIVE
POUNDS DIET

Remember, even if you have only five pounds of extra weight, you should not begin your P-Type Last Five Pounds Diet until you have followed the P-Type Weight Loss Diet for a week. The sequence of diets (see page 157) is vital for balancing your metabolism, as well as producing fast and efficient loss of weight.

The P-Type Last Five Pounds Diet is a very special diet. It has about 1,000 calories per day, about 200 calories per day less than the P-Type Weight Loss Diet; and the food you eat is specially programmed to get you off the periodic plateaus of dieting, as well as to assist you in losing the stubborn last five pounds of excess weight. If you were to begin this diet at the start of your program, you would probably find it difficult. But since you have been on the Basic P-Type Weight Loss Diet for at least a week, your metabolism is strengthened and in better balance, and you should be able to handle the Last Five Pounds Diet comfortably.

This diet is only to be followed for a week at a time. If, at the end of a week, you have not reached your ideal weight, return to the P-Type Weight Loss Diet for one, two, or three weeks, depending on your remaining extra weight. You may use the Last Five Pounds Diet every fourth week until you reach your weight goal. And as soon as you come within five pounds of your ideal weight, change to the Last Five Pounds Diet. Once you have reached your ideal weight, you are ready for the P-Type Health and Weight Maintenance Program (see page 168 for the complete program).

Note that the interval of time between meals has been increased on the Last Five Pounds Diet. Be sure to observe the full interval, as the hours between meals are the periods when your body is most active in burning fat.

THE P-TYPE LAST FIVE POUNDS DIET: GENERAL GUIDELINES

Breakfast

2 eggs, any style
1 teaspoon of vegetable oil
1 slice of whole-grain toast
1 cup of decaffeinated coffee or tea, or fenugreek tea (no sugar or honey)
WAIT FIVE HOURS

Lunch

Your choice of fresh fruit
Your choice of 4 ounces of lean beef, lean pork, lamb, dark poultry meat, or organ meat (liver, heart, or kidneys)*
P-Type Vegetable Soup,* as much as you like
Fenugreek tea
WAIT SIX HOURS

Dinner

4 ounces of fish or shellfish
1 slice of whole-grain bread
P-Type Vegetable Soup,* as much as you like
Fenugreek tea

THE P-TYPE LAST FIVE POUNDS DIET: A WEEK OF SAMPLE MENUS

Monday

BREAKFAST:
2 poached eggs
1 teaspoon of vegetable oil

1 slice of whole-grain toast
1 cup of decaffeinated coffee or tea, or fenugreek tea

LUNCH:
One piece of fruit
4 ounces of grilled lean hamburger
P-Type Vegetable Soup★ (as much as you like)
Fenugreek tea

DINNER:
Baked Halibut Steak★ (or use your own fish recipe, as long as fish is
     not breaded and you use only 1 teaspoon of vegetable oil)
1 slice of whole-grain bread
P-Type Vegetable Soup★ (as much as you like)
Fenugreek tea

Tuesday

BREAKFAST:
2 scrambled eggs
1 teaspoon of vegetable oil
1 slice of whole-grain toast
1 cup of decaffeinated coffee or tea, or fenugreek tea

LUNCH:
One piece of fruit
4 ounces grilled pork chop
P-Type Vegetable Soup★ (as much as you like)
Fenugreek tea

DINNER:
Marinated Sole★ (or use your own fish recipe, as long as fish is not
     breaded and you use only 1 teaspoon of vegetable oil)
1 slice of whole-grain bread
P-Type Vegetable Soup★ (as much as you like)
Fenugreek tea

Wednesday

BREAKFAST:
2 fried eggs
1 teaspoon of vegetable oil
1 slice of whole-grain toast
1 cup of decaffeinated coffee or tea, or fenugreek tea

LUNCH:
Your choice of fruit
4 ounces of dark-meat chicken
P-Type Vegetable Soup★ (as much as you like)
Fenugreek tea

DINNER:
Stir-Fried Fish Fillets★ (or use your own fish recipe, as long as fish is
     not breaded and you use only 1 teaspoon of vegetable oil)
1 slice of whole-grain bread
P-Type Vegetable Soup★ (as much as you like)
Fenugreek tea

Thursday

BREAKFAST:
2 soft-boiled eggs
1 teaspoon of vegetable oil
1 slice of whole-grain toast
1 cup of decaffeinated coffee or tea, or fenugreek tea

LUNCH:
Your choice of fruit
4 ounces of grilled lamb chop
P-Type Vegetable Soup★ (as much as you like)
Fenugreek tea

DINNER:
Salmon Steak Florentine★ (or use your own fish recipe, as long as
     fish is not breaded and you use only 1 teaspoon of vegetable oil)

1 slice of whole-grain bread
P-Type Vegetable Soup★ (as much as you like)
Fenugreek tea

Friday

BREAKFAST:
2 poached eggs
1 teaspoon of vegetable oil
1 slice of whole-grain toast
1 cup of decaffeinated coffee or tea, or fenugreek tea

LUNCH:
Your choice of fruit
4 ounces of grilled lean steak
P-Type Vegetable Soup★ (as much as you like)
Fenugreek tea

DINNER:
Sole Provençal★ (or use your own fish recipe, as long as fish is not
    breaded and you use only 1 teaspoon of vegetable oil)
1 slice of whole-grain bread
P-Type Vegetable Soup★ (as much as you like)
Fenugreek tea

Saturday

BREAKFAST:
2 scrambled eggs
1 teaspoon of vegetable oil
1 slice of whole-grain toast
1 cup of decaffeinated coffee or tea, or fenugreek tea

LUNCH:
Your choice of fruit
4 ounces of broiled liver★

P-Type Vegetable Soup★ (as much as you like)
Fenugreek tea

DINNER:
Broiled Shrimp with Lemon★ (or use your own shellfish recipe, using only 1 teaspoon of vegetable oil in preparation)
1 slice of whole-grain bread
P-Type Vegetable Soup★ (as much as you like)
Fenugreek tea

Sunday

BREAKFAST:
2 hard-boiled eggs
1 teaspoon of vegetable oil
1 slice of whole-grain toast
1 cup of decaffeinated coffee or tea, or fenugreek tea

LUNCH:
Your choice of fruit
4 ounces of grilled lean hamburger
P-Type Vegetable Soup★ (as much as you like)
Fenugreek tea

DINNER:
Marinated Fish with Vegetables★ (or use your own fish recipe, as long as fish is not breaded and you use only 1 teaspoon of vegetable oil)
1 slice of whole-grain bread
P-Type Vegetable Soup★ (as much as you like)
Fenugreek tea

THE P-TYPE HEALTH AND WEIGHT MAINTENANCE PROGRAM

The formula for keeping the ideal weight you've achieved through your Body Type Diet is to have a continuing awareness of your body type and its special needs. Your P-Type Diet has brought about a state of balance in your metabolism; the P-Type Health and Weight Maintenance Program is designed to make it easy for you to *maintain* that balance, as that is the only way you will keep your ideal weight.

"Plenty," "Moderation," and "Rarely" Foods and the P-Type Food Pyramid

To make it as easy as possible for you to keep your body type requirements in mind, your program includes a *short, simple set* of guidelines for you as a P-Type. You need only remember 1) your Plenty foods (foods you can always eat, which will always be good for you); 2) your Moderation foods (foods you can eat as long as you don't overdo them); and 3) your Rarely foods (ones you should save for special occasions only, because eating them will tend to revive your old cravings and make it harder for you to keep to your guidelines).

Continue to use your herbal tea and your vegetable soup. They will continue to strengthen your metabolism and are the best possible means for you to maintain the healthy balance you have achieved.

To help you internalize your Plenty, Moderation, and Rarely foods, I have arranged them into a Food Pyramid. The Plenty foods are on the bottom—they create a solid foundation for your continued balance. Moderation foods appear next; these are foods that are balancing for you in moderation but that have the *potential* to become overstimulating or unbalancing unless you keep half an eye on them. Finally, the Rarely foods are at the top of the pyramid. No food is absolutely forbidden; but if you eat these foods often they can certainly make life harder for you by reviving your cravings.

Patients often ask me about the right quantities of the Plenty, Moderation, and Rarely foods. My advice to them, and to you, is that by the time you have become balanced through your Body Type Program, *you* are a much better judge of quantities than I am. Consult yourself, your feelings, your energy level, your emotional stability. Check your cravings (any food that revives your cravings should come under suspicion that you are eating too much of it). Finally, adjust your own quantities yourself. The ability to do this is very much a part of being balanced.

If You Forget the Guidelines and Gain Weight

If you stay with your guidelines you will not find yourself putting on weight. But if you let your guidelines go for any reason and you find yourself three to five pounds above your ideal weight, then go back to your original P-Type Weight Loss Program. With five extra pounds, you will need only a week of the P-Type Weight Loss Diet and a weekend of the P-Type Last Five Pounds Diet to be right back at your perfect weight.

THE P-TYPE HEALTH AND WEIGHT MAINTENANCE PROGRAM: GENERAL GUIDELINES

1. YOUR PLENTY FOODS:

Beef, lamb, and pork (without visible fat)
Organ meats: liver, kidneys, heart
Fish and shellfish
Eggs and poultry
Fresh vegetables
Fenugreek tea

2. YOUR MODERATION FOODS:

Fruits
Legumes and whole grains
Yogurt
Vegetable oils

3. YOUR RARELY FOODS:

Sugar
Dairy products other than yogurt
Caffeine

4. YOUR IDEAL EATING SCHEDULE:

A substantial, protein-rich breakfast
A moderate lunch, with vegetables and some protein
A light dinner
Avoid late-night eating

Breakfast

Your choice of 2 eggs, any style OR a small steak or broiled organ
    meat
A slice of whole-grain bread
Decaffeinated coffee, tea, or fenugreek tea

Lunch

Vegetables of your choice, cooked or raw
Two servings of whole grain (2 slices of whole-grain bread, or 1 cup
    of other whole grains)
A serving of fish, poultry, or meat. You may substitute yogurt occa-
    sionally (about every 2 weeks) if you feel good and do not have
    cravings for other dairy
1 piece of fruit
Decaffeinated coffee, tea, or fenugreek tea

Dinner

A serving of fish, poultry, or eggs. Plan to eat eggs several nights per
    week, fish or poultry on the remaining nights.
Vegetables, cooked or raw, as much as you like
A serving of whole grain
A piece of fruit, or a small dessert
Fenugreek tea

Pituitary Type Pyramid

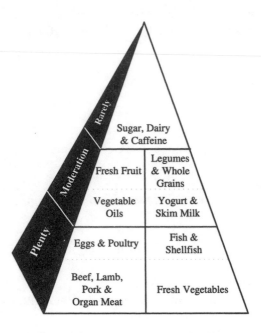

ADDITIONAL NOTES ON THE P-TYPE DIET

If you have just determined you are a Pituitary Type, whether by double- and triple-checking your answers on the Body Type Checklist or by consulting the Body Type Institute, I imagine you are wondering whether I could possibly be serious about this diet.

I am, but of course I am very aware how unusual and out of step with the times the P-Type Diet is. Recommending organ meat for breakfast is not the kind of thing you normally find in diet books these days, and there are those who might shudder at the thought. The fixed belief of most nutritionists, that bran flakes with milk are the right breakfast for everyone, may be overly influential here.

If you really are a P-Type, though, you will find the way of eating I recommend creates a real transformation. But you must really be a P-Type! P's are the rarest of the body types, perhaps no more than 5 percent of the population; and there are more P-Type men than women. Over the years I have received a significant number of inquiries from people who begin, "I'm a Pituitary Type, and . . . ," but if I see them in person or if their letter is accompanied by a photograph, I stare in amazement, because I am looking not at a P but an Adrenal or Gonadal Type! And of course, the P-Type way of eating is completely wrong for them.

I have come to two conclusions. One is that A- and G-Types sometimes believe they are Pituitary Types from wishful thinking—because all that meat sounds pretty good to them. So if you feel strongly attracted to the P-Type Diet before even trying it, you may be reading the wrong chapter. The other conclusion is that there may be something in my description of the Pituitary Type that makes people want to be P-Types. Maybe it's because I describe P-Types as intellectual, cool, detached, spacy, uninterested in sex, and so on. If these are your main reasons for believing yourself to be a P-Type, and if your body does not remotely fit the physical description, again, you may be reading the wrong chapter.

But if you are, indeed, a P-Type, and if your initial reaction to the diet is "Dr. Abravanel, I could *never* eat all that meat," then I urge you just as strongly to give it a try. I well remember a P-Type patient of mine, years ago, who was living at an entirely vegetarian ashram in Southern California. Cooking liver for her breakfast in the ashram kitchen was totally out of the question. So my patient took a camping stove out into the parking lot every morning and made her liver or her breakfast steak, and ate it out there. She said, "I wish I didn't have to do this, but this food is my medicine. It's so obvious to me now that my body needs it; and I don't feel I follow my spiritual path if I don't take care of my body." I always think, if she could do it, anyone can.

COMMONLY ASKED QUESTIONS ABOUT THE BODY TYPE DIET

Question: I don't understand why I need to know my body type. Isn't it true that if I eat fewer calories than I'm using up, I'll lose weight? Isn't all dieting just a matter of eating less?

Answer: Yes, of course it is—in a sense. To lose weight you *must* take in fewer calories than your body burns. The laws of physics haven't been suspended by the Body Type Diet. But if you think about it, losing weight is just a small part of what you hope for when you diet. At the very minimum, you want to lose weight in the right places, you want to look and feel great, and you want to keep off the weight you lose. (In fact, you should realize many more benefits than these—check them out in Chapter 16.)

Reaching these goals requires more than just reducing calories. It requires a diet that is right for your metabolism—for your body type. If you need proof, just ask yourself how many diets you've been on before. Maybe you even lost weight on some of them. But was that enough? Somewhere, these diets failed you. Your Body Type Diet won't.

Question: Is it possible to be a "mixed" body type? For example, could I be a mixed Thyroid-and-Adrenal Type? I did the Checklist, and I have some characteristics of both these body types.

Answer: No, not really. Of course, in one way, *everyone* is a "mixed" body type, because we all have all four glands (unless one has been lost through injury or surgery), and we all have *some* characteristics of all four body types. If you're a Thyroid Type, it doesn't mean that you *only* have a thyroid gland. You also have adrenals, a pituitary, and gonads, and each has contributed something to your body's structure and style of functioning.

But you always have one gland that is stronger than the other three, and that is your dominant gland. Even if you are very well balanced, and your dominant gland dominates your system by only a little, it is still your dominant gland. That is what gives you your body type.

It may be that you have a well-balanced metabolism in which the difference in activity among your four glands is not extreme. If so, you may have an "unusual" or hard-to-determine body type (check back to Chapter 5 for more on this). If so, you may want to consult the Body Type Institute for assistance in determining your body type.

Question: I read the first edition of your book and ever since I've been wondering how you came up with the body type concept. Did it come from your Western medical background? Or were you inspired by some other medical system, like Ayurvedic medicine, which I understand also has body types?

Answer: I came up with the body type concept very much in response to the need I saw to help my patients find a way of eating that was right for their own particular metabolism. The concept of the four body types comes partially from my Western medical training, and partially from the unusual and holistic background I had acquired in my years as medical director of Maharishi European Research University. During my years there, in the seventies, I did a great deal of research on consciousness and enlightenment, especially in relation to overall health and longevity.

But in fact, the most important part of the Body Type Program—the nutritional plans, the exercise programs, the supplements for each body type, and all the rest of it—did not come out of Western medical literature. It is original work based entirely on my clinical research in my practice. It is supported by everything known medically about food, exercise, and the glandular system. I was the first to use this knowledge to create diets, and other health programs for individuals, based on body type.

On the other hand, there have been medical descriptions of glandular body types in the past, some of them going back to the very earliest scientific knowledge of what the endocrine system does. My immediate predecessor in developing the body type concept was Henry Bieler, M.D., author of *Food Is Your Best Medicine*. I feel a kinship with Dr. Bieler. We graduated from the same medical school, we both went on to have nutrition-based medical practices, and when we became authors we even shared an editor—Charles Bloch, my first editor at Bantam, edited several of Dr. Bieler's books.

But I did not actually use Dr. Bieler's description of the body types—in fact, I hadn't even read his work on body types when I developed my system. My description of the four body types comes from my own close observation of thousands of patients in my practice, and it differs from Dr. Bieler's in a number of ways. And neither Dr. Bieler nor anyone else who wrote about body types ever related them to their specific dietary and health needs. I feel that that is where my real contribution has been made.

To me, the description of the four body types, while obviously very important, is not *the* most important aspect of my work. I've seen over the years that readers and even health practitioners tend to get very caught up in the Body-Typing aspect, and that's understandable. You want to find your own body type, of course. Then you want to find the body types of your family, your friends, and your patients. Fine, but just knowing your body type isn't as important as *applying that knowledge to your daily life.* In other words, I want you to create balance in your system—that's what this program is all about.

Question: Speaking of that, I've seen several other works on body-type dieting on the bookstore shelves. How do they relate to your work?

Answer: There are several recent books that promote various diets based on glandular or metabolic body type. Many of these have been written by individuals trained at the Body Type Institute, or by people who have studied my work and tried to build on it. Of course, I can't comment on their specific advice—it would take a whole book to do that. I'd rather give you the tools to evaluate it for yourself.

When reading any advice based on your body type, think about what you've learned about the influence of the various foods on the glands. Ask yourself whether the foods would be balancing or un-balancing for your body type; then proceed accordingly. Question what you read, and always use the standard of your own body's needs when judging any advice. Always remember, what's right for your friend may not be right for *you*.

By the way, don't be confused if you see different names used for the body types in some of these books. Some of the writers may feel that terms like "thyroid" and "adrenal" are too technical, and instead prefer descriptive terms like "spoon-shaped" and "stick-shaped," or fruit names like "the apple-shaped" and "the pear-shaped." Or they use terms like Metabolic Profile #1, #2, #3, and #4, or personality terms like The Communicator and The Warrior. One writer changed the glandular names slightly, and calls the four types the Thyroid, the Android, the Gynecoid, and (for some reason) the Lymphatic. Or they add additional body types (in some cases, a *lot* of additional body types), but the "additional" types are only variations of the four actual body types—possibly ones that the author was not able to identify without more training.

None of these changes actually alters the nature of the body type in question, and it's usually quite easy to bring these back to the original terms: Thyroid, Adrenal, Gonadal, and Pituitary Types. I feel that the glandular names are most helpful because they indicate most clearly *what* is going on in your body, *why* you need what you need, and *how* you can use this knowledge for health and balance at your best weight.

Question: Suppose I make a mistake in the Body Type Checklist and decide I'm the wrong body type. Will it hurt me to follow the wrong diet?
Answer: No. All the Body Type Diets are healthy, balanced, and nutritionally sound. They can't possibly hurt you. You will probably even lose weight, at least at first. It would be just as if you went to the bookstore and bought a book with an ordinary, well-balanced "for-everyone" diet.

What you *won't* get, though, are the special benefits of a diet that's right for your body type. You won't get the reduction of foods that stimulate your dominant gland, and the extra support to build up your less active glands. You won't find your cravings disappearing, and you won't lose weight in your trouble spots. But that's the worst that can happen.

However, these are important benefits you don't want to miss! So be very careful doing the Body Type Checklist.

Question: A friend of mine lost a lot of weight on a high-protein diet, without knowing the first thing about body types. This shouldn't have happened, should it?

Answer: Your friend is probably either a Pituitary or a Thyroid Type. These two body types do fairly well on high-protein diets. There are problems with them even for these body types, however. For example, if they allow caffeine drinks, the Thyroid Types will use them to overstimulate their thyroid. If they encourage dairy products, the Pituitary Types will use those as pituitary stimulants. But even at the worst, the higher-protein diets are better for T's and P's than the very low-fat, high-carbohydrate programs.

Some people are lucky enough to find acceptable diets for their body types by accident. But even so, it will be to their advantage to know their body type, to understand how to keep off the weight they lose. The more knowledge we have about our bodies, the more intelligently we can care for them and maintain our weight and health.

Question: I tend to eat a lot through nervousness. Is there anything I can do to relieve my tension and anxiety? So many times I find myself eating out of tension even though I'm not really hungry. And I get especially nervous when I'm dieting, because I know I'm not supposed to eat.

Answer: For true relief of stress, there is no technique I have found to be more effective than transcendental meditation. It is a simple and easily learned technique and requires no particular belief or change in life-style. As a physician, I have been impressed by the well-done scientific studies showing that twenty minutes of transcendental meditation, twice a day, gives rest that is much deeper than sleep and relieves a wide range of physical and mental symptoms. It's especially helpful for general tension and anxiety.

I practice TM regularly myself, and my experience bears out the scientific evidence. It is invariably refreshing and energizing. I have also found in patient after patient that those people who practice the transcendental meditation technique have a far easier time losing weight and keeping it off. This is undoubtedly because stress does play such a considerable role in overeating. Feeling rested and less stressed, people who meditate find they are far less likely to eat when they feel tired or tense. To learn more about this valuable technique, I suggest you consult one of the many books on the subject, such as *The TM Book* by Denise Denniston and Peter McWilliams, or call your local transcendental meditation center. Remember, though, that any technique that reduces stress is fine. There may be a form of meditation that is encouraged by your religion, or another kind of practice with which you feel very comfortable. The point is to find something that works for you—and use it.

Question: Do I need to drink lots of extra water on my diet?
Answer: How much you need to drink depends on many factors, including your activity level, the temperature and humidity in the environment, and how much water is intrinsic to the food you eat. In general, your hypothalamus is very reliable in telling you when you should drink; just be sure to pay attention and to drink when you feel thirsty. You should drink all the liquids called for on your diet, especially your body type herbal tea. Any additional liquid that you drink should preferably be plain water at room temperature.

The only exception to this is when you are exercising. Thirst is not a completely reliable guide to how much water you need when you are working out, so most experts recommend that you drink water every twenty minutes or so during a workout.

Question: I've heard some experts say that caffeine can interfere with weight loss, but other diet books say you can drink all you want. Personally, I can't think straight unless I've had a cup of coffee in the morning. Do I have to give it up to lose weight? What's the story, anyway?
Answer: The ability to tolerate caffeine varies among the body types. Thyroid Types must be very careful with caffeine, since it is so stimulating to the thyroid gland. Many T-Types do indeed have to eliminate it to reach their ideal weight. Gonadal and Adrenal Types, by contrast, can actually *benefit* by the thyroidal stimulation it pro-

vides. They are allowed moderate amounts of caffeine in their Body Type Diets.

Question: Speaking of Thyroid Types, I'm an overweight T-Type and I feel tired all the time. Does that mean my thyroid is exhausted? Should I be taking thyroid hormone?

Answer: This is a question that can only be answered by your physician. Supplementary thyroid hormone is a medicine, and whether you need it is a medical question, not one I can answer generically in a book. But I will tell you what I have experienced with my T-Type patients.

Many of them do in fact begin the Body Type Program with some depression in their thyroid function. Some of them are actually clinically hypothyroid and should take some hormone until they recover; others are already on Synthroid and have been for many years.

I was quite aware of this problem when I designed the T-Type Diet. The central strategy is to have you stop overstimulating your thyroid with sugar, refined carbohydrates, and caffeine. This allows your thyroid gland to rest and, hopefully, to recover. Many T-Types who have been on the T-Type Diet for some time find they are able to reduce, and in some cases actually eliminate, their need for Synthroid. This is not supposed to happen, but it does—not always, but often enough to make it worth mentioning.

Of course, if you're on Synthroid you should not stop taking it just because you're on the T-Type Diet! Thyroid recovery takes time. You should work closely with your doctor to monitor your need for thyroid hormone, and you may find you can reduce it bit by bit over a period of time. If this happens, be sure to write to me and let me know about this good result.

Question: What about salt and sugar? I've heard they're both terrible for you. Do your Body Type Diets eliminate them?

Answer: Not necessarily. Again, like so many elements of diet, it depends upon your body type. Sugar and salt are both stimulating to certain glands, but the two substances create their effects in different ways.

Sugar stimulates the thyroid and indirectly raises the blood glucose level—and thus gives an immediate energy lift. Salt acts to contract the blood vessels and drive water out of the cells, causing a feeling of fullness and power. Thus, the body types tend to use these substances in different ways. Pituitary and Thyroid Types eat sugar because they enjoy the feeling of quick energy, while Adrenal and Gonadal Types are more apt to use salt for the powerful feeling it provides.

In my Body Type Diet, I use the effects of sugar and salt in a controlled way to offset certain tendencies of the body types. I allow a small amount of sugar to Adrenal and Gonadal Types, who benefit from the thyroidal stimulation it provides. And I allow Pituitary and Thyroid Types to have a small amount of salt with their foods, because the tightening of the system and the increased rigidity that salt produces counteract the tendency to the slight vagueness and lack of focus that are characteristic of these types.

Certainly, sugar and salt in excess are harmful. I would not want you to have more than a small amount of either one—but in small quantities these substances can be used with great benefit, provided you take your body type into consideration.

Question: What about artificial sweeteners? Is it true they're bad for you?
Answer: One thing is certain: They aren't foods. They can't possibly provide nourishment to the body in any way. The question, then, is whether they are harmful. The evidence at this point is inconclusive, but I am conservative and prefer to avoid risk. I don't recommend them.

Question: I know you don't recommend artificial sweeteners. But what about all the other new "diet" foods on the market? For instance, there's diet margarine, diet mayonnaise, fat-free cheese, even fat-free oil. Is there any harm in eating them?
Answer: My advice is to examine the individual product before you buy it. In many "diet" foods the reduction in calories has been caused very simply, by adding water; this is the case with most margarines and mayonnaises. There is no harm in them, and they enable you to conserve calories while enjoying at least an approximation of the original food.

You have to be careful about salad dressings, however. Many of them contain fewer calories than the equivalent nondiet dressing but are nevertheless quite calorie-laden; e.g., "diet" blue cheese dressings may contain forty calories per teaspoon—hardly a "diet" food. For this reason, I specify that you use only clear diet dressings on your salad while on the Body Type Diet.

Fat-free cheese is another issue. If you look at the list of ingredients, it seems to be barely a food. I don't like you to eat food in which most of the ingredients are numbers. And I would be very cautious about Olestra for the same reason that I am cautious about artificial sweeteners: I am conservative and like to wait until more is known before making a recommendation.

Question: I've been thinking of going on your Body Type Diet with my teenage daughter, who is already a few pounds overweight. Is it all right for a teenager to follow this diet?

Answer: This is a complicated question. On the one hand, it's an excellent idea to acquaint your children with good eating habits for their body type. You can help them avoid many problems later on. And usually children are fascinated with the concept, and can often learn to spot body types more easily than adults.

On the other hand, a teenage girl is already under a lot of pressure to be thin—sometimes unreasonably thin. Your daughter doesn't need more pressure from you—she needs love and acceptance. So you need to approach this with care. It may be better to simply share with your daughter the idea of eating right for her body type, rather than have her go "on a diet" with you per se.

Question: Doctor, I'm overweight but also pregnant. Can I go on my Body Type Diet anyway?

Answer: I feel, as do most doctors, that it's not a good idea to try to lose weight while pregnant. After you have your baby, by all means go on your Body Type Diet. In the meantime, follow your doctor's advice about diet.

If you are not yet pregnant but thinking about having a baby, the best thing for you is to get your body in balance through the Body Type Diet before you get pregnant. Your pregnancy will be much easier if your body is balanced.

Question: Doctor, do you believe in fasting? I've always heard it's the best way to lose weight, if you can do it.

Answer: Fasting has a strange fascination for many people. I have concluded that if you are driven by cravings, and do not know how to use food to create balance and harmony in your system, then food becomes such a problem to you that it seems easier not to eat at all. Yet fasting is not the ultimate answer to weight control, since sooner or later we must learn to eat right. You can't fast forever, and eventually you'll have to deal with food.

To the question of whether fasting is useful as a temporary means of losing weight, my answer is yes, but up to a point. I have occasionally allowed some of my patients to fast for a couple of days. However, there are problems with fasting. Deficiencies of vitamins, minerals, or proteins may develop, for example. Many people feel weak or irritable, or have headaches while fasting, although some do not. It is even possible to do great harm to the body on extended fasts, if you fail to provide yourself with some vital element that your body needs to keep on functioning.

On the other hand, I believe that the theory of fasting is sound. The theory says by resting the machinery of digestion, we restore our bodies more completely than if we continued to eat as we normally do. So there is a contradiction: Fasting could be helpful, yet it has the potential to be harmful. What to do?

I believe I have solved this problem with the Last Five Pounds Diet. The Last Five Pounds Diet for each body type provides what I consider to be an optimum balance between the values of fasting and its potential dangers.

These diets are more restricted than the Weight Loss Diets, to the point where they can be considered as partial fasts. They "fast" the dominant gland by eliminating completely each body type's dominant gland stimulators. At the same time they provide nourishment for the less active glands, which relieves some of the negative side effects of fasting.

By allowing some food, the Last Five Pounds Diet has a positive value that total fasting lacks: that of helping you learn how to eat—how to handle food—so that once the fast is over you are not thrown back into the world of food as helpless as when you left it!

Question: Doctor, you say that your Last Five Pounds Diet helps get rid of cellulite. It sounds wonderful—I've got it and I hate it. But

I read somewhere that there's no such thing, that it's just regular fat. Is cellulite any different from ordinary fat?
Answer: Yes, it is. There are people who doubt the existence of cellulite, but I've seen too much of it—and seen how differently it behaves from ordinary fat—to say there's no such thing!

Of course, it looks different from ordinary fat. But more important is the internal difference. Cellulite gets its distinctive, wrinkly appearance by being more toxic than ordinary fat. That is, it contains more of the toxic by-products of faulty digestion, bad diet, or illness than ordinary fat. This is what makes it so hard to lose.

When cellulite (or any fat, for that matter) is lost, it is burnt up by the body, used as food. The body has more trouble using toxic fat. As thousands of dieters have told me, when they are losing toxic fat they actually feel toxic; that is, irritable, fatigued, weak—the negative feelings so often associated with dieting. These feelings make dieting so difficult that many dieters will simply stop dieting, preferring to keep the five extra pounds rather than go through the feelings involved in losing them.

I have designed the Last Five Pounds Diet for each body type to combat the effects of losing toxic fat. The most important means is through the balancing of the metabolism that the entire Body Type Weight Loss Program provides. A more rested dominant gland, and strengthened support glands, handle the burning of cellulite much more effectively than a weakened metabolism.

Also, the herbal teas, the snacking strategies, and the vegetable soups for each body type are designed to ease the process of digesting toxic fat. My patients tell me that they have so many strategies available to them for overcoming the "negatives" of dieting that, in fact, they never feel negative at all!

Question: What do you think about alcohol? Some diets let you drink white wine or even liquor. What about yours?
Answer: Mine doesn't. Alcohol has no place on a weight loss program. Not only does it add calories without adding nutritive value, it also makes you hungrier and less alert—which means less able to remember the principles of Body Type Dieting!

Of course, I know that even if you stop drinking while you're losing weight, you may enjoy alcohol and will continue to do so after you've reached your ideal weight. My caution would be that alcohol has a stimulating effect on the adrenal glands. A-Types are more susceptible to overdoing alcohol and putting on weight as a result.

Question: Can laboratory tests be used to determine my body type? I think I'm a Thyroid Type, but I'd like to have a blood test of my thyroid levels to be sure that I'm right.

Answer: I had a patient once who heard that I prescribed diets on the basis of the dominant gland, so she came to see me bearing a complete folder of lab tests she'd had done. She'd spent several hundred dollars on the work. I looked at her without opening the folder and told her that she was an Adrenal Type. I was sorry she'd spent that money; it was completely unnecessary.

Laboratory tests are neither necessary nor helpful in determining the body type. In the first place, they are unnecessary. Your dominant gland shows itself in the way your body looks, as long as you understand clearly what to look for.

Body shape is glandular chemistry writ large. The glands are artists who work quietly in their studios behind the scenes, producing their works. The body is a work of art produced by all the glands together, masterminded by the dominant gland. Just as every artist has some characteristics by which his work can be recognized, so each of the glands has key characteristics that it imparts to the bodies it dominates. As a result, every individual has features that point to his or her dominant gland.

In the second place, using lab tests to find blood hormone levels is not as simple as it sounds. There is a great deal of fluctuation in hormone levels in the body, both on a daily basis and in the course of longer cycles, such as the menstrual cycle. A "high" level of pituitary hormone and a "low" level of a female sex hormone at any given time would not necessarily indicate that the person was a Pituitary Type; it might just as well indicate a particular point in that woman's monthly cycle. So laboratory tests do not tell the story; close observation of the body reveals much more.

Question: I have gone through the Body Type Checklist and have no doubt about which body type I am. But I don't have the cravings I should. I'm a G-Type, but I crave sweets. What does this mean?

Answer: To answer this question fully, I'd want to ask you another question or two in return. What kind of sweets do you crave? It may be that you crave chocolate, which is indeed sweet but which is also fat—and it may be the fat that you are craving, not the sweetness. There are many foods that are sweet, but predominantly fat. Mall cookies are another example.

But if I found that you actually did have a sweets craving in addition to your normal fats craving, it would tell me that the cravings natural to your body type have been either joined or supplanted by another craving that normally belongs to another body type. I call these "crossover cravings." They obviously do occur, and there are several possible reasons why they do.

One reason is early childhood conditioning. There are some families and some cultures that emphasize a particular kind of food very strongly. For example, there are families who insist on having meat at every meal, and who tell the children how healthy, nourishing, nonfattening, and generally desirable meat is. People with such a background sometimes develop a craving for meat, even if they are Thyroid or Pituitary Types. Other cultures place a strong value on certain carbohydrates such as rice or pasta.

Some families emphasize sweets heavily. A sweet is a reward for every good deed and the prize at the end of every meal. This may have been how your sweets craving came about. Since sugar does have such a strong thyroid-stimulating quality, and since you do, after all, have a thyroid gland, it is possible that you have developed a sweets craving on the basis of this constant exposure to sweets, along with the psychological value of sweets as a highly desired reward food.

This would be even more common than it is, except for the fact that most of us have psychological associations with many types of food. Naturally, we tend to select our craving foods from the foods that are most stimulating to our dominant gland. I remember two patients, a brother and sister, whose case illustrates how this works. They came from a warm Italian-American family, and both were deeply attached to the foods of their childhood. But the brother, a Thyroid Type, was attracted mainly to the pasta—a typical T-Type craving. The sister, by contrast, who was a Gonadal Type, all but dreamed of the spicy sausage dishes her mother used to make. Both had selected, from the identical background, foods that were stimulating to their own dominant gland. They told me they had spent their childhood finishing what was on each other's plates!

Another reason for "crossover" cravings is dominant gland exhaustion. Here's how that works. Let's say you're a Thyroid Type, and you've been overeating sweets and drinking lots of caffeine for years. Your thyroid is by now so tired that when you drink a cup of coffee or eat a candy bar, it can hardly respond at all. So eating these foods doesn't have the payoff—the kick—that it used to have. So in order to get any additional energy out of your craving food, you have to add another craving food to it, one that stimulates another, not yet exhausted, gland.

This is the way cravings for very rich, greasy sweets develop. T-Types who have exhausted their thyroid begin to eat very rich mall-style cookies, which give them an adrenal rush in addition to kicking their poor tired thyroid. The same thing can also happen in reverse: An A-Type or a G-Type like you can have such tired adrenals or gonads that a greasy snack doesn't do much for them anymore. So you begin adding sugar to your list of craving foods, in order to at least get *some* response out of your body.

This is why cravings are not an absolute guide to body type. There are questions about cravings on the Body Type Checklist, but the main emphasis is on your body's shape. While your cravings and your body type will correspond most of the time, body shape is a much more reliable guide to body type.

EATING OUT ON THE BODY TYPE DIET

We all feel certain time pressures in our busy lives. As such, eating out is a way of life for most of us today. And of course, eating out is not entirely bad. Eating out is relaxing and fun—someone else does the dishes—but when you're working on becoming balanced, it can present certain challenges.

While eating out, what you gain in convenience, you give up in control. And of course, the degree of control you have over your food varies—there are many different eating-out experiences. If you go out to a restaurant you select yourself with your body type in mind, that's one thing. And restaurants are more accommodating than you might think. A 1993 National Restaurant Association survey found that nearly ninety percent of all table service restaurants (that is, ones that aren't either fast-food places or serve-yourself buffets) will alter food preparation for you—you just have to ask.

If you go to dinner at the home of a friend or relative who has selected the menu in accordance with needs of her own, that's something else. You can't exactly place an order at your mom's. This is an area in life that is a compromise; just do the best you can, and resolve to go back to your body type guidelines at the very next meal.

FOR ALL BODY TYPES
TO KEEP IN MIND

PLAN AHEAD

The first decision when eating out is where to go. For each body type, there are some kinds of restaurants you should just forget about. For A-Types, it's steak houses where that's all they serve, and they look at you funny if you even mention the word "chicken." For T-Types, it's bakeries, where the highest-protein item available is the croissant. For G-Types, it's barbecue places. Don't even think about the ribs, at least for now. For P-Types, it's yogurt shops and pizza places (unless you can find pizza without cheese).

On the other hand, there are plenty of places where you will be able to enjoy yourself and stay with your body type guidelines easily—healthy soup-and-salad places, for instance. Ethnic restaurants of all kinds, where the cuisine is based on fresh vegetables, whole grains, and small amounts of meat are a great choice for all types. Family-style places whose menus have lots of entries with the "heart-healthy" symbol beside it offer plenty of options. You have a lot of choices, so give your decision some thought.

Once you've chosen the place, take a moment to think about what you will eat. Review the Plenty and Moderation foods for your body type. These will be the basis of your meal, and will help you avoid falling for your Rarely foods. If you have thought through your eating plan, you will have less trouble resisting the danger foods for your body type.

START OFF RIGHT

Once you're in the restaurant, act immediately to take the edge off your hunger. Order an appetizer even before you peruse the menu. G's and A's can order a big salad (oil and vinegar on the side) or a bowl of vegetable soup. T's and P's can ask for a seafood cocktail. You can avoid a lot of cravings this way. By the time you've enjoyed your appetizer, you'll be able to eat moderately and happily according to your eating plan.

ORDER WHAT YOU REALLY WANT

There's absolutely no point in ordering something you dislike. Within your Plenty and Moderation foods are lots of delicious foods. Pick one—otherwise you'll feel so dissatisfied you may go home and eat craving food just to feel satisfied.

EAT SLOWLY AND SAVOR YOUR FOOD

A restaurant meal is a treat. Enjoy it! The more you enjoy the food you order, the less it will take to satisfy you. Even in a fast-food restaurant, the food can be fast but you don't have to be. Sit down, eat, and appreciate. Focus on the food for maximum pleasure from minimum calories.

DRINK PLAIN WATER (NOT ICE WATER) AT THE TABLE

It's surprising how much of what we think is a desire to eat is actually a combination of thirst and the need to do something with our mouths. Having a glass of water to sip is a major way to avoid constant eating. But drinking ice water, especially during meals, is not a good idea. It inhibits your stomach's ability to digest your food, which means that you may eat enough yet still feel unsatisfied. Warding off the ice in your water can be a challenge, but it's worth it.

BRING A TEA BAG OF YOUR BODY TYPE HERBAL TEA

It's smart always to carry several tea bags with you in your purse or briefcase. Ask for hot water and make yourself a cup of tea. It will soothe your body and take away cravings instantly!

TAKE HOME HALF YOUR MEAL

One of the biggest problems with restaurant meals is portion size. Many popular restaurants should be called "A Lot for Cheap," because that's what they are selling. I appreciate their generosity, but it's not in our best interests to be served eight-ounce pieces of meat, huge potatoes, and half-cups of sour cream.

If your restaurant offers a half-portion at a reduced rate, as many do, order it—it will be *plenty* of food. Or just ask for a box and take half the meal home. If you have trouble leaving food on your plate (as many people do), ask for the take-home box at the beginning of the meal, and put half in immediately. Then slowly savor the other half—you will never miss the part in the box, and you'll enjoy a second meal at home for the same price. Never be embarrassed to do this—you'd be amazed how many people do.

SPECIAL GUIDELINES FOR GONADAL TYPES

THE STRATEGY TO AVOID YOUR WORST TEMPTATION in a restaurant—spicy dishes that will stimulate your appetite and make you lose control over your eating—is to carry a piece of fruit with you and eat it shortly before you go into the restaurant. The fruit will help balance your system so that resisting spicy foods becomes easier, not harder. In any case, it is psychologically difficult to eat spicy foods after cool, fresh fruit.

YOUR BEST ORDER for your main course is fish. Ask that it be broiled, baked, steamed, poached, or cooked in its own juice. Chicken is also an acceptable choice, but not barbecued chicken— the sauce is too salty and, of course, too spicy for you. Avoid red meat and casserole-type dishes (things like beef Stroganoff), which are made with creamy sauces. Also avoid most ethnic dishes (Mexican, Indian, etc.)—again, too spicy. In Chinese restaurants, do not select a Hunan- or Szechwan-style dish. Choose Cantonese-style dishes based on chicken, fish, and vegetables.

AT A FAST-FOOD RESTAURANT, be aware that the main problem for you is the excessive oil used in cooking. In a hamburger place, the trick is to order a fish sandwich, remove the tartar sauce, throw away the top piece of bread, and blot the fish with your napkin, on both sides. Don't order fries. Some fast-food places have a salad bar; if available, a big salad is your best bet. Another good choice for fast food for you: frozen yogurt. Avoid pizza restaurants and Mexican-style fast food (too spicy).

SPECIAL GUIDELINES FOR
ADRENAL TYPES

THE STRATEGY TO AVOID YOUR WORST TEMPTATION in a restaurant—ordering a big steak with salad and pretending you had a healthy diet meal—is to have the salad, but with tuna fish or cottage cheese instead. Before-meal appetizers (peanuts, salty snacks) are also a temptation for you, so if these are on the table in a restaurant ask that they be taken away immediately, before you have a chance to weaken. If you eat one, you'll eat a lot of them. Drinks can also be a temptation. Order a club soda or mineral water, with a twist of lemon for eye and taste appeal. If you simply can't resist a drink, you might have a wine spritzer—white wine mixed with lots of club soda. Sip it slowly and make it last.

YOUR BEST ORDER for a main dish is breast of chicken or turkey, but be sure to request that it is baked, broiled, steamed, or poached, not fried. The classic "dieter's plate" in many restaurants consists of fruit, cottage cheese, and a hamburger patty. This is a good choice for you if you ask them to leave off the hamburger. Fruit salad with cottage cheese is another good choice at either lunch or dinner.

IN A FAST-FOOD RESTAURANT, the main thing to avoid is the hamburger. Look for something without red meat—for example, a chicken taco or a mostly lettuce burrito in a Mexican-style place. A slice of one of the newer "heart-healthy" pizzas once in a while is acceptable, although pizza in general is too salty for you to make a habit of it. In a hamburger restaurant, a fish sandwich is a possible choice. Or you can have frozen yogurt with a granola topping. For really fast food, carry a covered mug full of granola with you and order a carton of milk to pour over it, perfect for your body type.

SPECIAL GUIDELINES FOR
THYROID TYPES

THE STRATEGY TO AVOID YOUR WORST TEMPTATION in a restaurant—the bread basket—is to ask to have it taken away immediately, before you start to nibble on it. Then order a seafood cocktail right away. The protein in the shrimp or crab will strengthen your body and your willpower by keeping your thyroid gland cooled off.

YOUR BEST ORDER for a main dish in a restaurant is broiled or baked chicken. An omelette is another good entrée if you did not have eggs for breakfast. At the end of the meal, if you've eaten a good, high-protein entrée, you'll be in a good position to resist your second major temptation, dessert. If you feel you may not be able to resist, excuse yourself and go to the bathroom while the others at your table are ordering dessert. Then, while the others eat, call for hot water and make your raspberry leaf tea. You might order the cheese plate for dessert, but if it comes with fruit, restrict yourself to half a piece at most. Avoid the bowl of mints at the register by having someone else pay the bill.

IN A FAST-FOOD RESTAURANT, you are in relatively good shape, since protein foods are readily available. A hamburger or a chicken or fish sandwich are all acceptable—as long as you throw away the top piece of bread and blot the meat with your napkin. Also, many places have a variation of eggs Benedict, consisting of an egg with a slice of meat and cheese. Again, throw away the top piece of bread and have the rest. In some fast-food restaurants there are sandwiches served on whole-wheat bread. You may be tempted by a cola drink, but you must resist. The best strategy for this is to order water—no ice, remember. Drink it right away; if you're not thirsty, your temptation to drink a cola will be much less.

SPECIAL GUIDELINES FOR PITUITARY TYPES

THE STRATEGY TO AVOID YOUR WORST TEMPTATION in a restaurant—a cheeseburger, or anything au gratin (with cheese)—is to order something high-protein immediately, like a shrimp cocktail. The protein will help you feel strong enough to resist those cheesy, creamy dishes that no P-Type would dream of making at home, but that always seem to appear on restaurant menus. Another temptation for you: the desire to eat a heavy meal at night when dining out. Avoid it by concentrating on protein.

YOUR BEST ORDER in a restaurant is a shrimp or crab salad, or an omelette. Stay away from dishes with sauces; they are invariably too creamy for your metabolism. In a really elegant restaurant you can order steak tartare—raw chopped meat with seasonings. Perfect for you! In a Japanese restaurant, have sashimi (raw fish) rather than sushi, which has too much rice. Avoid tempura; it's too greasy.

IN A FAST-FOOD RESTAURANT, order a hamburger (but not a cheeseburger). Throw away the top piece of the roll and blot the burger with a napkin, twice. No shakes for you, ever—and no cola drinks while you are dieting. Request a cup of water, or ask for hot water and make fenugreek tea. Stay away from most pizza places—no pizza with cheese has ever agreed with a Pituitary Type. In a Mexican-style restaurant, skip the enchiladas (they have melted cheese on the top and sour cream on the side). If you order a taco, be sure to request that they leave off the grated cheese. Fast-food rotisserie chicken is a good choice, but pull off the skin before you eat it.

THE BODY TYPE EXERCISE PROGRAM

Since the 1983 edition of this book, new health research on exercise has provided us with a clearer picture of how much our bodies need physical activity. We now have a better idea of what exercise can do—from preventing disease to speeding up the metabolism so that extra weight comes off and stays off. We now know that exercise is more beneficial than was suspected twenty years ago or, to put it another way, that *not* exercising is far more of a health risk than had been realized.

In fact, the American Heart Association in 1996 added "not exercising" to its list of known risk factors for heart disease. The other risk factors are high blood pressure, elevated cholesterol, and smoking. Being a couch potato is as risky as having high cholesterol! It's as risky as *smoking*! That's quite an insight, and one that deserves our total attention.

SO WHY AREN'T WE EXERCISING?

It's obvious that while the research on exercise has shown us what we should do, we haven't begun to do our part and put the research into practice. A recent study at the Centers for Disease Control and Prevention showed that 68 percent of Americans aren't exercising enough to get the benefits—that's 120 million people. My own experience bears that out. When I question new patients about their exercise program, most are not doing any exercise at all. (When I ask what they do, they say "I walk to the car.") Others tell me that they have started, but quit, an exercise program in the past or have a roomful of exercise equipment that they never touch. Very few are on what I would regard as an ideal program.

Some patients tell me they are trying to exercise faithfully, but their commitment is weakening because they aren't seeing the kinds of changes they hoped for or have been led to expect. Still others are actually *overexercising*—working out for hours each day to the point of exhaustion—and still not feeling that they're doing enough, or that the results are what they wanted for themselves. They feel caged and exhausted behind taut strings of muscle.

If you were caught up in an exercise wave that has now departed and left you panting on the shore, or if you're one of those who exercises intensely but incorrectly, you may also have experienced some of the negative effects of exercise. Exercise certainly does carry the possibility of injury (or else why would sports medicine be one of the fastest-growing fields in medicine today?). It can also be *unbalancing*—that is, it can *increase* the imbalance typical of your body type, as I'll explain. And of course, there is also the frustration of using your time and energy in something that doesn't seem to pay off in the way you wanted.

In this chapter, I want to give you the missing key to enjoying the wonderful benefits of exercise. The right exercise program really is a health gold mine: It can make you stronger, more energetic, more attractive, and healthier. The enrichment is really indescribable. In time, it will give back far more in benefits than it takes. But to get all this, you have to understand your own body and what it needs.

On the most basic level, you first have to find an exercise program you will actually *do*—not just start, but continue as an enjoyable practice for the rest of your life. Then, you have to be sure that the program you choose gives you the results you want—because otherwise you will certainly not stay with it. It's not the case that any exercise is right for you, or that just because you begin a program you're going to be getting the right results. Unless you have a clear idea of what you're doing, the results may be all wrong!

The missing key, of course, is knowing how to choose an exercise program that fits the needs of your body type. An exercise program that you will feel good about starting and better about continuing is one that *invigorates the abilities your body lacks.* In other words, the right program for you does not simply use your body's natural abilities. Rather, a body type exercise program works to create balance and harmony in your system by developing other abilities—ones that your system needs to be whole. Exercise, like diet, can either overstimulate and stress aspects of your nature, or fill in gaps and make you more balanced and whole. It can actually offset and reduce your vulnerabilities while it gives you a stronger and healthier body—and indeed a stronger and healthier mind and spirit as well.

THE NEEDS OF THE EXERCISER

Exercise is intense activity. Because of its intensity, its effect is never neutral—if it's not extra positive for you, it's extra negative. If you choose the right exercise, you can produce genuine and profound improvements in your total metabolic system. But exercise, like diet, has to be considered in the context of the *needs of the exerciser.* You now know that you can't figure out the best diet for yourself without considering what your body type requires. No food is good or bad in itself—it can only be judged by the effects it produces, for good or ill, on your own system. Exercise must be judged in exactly the same way. Everything we do has holistic impact—there are never any purely "local" effects.

Exercise, by its character, stimulates different organs and different parts of the spinal cord. These varying stimulations change the chemical balance of the body. Similarly, the fact that exercise does affect the spinal cord on different levels means that it also affects the character of arousal of the brain. We're all familiar with beta-endorphins and the "runner's high," but that's only one, well-advertised aspect of the complex chemical changes that exercise produces. These include the glandular balance, the balance of the sympathetic and parasympathetic nervous systems ("fight or flight" versus "stay and play"), and the balance of mental functioning. With all these complex variables, it's essential to take into account your body type in deciding which exercise to do.

Far too many people today are pinning all their hopes for perfect health on an exercise program that might be good for someone else, but completely wrong for them. This can be disastrous. It's vital to stop and look at the map—the one that indicates the direction *you* need to go. If an exercise program is having a positive holistic impact, it's the right one for you. If not, it isn't—no matter what the most buffed trainer at the gym might have to say.

Signs of the Wrong Direction

Like the wrong diet, the wrong exercise program results in strain, fatigue, cravings, and imbalance. Yes, doing a form of exercise not suited to your body type will *actually increase your cravings* for your downfall foods. This is the worst, and a common, nightmare. If you are a T-Type and crave sweets after a workout, or a G-Type who needs a creamy lunch after exercise class, you're almost certainly doing the wrong exercise and stimulating your nervous system and body chemistry in the wrong way. The craving is a tip-off you shouldn't ignore.

The wrong program can also produce a craving for *the exercise itself.* If you are, for example, an Adrenal Type and find that you actually crave a session with your weights, a T-Type who craves tennis, a P who craves long-distance running, or a G who craves horseback riding, you are doing the wrong kind of exercise. Think how many people you know like this. Exercise should not have the features of an addiction.

Another sign that you're not on the right program is if you don't find any improvement in your health, only superficial improvement in your muscles. Swami Vivikananda, an expert on the yoga system of integration of mind and body, says, "Muscular development of the body does not necessarily mean a healthy body, as is commonly assumed, for health is a state where all organs function perfectly under the intelligent control of the mind." I certainly agree.

This is not to degrade strength training. Developing your muscles has many benefits in itself, but an exercise program should provide much more. It's important not to consider exercise only in terms of its superficial effects—such as the way your pectoral muscles show off the logo on your shirt—and to ignore what it does to the functioning of the organs, the organ systems, and the body as a whole.

We need to use a better yardstick than just looks in judging the success of an exercise program. But even judging by looks, the wrong exercise program won't give you what you want. On the contrary, most of the overexercisers I see in my practice have a strained, out-of-balance look that is a direct result of the wrong kind of exercise for their body type.

Each of the body types has its own particular way of looking unbalanced. The Thyroid Types on the wrong program look stringy and gaunt, but retain pockets of cellulite on their upper thighs. The Adrenal Types tend to be heavy and muscle-bound. The Pituitary Types look overintense and fanatical and can also have a stringy look. Gonadal-Type women often look toxic and have exaggeratedly large (though muscled) rear ends. The results of the wrong exercise program, rigidly adhered to, are all too apparent to the practiced eye. Basically, if you're going to do the work, you should get the benefits.

Imbalance and Exercise: A Case History

To give you an idea of what imbalance in exercise means, let me tell you about a young computer designer named Carlos E. Originally from Argentina, Carlos became a patient of mine when he took a job with a prominent computer company in Los Angeles. He was a classic Adrenal Type: strong, solid-looking, perhaps just a little too red in the face but, by the usual outward signs, a healthy man.

When he came in for his annual physical, I found that his cholesterol was too high, and we talked about diet and exercise. I recommended the A-Type Diet. This meant that Carlos would be cutting down on the steaks and other rich, adrenal-stimulating meats that he was accustomed to eating, and increasing fresh vegetables, fruit, and whole grains.

Like most of us, Carlos ate what his South American mother had taught him to eat. I mean no criticism of anyone's tradition; I'm sure every mother in every culture does her best to feed her kids correctly, but there comes a time when change is truly necessary. At this point, changing to the Adrenal Type Diet was, for Carlos, of vital and urgent importance.

However, he was dubious. He didn't see why he needed to make changes, even with his cholesterol as high as it was, because, he said, "I'm taking care of that problem with exercise." What he had chosen to do was to keep up his muscles by lifting heavy weights six or seven days a week. This, he felt, was giving him the cardiovascular insurance he needed.

It wasn't. Its overall effect on his system was very similar to that produced by his steak-and-buttery-potatoes diet: It acted to stimulate his dominant adrenal glands. I wanted him to change to a diet that would increase balance in his system by resting his adrenals and stimulating his thyroid and pituitary glands. I also wanted him to do a kind of exercise that would reduce adrenal stimulation and give a workout to his other glands, so as to create balance in his metabolism through activity.

What Carlos Needed

Let's go back to the idea that the right exercise program should increase the abilities your body lacks. I explained to Carlos that the form of exercise he was doing—weight lifting, which is aimed primarily at building a solid musculature—was the very opposite of what he should be doing. What he needed was to focus on the ability his body lacked, which for an A-Type like Carlos was flexibility, not strength. I told him that flexibility means more than the ability to touch his toes. It refers primarily to inner flexibility, especially of his cardiovascular system, which in A-Types tends to be stiff and congested. He needed a varied cardiovascular workout that would exercise his heart and increase his coordination. I recommended handball and thought he would enjoy it.

Carlos just didn't see it. "Exercise is exercise, Doctor," he argued. "Sure, I could play a little handball, but I *like* lifting weights. Why should I stop?" I told him that I had no objection to his doing one or two sessions a week with lighter weights, which would be less stimulating to his adrenals, but that the heavy weight lifting so many times a week was acting like a drug on his system, just like the steaks. I couldn't persuade him. However, I didn't worry too much about his skepticism. I didn't want to overwhelm him with too many changes at once, so I decided to focus on the A-Type Diet at the beginning, planning to return to exercise when his diet changes had taken hold.

I assumed I would have plenty of time to get to Carlos's exercise program. I didn't. The next week I received a call from the hospital, where Carlos had just been admitted to intensive care with a heart attack. He was thirty-one years old.

Despite this catastrophe, Carlos emerged more or less okay. His attack turned out to be fairly mild, and since it happened when he was young and otherwise robust, his recovery was rapid. He should not have had to endure a heart attack, but at least he was now motivated (to put it mildly!) to get serious about a plan for his own health. I connected with his cardiologist, and we put him on the A-Type Exercise Program as soon as we agreed he was ready for it.

By the time a year had elapsed, he was in far better shape—in terms of cardiovascular condition and overall health—than he had ever been. There is no doubt that his condition was serious, entailing as it did loss of heart tissue that he will never get back. But his motivation is still strong, and his prognosis for the future is excellent.

The Garden Path:
Imbalance in Each Body Type

Luckily, Carlos's case was unusual. Few people, even strong, A-Type men living on steak and stress, are going to experience the catastrophe of a coronary occlusion at so early an age. But Carlos was typical in one respect: his tendency to choose a form of exercise that contributed to imbalance, rather than balance, in his metabolism.

Each body type, in its own characteristic way, does precisely this. "I love horseback riding," says Sarah H., a G-Type woman I know. Certainly she does—but the effects on her G-Type rear are unfortunate. It's hard and muscled, but her cellulite gives it a marbled quality, and it's entirely out of proportion to her body. The rest of her reflects the same imbalance as her rear end. But riding makes her feel good, and she misses it intensely when she doesn't spend every weekend on her horse. It works out her body mainly below the waist, giving plenty of blood flow and stimulation to her sex glands. Other G-Type women ride bicycles, or do intense lower-body calisthenics or high-kicking jazz dancing. Clearly, these forms of exercise use their strengths, but do nothing to invigorate the abilities their bodies lack.

Sarah's husband Gerald is a Pituitary Type, and he's into compulsive, long-distance running. Never mind that he's exhausted and fanatical—he's got an elaborate theory on the philosophy of running and doesn't really care what he's doing to his body. For him, as for most P-Types, exercise is primarily a *mental* stimulant—and a stimulant to his dominant gland. What he really needs is to feel more connected to his body and more coordinated, but what he does is put his legs on automatic pilot and go for the "runner's high."

Louanne B. is a Thyroid Type, and her sport is tennis. Tennis fits in with the thyroidal way Louanne always does everything: in short, intense bursts of energy that leave her totally wiped out. Every Saturday morning Louanne breakfasts on four cups of coffee and a marzipan croissant, goes out on the courts, and runs around like a madperson for a couple of sets. Then she falls into a chair, where she drinks iced tea and talks nonstop until she's ready for her afternoon nap. She can never figure out why her game doesn't seem to improve from one weekend to the next. She needs to realize that she's making her T-Type instability worse with exercise that is intermittent and unsustained.

Like Carlos, each of these people has chosen a form of exercise that fits into, and amplifies the discordancies of, his or her typical body type energy pattern. All of them have chosen what I call the garden path of exercise: the form of exercise that confirms imbalance rather than corrects it. Exercise like this lets you think that you're healthy ("I exercise, don't I?"), but is really a form of dominant gland punishment.

What each of these people needs to do is just what we all must do: change from a form of exercise that accentuates bodily disharmony to one that increases balance. The Body Type Exercise Program is one that gets you off the garden path and onto a new path: the path of superfluidity.

Some Things Exercise Can't Do

Before we go on to the benefits of the right exercise program for your body type, I want to point out that even the best program does have certain limitations. For example, patients often tell me that they would like to exercise to reduce stress. Sometimes stress actually does accumulate in the muscles and tendons, and exercise moves the parts around and dissolves the knots. But once dissolved, they must still be removed—which exercise cannot do.

It is not truly in the province of exercise to undo the results of stress in your body. The key to reducing stress (which may be defined as the accumulated fatigue of our activity, which may be mental, physical, or emotional) is not further activity but *rest*. Obviously, we cannot be at rest and exercising at the same time, and we should not expect to accomplish the goals of rest and activity at once. If you wish to rid yourself of the fatigue of a stressful day, what you need is a period of deep rest.

Fatigue, stress, and tension have results in the body that are similar to disease (in fact, they are disease). These effects are the opposite of energetic good health, which can be restored only by rest. Exercise gives us a break from a certain kind of mental stress, and it can dissolve knots of fatigue, but it cannot get *rid* of the stress—only take our attention away from it for a time. The truth is that to *cure* stress and fatigue, actually throw it off, we must turn to something that gives rest.

For this, I have always recommended the technique of transcendental meditation. The regular practice of transcendental meditation, or TM, produces a general and very beneficial reduction in stress throughout the entire system. Research has shown that TM also increases our ability to deal with difficult situations, so that stress does not build up as rapidly in the first place. For general relief of stress, then, the practice of transcendental meditation is incomparably preferable to exercise.

Another thing that exercise can't do is enable you to disregard your body type nutrition guidelines and indulge yourself freely in your downfall foods. On the contrary. A T-Type patient of mine once came back from a hiking trip around the High Sierra camps in Yosemite National Park having gained five pounds in seven days. "But I walked at least ten miles every day!" she said. "If I can't eat all the candy I want to then, when can I?" She might also have asked why she wanted to eat so much candy—obviously, it was a craving.

I had to tell her, sadly, that she *never* could, if what she was talking about was unlimited quantities of a food that would overstimulate her dominant gland. Hiking ten miles a day might have let her sneak in an occasional protein bar, but there's no exercise program in the world that allows you to live on your craving foods. It just doesn't work that way. Exercise has a lot of benefits, but not that one.

The fact is that any exercise, even one that's perfect for your body type, is still something of a mixed blessing. By raising your metabolism it does, in fact, increase wear and tear—aging—of your system. There is only a narrow corridor in which the benefits outweigh the costs. In a car, we talk about "wearing in" an engine so that the parts mate more perfectly and, ultimately, function more efficiently. But a body isn't quite like a car, and we can accept this kind of breaking in only up to the point where it results in truly better overall functioning. Besides, in a car we can change the oil and get out the gunk that wear and tear put there. Doing the same thing for the body would also be desirable, but exercise isn't the way. (What does work is the Long Weekend of Rejuvenation—see Chapter 15.)

Developing the Abilities
Your Body Lacks

But enough about what exercise can't do: Let's go back to all the amazing things it *can* accomplish for you. Remember, we're talking about exercise that specifically develops the abilities your body lacks, and offsets weaknesses that your body type has. What do you have to know in order to design this ideal program?

Choosing exercises to invigorate the abilities your body lacks is almost exactly like choosing foods to stimulate your less active glands. In choosing the right foods for your body, you first had to understand the effect of the various types of food on your glandular system. This told you which foods you needed to reduce, in order to stop overstimulating your dominant gland, and which foods you needed to increase, in order to nourish and support your less active glands. In effect, you were using foods to invigorate the abilities your body lacked.

You need the same kind of information about the different forms of exercise in order to design an exercise program with the same effect. Like the different types of food, each different exercise has a specific effect on your body. (As with Carlos, craving salt and craving weight lifting amounted to the same thing.) You need to know the abilities your body lacks and then match that with the kinds of exercise that are enlivening and invigorating to those particular abilities.

You also need to know the abilities that your body possesses naturally. You want to enjoy those abilities, of course, but you don't want to concentrate on exercises that use them. They will not be as balancing to your system as exercises that develop the abilities you *don't* have naturally.

WHAT EACH BODY TYPE
NEEDS FROM EXERCISE

The abilities that your body has naturally come from the character of your dominant gland. At birth, and during the time you were growing and developing, your dominant gland was the one that gave you your natural, inborn characteristics. If you're a Pituitary Type, your abundance of pituitary hormones provided you with a good cardiovascular system. It also gave you natural quickness. If you're a Thyroid Type, you also were rewarded with a healthy heart, along with a body that is naturally flexible and well coordinated. If you're an Adrenal Type, your abundance of adrenal hormones provided you with natural strength. If you're a Gonadal-Type woman you have naturally good endurance and a very strong sense of connection to your body. These natural abilities are never fully lost, even though in later life you may overstimulate and even exhaust your dominant gland.

You also tend to *lack* certain characteristics by nature—those that belong to your other, less active glands. If you're a Thyroid Type, you did not get the benefit of having lots of adrenal hormones, either during your development period or later. As a result, you do not have the natural muscular development that Adrenal Types do. (As long as your thyroid gland was strong, you did have good muscle tone, but that goes down as the thyroid becomes fatigued, leaving you with little strength *or* tone.) So strong muscles are usually an "ability that your body lacks." They are not yours by nature—but you can absolutely develop them through the right exercise program. You could say that they are dormant qualities, just waiting to be awakened by the right exercise program.

If you're an Adrenal Type, you are naturally strong, but tend to lack the springy quickness of pituitary hormones and the flexibility conferred by the thyroid. You can be stiff in the sense of not being able to touch your toes; you can also be stiff internally, in the sense of having poor cardiovascular health and increased risk of heart disease. Usually you are stiff in both these ways. There is a lack of variety in your movements. So your program focuses on giving you the inner and outer flexibility you need.

If you're a Pituitary Type, you are not as influenced by hormones from the thyroid, adrenals, or gonads. So while you have the natural quickness that comes from pituitary hormones, your body lacks a strong sense of *presence* that causes you to be strongly aware of it at all times. Or, to put it another way, you as a person tend to feel disconnected from your body, because the thyroid, adrenal, and gonadal hormones that create strong bodily awareness are not as abundant in your metabolism. Your program is specially designed to create integration between your mind and body: to get you to come down out of the attic.

If you're a Gonadal Type, you have a special set of vulnerabilities, arising from the nature of your metabolism. The influence of your abundance of ovarian hormones shows up mainly below the waist. Ovarian hormones give you a strong lower body and good natural endurance; but above the waist your body is characterized by the vulnerability of your secondary gland.

The most common secondary gland for G-Types is the thyroid; so many G-Types with secondary thyroid are strong below the waist but are flabby and weak (the way T-Types often are) in their upper body. If you're a G-Type with secondary pituitary, you have a slightly different problem. This combination builds a conflict into your system. On the one hand, you identify strongly with your body as a result of abundant ovarian hormones. On the other hand, your pituitary gland creates a sense of detachment from physical things. The conflict this entails can be disturbing. (Incidentally, this is a rare combination, but it does occur. Your feeling of internal conflict can be greatly lessened by the right exercise program, which will help you find a better balance between your dominant and secondary glands.) If you're a G with secondary adrenals, there is less difference between your upper and lower body, and you will have good natural strength and endurance but be quite lacking in flexibility. But regardless of your secondary gland, the G-Type Exercise Program creates balance and proportion between your upper and lower body so that you feel like one whole person, without the vulnerability that imbalance implies.

Exercises for Invigoration

An exercise program that is complete and balancing is made up of three basic types of exercise: cardiovascular exercise, strength training, and flexibility training. Each of them has its particular effect, or type of benefit, and each of them develops abilities that one or more body types lack.

Cardiovascular exercises are all forms of exercise that raise your heart rate for a sustained period—walking, jogging, swimming, biking, dancing, skiing, using a fitness flyer, taking an aerobics class. The benefits of cardiovascular exercises are a stronger and healthier heart and lungs, better endurance, a higher metabolism for fat burning while you are exercising, and, if the exercise is weight-bearing, stronger bones.

Strength training uses weights (free weights or exercise machine weights) or resistance to increase muscle mass. The benefits of strength training are stronger bones and muscles, a higher metabolism even while you aren't exercising (because even at rest, muscles burn more calories than fat), better balance, and a better ratio of muscle to fat.

Flexibility training uses a technique of stretching and holding to improve your body's range of motion. Flexibility training can be anything from a simple stretch routine to the most advanced, pretzel-bending yoga postures. In addition to giving you a wider range of motion, flexibility training gives you a more symmetrical body, better posture, and improved balance.

To enjoy the total benefits of exercise, your program must include all three kinds—but don't worry, it won't take as long as you think. Depending on your body type, the amount of time you spend on each will vary. Adrenal Types will spend *less* time on strength training and *more* time on cardiovascular workouts. Thyroid and Pituitary Types will spend *more* time on strength training and *less* time on cardiovascular. Gonadal Types will spend *more* time on a combination of cardiovascular workouts and strength training for their upper body, and *less* time on strengthening their already strong lower bodies.

Yoga for Flexibility

For all body types, I have found that the most effective way you can get the flexibility your body needs is through a short (five- to ten-minute), daily routine of yogalike positions. As a matter of fact, the value of yoga goes beyond flexibility and into the area of profound effects on the internal organs.

Yoga and other ancient and modern systems of health development through body positioning have definite medical effects on many bodily organs. When you reach the section of recommended exercises for your body type, you'll see that I have selected, from the literature on such postures and their effects, a brief routine for you that will give you flexibility and exactly the form of internal invigoration that you need. I recommend these postures to the patients who come to my office, and I do them myself every day and have for many years. The fact is that you'll be amazed at what a pretzel you'll become in just a short time, and what a soothing and balancing effect the postures have on you when you do them regularly. Yoga positions seem very simple, but their effect is cumulative and extremely profound. They actually direct the energy of your body, and the effect is felt on your internal organs even more than it is on your outer flexibility and tone.

Start Slowly and Get Help!

You'll notice that in your exercise recommendations I have not included detailed instructions. Whether you are already exercising or not, it is wise to check with your doctor and get his or her approval for what you want to do. Especially if you're over forty or have any doubts at all about your ability to exercise, be sure to check with your physician before beginning the program.

If you aren't currently doing any exercise, it's also important that you start easily and work into your full Body Type Program. You don't want to overdo, especially at the beginning. Of course, if you are on a program of exercise already, you may only need to shift your current exercise over to the exercises for your type. You may even find that your Body Type Exercise Program takes less time than you are spending now.

With your cardiovascular workouts, if you have not been exercising you must start by doing no more than ten minutes of your exercise three times a week. After a week at that level, you can work up gradually to your specified times, adding time little by little as you feel comfortable.

Strength training can begin with the suggested time periods, but of course you will start with very light weights and increase gradually. In the area of flexibility training, it's just as important to begin slowly as it is with the other exercises.

In the following section are instructions for a simple routine of stretching and a series of strength-building exercises. For more detailed instructions I strongly suggest you consult a certified trainer or exercise instructor. Even if I had room in this chapter for extensive instructions, I feel that exercise instruction is much better done in person. This is particularly true of strength and flexibility training. You can begin walking without instruction (you acquired that skill very early) but weight lifting and stretching may be brand-new skills.

It is very helpful to have someone watch you as you learn to lift free weights or use weight machines. A good trainer will observe your form and give you corrections as needed so that you strengthen your muscles without fear of injury. The same is true with flexibility. If you choose to do the yoga positions I suggest for flexibility, a yoga instructor is of vital importance to show you the positions.

In addition to these exercise professionals, certified Body Type Counselors have a great deal of information to share with you on exercising right for your body type. They can coach you through that critical early stage until the habit of exercise takes hold and you'll never want to stop.

Now you're ready to begin. Good luck, and enjoy yourself!

THE G-TYPE
EXERCISE PROGRAM

The G-Type Exercise Theme is *Upper/Lower Body Proportioning.*
Your typical G-Type shape can make you look like two different
people above and below the waist. Your legs are strong and put on
muscle readily, while your arms, face, neck, and chest are smaller,
less developed, "chickeny," and not nearly as strong. The dispropor-
tion is accentuated by the wrong exercise program. Your Exercise
Theme tells you that balance between your two halves is not only
possible, it's a certainty with the right program.

Your Natural Abilities and the Abilities
Your Body Lacks

As a G-Type, you have great natural strength in your lower body, but
your much smaller upper body tends to be weak. And your lower
body, while strong, tends to have poor circulation, and toxins may
accumulate there as a result.

Your body as a whole has a great deal of natural coordination
and intelligence; you love to dance, for example, and have the ability to learn dances or exercise routines very easily. However, your
eye-hand coordination may be less than ideal. This is because you are
so firmly connected with and "in" your body that you can actually
lose connection with the outside world. Your exercise program includes exercises to improve this area of slight weakness.

The G-Type in Shape

You have reached your ideal development when you see that your
upper body is in proportion with your hips, thighs, and rear. You will
accomplish this by increasing upper body strength and improving
circulation below the waist. You can never change your bone structure, but you will absolutely improve your energy structure.

A persistent myth used to hold that the average woman could
never develop her upper body as well as the average man. Observing G-Type women was probably what gave rise to this myth. You

know yourself that when you're out of balance your arms don't seem to have much potential for strength or shapeliness. But in a recent study William Kraemer, a researcher at Penn State, found that women doing a moderate amount of strength training increased their upper body strength by 10 to 37 percent in just six months, which is just about what men do. G-Types on the Body Type Program end up at the upper end of this statistic, exploding that myth once and for all!

You will love it when people say, "Are you sure you're a G-Type? You look more like a really balanced Thyroid Type to me. Your rear's not big, just nice and curvy!" The G-Types I know treasure these remarks—a major benefit of the G-Type Exercise Program.

Your Ideal Program

Overall, your program is a combination of a moderate amount of cardiovascular conditioning (more than T's and P's but less than A's), full-body strength training, and additional strength training for your upper body. A special five-minute routine of yoga positions, done daily, will keep you totally flexible and integrated in your mind and body.

Cardiovascular recommendation: Do a workout that raises your heart rate to 70 to 75 percent of your maximum (see chart on page 221) four times a week. Increase eye–hand coordination by choosing cardio workouts that make you think about what you're doing: jazz dancing, complex aerobic routines, or martial arts like kung fu. You can also walk—walking is recommended for all body types—but be sure to walk fast enough to raise your heart rate, and to keep some mental focus on your body while you are walking.

Strength recommendation: Do the upper-body strength exercises three times a week and the lower-body strength exercises twice a week. When working your upper body, increase the weights so as to continue to challenge your muscles to further development (consult a certified trainer for the right level for your age and degree of fitness). When working your lower body, deliberately limit the weight you use to a maximum of five to six pounds, to avoid disproportionate development below the waist.

Flexibility recommendation: Do the following set of yoga positions, or consult a certified Body Type Counselor for a simple stretching routine.

1. Body Toning
2. Back Stretch
3. Modified Shoulder Stand
4. Fish Position
5. Twist
6. Locust Position
7. Relaxation Position

EXERCISES THAT DON'T WORK FOR G-TYPES

Horseback riding, bicycling, skating, or moves that focus mainly on your lower body such as step class or power lunges, or swimming with a kickboard, are not recommended.

A Special Note for G-Types

You must drink at least two full glasses of warm water after each exercise session to help eliminate the toxins you'll be releasing from your system. The water helps liquefy the lymph and pump it to where the toxins are being removed. Also, spend a few minutes after each session massaging your legs, thighs, and buttocks, working from the feet toward the head. Then rest for a moment or two with legs elevated. (Get your husband to do this for you if you can. Again, this will help the toxins move on out.)

THE A-TYPE EXERCISE PROGRAM

The A-Type Exercise Theme is *Cardiovascular Conditioning.* This form of exercise, the basis of heart health, is your primary need, because of all the body types you have the highest risk for heart disease. The A-Type shape, with extra pounds on the belly, is now widely recognized to be associated with this risk, although it is not actually the shape but your underlying metabolism that creates the risk.

An out-of-balance middle-aged male A-Type whose once muscled physique has sagged and whose fine chest has sunk to below his belt is the prime candidate for the great benefits of this exercise program. If you're an A-Type woman who has put on weight in front and who is so caught up in work you have no time to exercise, you need to pay attention, too. Your risk of heart disease may not be as high as that of an A-Type man but it's still significant (and the gap closes after menopause). The increase in balance and loss of belly fat that this program will bring are just what you need.

Your Natural Abilities and the Abilities Your Body Lacks

You have great natural strength, which manifests itself in good musculature when you are young. Whatever your age, you put on muscle readily. You also start with strong bones and hence a lesser risk of osteoporosis than the other body types.

However, your strong body lacks flexibility, both inside and out. Internal inflexibility refers to your heart and circulatory system, especially your arteries: "Hardening" is the very opposite of being supple and flexible. Outer inflexibility means that your entire body tends to be stiff; your joints have limited range of motion and your shorter, though stronger, muscles also limit how much you can bend.

You are not strong in eye-hand coordination, mainly because your inherent stiffness prevents a smooth flow from the information coming in at the eye, and the resulting action in the hand.

The A-Type in Shape

You'll know you are an ideal Adrenal Type when you have a streamlined look with no bulging muscles and no pockets of fat on your stomach or upper back. If you're a man, people will have a hard time figuring out if you're an Adrenal or a buffed-out Thyroid Type, because you'll look so flexible and loose. If you're an A woman, at your ideal shape you'll have created a slight curve to your rear in place of the flat boyish one you started with, and you will have a waist! Both men and women will have better coordination and quicker physical responses, with more fluidity to their movements.

Your Ideal Program

Your program has a strong focus on cardiovascular conditioning with a small amount of strength training. Notice that I do not suggest you do no strength training at all, even though good strength is a natural ability of yours. Everyone, and this does include Adrenal Types, needs to do some strength training to keep their muscle integrity into middle age and beyond. But I strongly advise you not to get involved in strength training with heavy weights as your primary form of conditioning. Remember Carlos! As pleasant as the temporary feeling of power may be, it may hide a catastrophic outcome.

Cardiovascular Recommendation: Do a workout that raises your heart rate to 70 to 75 percent of your maximum (see chart on page 221) five times a week. Increase your eye-hand coordination by playing strenuous games like handball, squash, or one-on-one basketball; this will also give a good outlet to your strong competitive urges. You can also walk—walking is recommended for all body types—but be sure to walk fast enough to raise your heart rate.

Strength recommendation: Do a complete set of strength exercises twice a week, using light weights (six pounds or less for women, ten for men) and a larger number of repetitions.

A 1998 study by fitness expert Wayne Westcott has shown that doing strength training exercises twice a week is extremely beneficial and produces almost the same effect as doing the same regimen three times a week. Remember that, if you should feel a craving to do more weight training or use heavier weights. The twice-a-week level, with light weights, will give you the health benefits you want and is much more suited to the needs of the A-Type metabolism.

Flexibility recommendation: Do the following set of yoga positions, or consult a certified Body Type Counselor for a simple stretching routine.

1. Body Toning
2. Back Stretch
3. Fish Position
4. Cobra Position
5. Modified Shoulder Stand
6. Locust Position
7. Bow Position
8. Twist
9. Relaxation Position

EXERCISES THAT DON'T WORK FOR A-TYPES

Heavy weight lifting, which overstimulates the adrenal glands, is not recommended. (If it has the potential to make you grunt, it's *out.*) Also avoid rowing, which is also overstimulating to the adrenals due to the position in which you row. Games like football and rugby in which you crash into things are also not good.

THE T-TYPE
EXERCISE PROGRAM

The T-Type Exercise Theme is *Strength and Endurance.* Your T-Type body may be slim, as nature and your strong thyroid gland intended, or padded out in the middle from thyroid overstimulation, but if you aren't paying attention to your exercise program you will never have the look of strength and integration it needs. Your Exercise Theme tells you that invigorating your very dormant strength and steadiness is the key to balance in your body type.

Your Natural Abilities and
the Abilities Your Body Lacks

You are blessed with good flexibility and very good eye-hand coordination. These make you a natural athlete, but many T-Types avoid sports because they don't feel strong enough or because they don't feel their energy is up to the effort of sustained activity. Strength and endurance are definitely the abilities your body needs to acquire. You do not put on muscle readily—but you can build up your muscles through strength training and your endurance through sustained cardiovascular workouts. You can reach a level of very satisfying and attractive tautness. The results are unbelievably balancing—you have to experience it to appreciate the difference it makes.

The T-Type in Shape

You'll know you have reached your ideal when your shape is both curvy and firm. T-Type women won't ever see a great deal of bulky muscle definition, but you'll acquire firmness and lose the "jiggles" and the cellulite on your thighs (eventually—be patient, it takes time). T-Type men can become moderately buffed, although you'll never be Arnold Schwarzenegger—it wouldn't look good on you anyway. There are T-Types in this world pumped up by steroids— they look absurd and they are.

The internal changes are even better than the external. With improved strength and constancy, your metabolism becomes much less prone to the fatigue that causes or exacerbates your sweets craving. The improved circulation you'll also experience means that your tissues can make better use of thyroid hormone. This is a key factor in maintaining clarity and preventing the lows that trigger cravings. Your exhausted thyroid does not have to work as hard, and this helps it rest and normalize—a key step toward balance.

Your Ideal Program

Your primary focus is on strength training. You do need cardiovascular conditioning, but your heart is generally healthy and you mainly need cardio work to improve your endurance. When you increase your muscle mass, your metabolism gets a boost via your adrenals, which is a very important point for T-Types who have overstimulated their thyroid gland in the past.

Muscle mass is the engine of your body; the more you have, the more calories you can eat and burn without gaining weight. A toned muscle at rest can burn a lot of calories even without doing anything.

But a tired, nonexercising T-Type gets none of this benefit. What thyroid hormone they do have available barely penetrates the cells well enough to stoke the fires. It is sad to observe what a small amount of food will put weight on an exhausted T-Type. The reason is that they have barely any muscle to burn up the food. My T-Type patients sometimes think I don't believe them when they tell me how little they have been eating, but I do. The T-Type Exercise Program changes that situation completely. Imagine the relief when you can eat like a human being and not put on several pounds in a single day.

Cardiovascular recommendation: Do a workout that raises your heart rate to 70 to 75 percent of your maximum (see chart on page 221) four times a week. Focus on workouts in which you put out sustained, steady energy, such as swimming, jogging, or rowing. You can also walk—walking is recommended for all body types—but be sure to walk fast enough to raise your heart rate.

Strength recommendation: Do a complete set of strength exercises three times a week. On all of the exercises, increase the weights so as to continue to challenge your muscles to further development (consult a certified trainer for the right level for your age and degree of fitness).

I always recommend backpacking to T-Types as it improves strength through carrying the backpack and endurance through hiking. It is also good for you to be out of doors. Many T-Types feel, like Woody Allen, that they are two with nature, instead of one. It's a sign that you are more balanced when you can contemplate dirt, and even bugs, with calm equanimity.

Flexibility recommendation: Do the following set of yoga positions, or consult a certified Body Type Counselor for a simple stretching routine.

1. Body Toning
2. Back Stretch
3. Fish Position

4. Cobra Position
5. Twist
6. Modified Shoulder Stand
7. Relaxation Position

EXERCISES THAT DON'T WORK

Exercises where the effort required is intermittent, not sustained, such as tennis, are not recommended. Avoid bicycling with underslung handlebars—the angle of your head with your neck is too acute and puts strain on your thyroid gland. You can, however, ride or use an exercise bike if it allows you to sit up straight.

THE P-TYPE
EXERCISE PROGRAM

The P-Type Exercise Theme is *Mind/Body Integration*. Your P-Type shape—youthful, childlike, soft, undefined—is an indication of an inner reality: Your body is not at the top of your priority list. It's "down there" and you are "up here." You can change your shape but only if your mind begins to engage actively with your body—it's your consciousness that is the source of change.

What this means in practice is that when you exercise, you must constantly consult your body and how it is feeling (or rather, how *you* are feeling). The last thing you need is exercise that is done repetitively to the point of exhaustion. Your theme will be realized when you actively *feel* your body, and enjoy the strong, centered feeling that comes to you from your body during physical activity.

Your Natural Abilities and
the Abilities Your Body Lacks

As a P-Type you possess good natural quickness, and a fairly high degree of natural flexibility. You have great potential as an athlete because you understand movement—in your mind. This potential is not often expressed, though, because of your lack of a natural ability to translate your theoretical understanding to reality. In other words, you know what you want to do—but you have a hard time just *moving* in a natural way. If you haven't learned mind-body coordination, the impression you give is anything but athletic; rather, you seem uncoordinated in the way that gawky children are. You are also not naturally strong, and you have the hardest time putting on muscle of all the body types.

Your endurance also needs work. P-Types who do go into sports are often long-distance runners, because they enjoy the spaced-out feeling they get when they put their bodies on automatic and let their minds trip on the runner's high. The fact that they run for long distances does not imply that their bodies have natural endurance, however. On the contrary, it shows that P-Types have the ability to drive their bodies to exhaustion by ignoring them. It's not a good thing. It causes peroxidation (rancidity) of fats, cross-linking, and free-radical formation. Achieving mind-body integration means that you are able to enjoy a more moderate form of exercise, in company with other people. Your body will enjoy it as much as your mind.

The P-Type in Shape

You will know you're at your best in muscular development when you can see that your head no longer seems a bit big for your body, but instead looks more in proportion. You will also enjoy looking like a grown-up instead of a child—you'll have a defined shape rather than the "Pillsbury dough boy" look. You will never have bulky muscles—it's just not in your metabolism to produce them—but you can have a finely muscled and supple look. Think Michelangelo's *David*. Think Fred Astaire.

Your Ideal Program

Your program combines a moderate amount of cardiovascular conditioning with a larger amount of strength training. A special five-minute routine of yoga positions, done daily, will keep you totally flexible and integrated in your mind and body.

Cardiovascular recommendation: Do a workout that raises your heart rate to 70 to 75 percent of your maximum (see chart on page 221) four times a week. To help integrate your mind with your body, choose an involved workout like aerobic dancing, jazz dancing, or ballet. Look for fairly complicated routines that make you really think about what you're doing. Karate, t'ai chi, and other martial arts also have this value of close mind-body involvement. You can also walk—walking is recommended for all body types—but be sure to walk fast enough to raise your heart rate.

Strength recommendation: Do a complete set of strength exercises three times a week. On all of the exercises, increase the weights so as to continue to challenge your muscles to further development (consult a certified trainer for the right level for your age and degree of fitness).

Flexibility recommendation: Do the following set of yoga positions, or consult a certified Body Type Counselor for a simple stretching routine.

1. Body Toning
2. Back Stretch
3. Modified Shoulder Stand
4. Fish Position
5. Cobra Position
6. Twist
7. Relaxation Position

EXERCISES THAT DON'T WORK

Anything repetitive or highly mechanical, such as long-distance running or repetitive calisthenics, is not recommended. (If you feel you must run, you will do better with a Swedish-style workout in which you vary your pace every few steps.) Avoid rowing—it's too mechanical and gives the wrong kind of muscular development. A handy rule of thumb for you: If you can get spaced out and start obsessive rumination during your exercise, it's the wrong one for you.

FINDING YOUR
MAXIMUM HEART RATE

For all the cardiovascular recommendations, I asked you to do a workout that raises your heart rate to 70 to 75 percent of your maximum heart rate. This is called your heart's "training zone" and is the number of beats per minute that will give you the most benefit from your cardiovascular exercise. To find your maximum heart rate, subtract your current age from 220.

This chart will help you estimate your heart's training zone using your age.

Your age	Approximate number of heartbeats/minute during cardiovascular workout
20	140–150
25	137–147
30	133–143
35	133–139
40	126–135
45	123–132
50	119–128
55	116–124
60	112–120
65	109–117
70	105–113
75	102–109

THE YOGA POSITIONS

Ideally, I would like you to find a yoga instructor and learn the positions in person. However, the positions I have suggested are relatively simple ones, and if you can't find an instructor or want to begin on your own, you can use these instructions.

The way to do each position is to move into it gently and hold it for about twenty seconds; then move, gently again, out of the position. When you begin, hold each position no more than ten seconds, and *gradually* increase your time to twenty seconds.

Never strain, even the least bit, as this is absolutely against the idea of yoga. Go only as far as you comfortably can in assuming a position. Without forcing, your body will gradually increase in flexibility, and you will be able to get closer to the ideal of each position. It's all right to feel stretch, but not strain. If you strain, you will have muscle spasms and become less flexible, rather than more.

You should do your positions every day. The best time to do your routine is in the morning before breakfast. If you wish to do it in the evening, the best time is at least forty-five minutes before your evening meal. If you need to do the positions after breakfast, wait an hour—they should be done with a mostly empty stomach.

Spread a light blanket or rug on the floor, and begin your routine by sitting quietly for a moment. Then start the positions in the sequence given for your body type, and do them one after another. Except on the Long Weekend of Rejuvenation, they are to be done only once each day.

Back Stretch

Lie on your back and raise your hands above your head. Slowly and gradually come up to a sitting position and then bend forward, still with arms extended, and reach toward your toes. Go only as far as it is comfortable, feeling a stretch but no strain. Remain in this position for ten seconds at first and gradually increase to twenty. Return to your original position (lying on your back).

Modified Shoulder Stand

Lie on your back. Slowly raise your feet to a half-vertical position. Continue raising your feet and legs, and when your waist begins to rise, support your hips with your hands and let your palms help you raise your waist into position. You do not need to straighten out your waist totally. Just let your legs go up far enough for your arms to support them from underneath. Hold the position for ten seconds, gradually increasing to twenty seconds. Slowly return to your original position by bending your knees to balance your trunk until your buttocks touch the floor. Then lower your legs slowly.

The Fish Position

Lie on your back. Stretch your legs and tuck your hands, palms down, under your buttocks. Raise your chest with the help of your elbows, and, bending your neck as much as possible backward, rest lightly on the top of your head. Begin by assuming the position in this way and holding it for ten seconds. After a few weeks, when you're used to the position, do it with your legs crossed in front of you, rather than extended. The technique is the same—tuck your hands beneath your buttocks and raise your chest with the help of your elbows.

The Cobra Position

Turn over and lie facedown on your blanket or mat, relaxing all your muscles. Place your palms next to your shoulders. Gradually raise your head and upper portion of your body, like a cobra raising its hood. Roll back your spine slowly, feeling each vertebra in turn. Your body from the waist down to the toes should still be touching the blanket. Go only as far as is comfortable, and do not strain. Do not press hard with your palms on the floor. Hold the position for ten seconds at first, gradually increasing to twenty seconds. Reversing the process, slowly lower your head until you are once again facedown on your blanket.

The Twist

Sit with your right leg stretched out in front of you. Raise your left leg and place your left foot next to your right knee. Then, in this position, turn your trunk to the left and reach with your right arm around your left leg to hold your right leg below the knee. Turn your trunk and head to the left so that you look over your left shoulder. At the same time, reach behind you with your left hand and, if you can, touch your right thigh from behind. Hold the position for ten seconds or less. Slowly return to your original position. Repeat with the other leg.

The Locust Position

Lie on your stomach with your arms at your sides, palms up. Let your chin rest gently on the floor. Raise your legs, one at a time, keeping them as straight as possible. Hold the position with each leg for a few seconds, then lower it to the blanket again. After doing the Locust for some time, you may raise both legs at the same time provided you do not feel strain in doing so. Repeat two or three times.

The Bow Position

Lie on your stomach, relaxing your muscles. Bend your legs at the knees and bring your feet backward over your thighs. Catch hold of your right ankle with your right hand and your left ankle with your left hand. Raise your head, body, and knees by tugging gently at your legs with your hands. Your back will be bent backward like a bow. Hold the position for ten seconds or less, but gradually increase your time to twenty seconds. Do not strain or use your legs to force your body backward. You may find at first that you can't lift your body very much. If so, just hold your ankles with your hands for a few seconds. Your flexibility will gradually increase.

Relaxation Position

Lie flat on your back with your arms at your sides. Let your mind and body be free and loose for a minute or two. For this minute, you have as much purpose in life as a puddle of water. Always end your session of flexibility training with the Relaxation Position.

BODY TONING

Body Toning is a two-minute procedure that is not for flexibility per se, but it is a good addition to your flexibility program. You can do Body Toning at either the beginning or end of your stretches, or at any time when you need a break during the day. It tones and conditions your entire body, helps to release stress, and is balancing for all body types.

Body Toning is done with the full surface of your palms and fingers. Press and then release your grip while moving your hands over each area of your body. Keep your hands in contact with your body until you complete each area, then release and move your hands to the starting place for the next area.

Begin by sitting comfortably on the floor, cross-legged if possible. Gradually begin to press and release in this order:

1. Head and neck. Press the top of the head; move your hands forward over your face and neck to the heart area. Then again press the top of your head and go over the back of the head and neck and over the shoulders, again finishing at the heart area.
2. Right arm. Grasp the fingertips of your right hand with the palm and fingers of your left hand (left hand palm is down). Gradually move the pressure upward along the arm. Go across the shoulder and chest, ending at the heart. Then grasp the fingertips of your right hand with your left hand (left hand palm is up). Gradually move the pressure up along the arm, under the shoulder, and to the heart. Repeat with your left arm.
3. Abdomen. Place both hands on your abdomen with the tips of your middle fingers meeting horizontally at your navel. Press and release, gradually moving your hands up toward your heart.
4. Back. Using both hands, begin to press and release the middle of the back and ribs, moving up toward the heart as far as you can reach.
5. Right leg. Grasp the top of your toes with your right hand and the sole of your foot with your left hand. Together, press and release, gradually moving your hands to the calf, thigh, up your waist to your heart. Repeat with your left leg.
6. Tone your back by lying on your back and drawing your knees up toward your chest. Clasp your hands over your knees and raise

226 Body Type Diet and Lifetime Nutrition Plan

your head slightly. Roll to the extreme right until the right wrist touches the floor; then roll to the extreme left by pushing off with the right elbow and moving your head to the left. Repeat several times in each direction.

7. Finish Body Toning by lying flat on your back and relaxing for several minutes.

THE STRENGTH EXERCISES

Resources

As with the yoga positions, I would much prefer that you learn the strength exercises from a qualified trainer, from a video, or from a Body Type Counselor. I'm including these instructions so that you can get started on your own, but be sure to be very cautious and careful and to begin with very light weights—one to three pounds, no more.

The program consists of eight exercises: three for the upper body, three for the lower body, one for the abdominal muscles, and one for the back. My primary resource is an excellent book, *Strong Women Stay Young,* by Miriam E. Nelson, Ph.D., with Sarah Wernick, Ph.D., published in 1997 by Bantam Books. If you do not have professional help available, I highly recommend this book. Dr. Nelson and Dr. Wernick have drawings of all the moves, along with many helpful hints about strength training. You will need to buy free weights (dumbbells) for the arm exercises, and ankle cuffs for the leg exercises. These are readily available in any sporting goods store and are not at all expensive. Dr. Nelson's book has several sources for ankle cuffs to which you can add weights as your strength increases. These are more expensive to begin with but will save you from having to buy more than one set of cuffs.

How to Begin

Before you begin your strength training, be sure to warm up your muscles for five minutes first. This can be done by walking around; by slowly standing up and sitting down in a chair ten times; or by doing all the exercises several times without weights. If you are doing your strength program right after your cardiovascular workout, you do not need a special warm-up session, as you are already warmed up!

On each of these exercises, the lift itself should take about nine seconds. Take four seconds to raise the weight, pause for one second, and take another four seconds to lower the weight. Pause for about three seconds between each lift. A "set" consists of eight to ten repetitions ("reps") of the lift. When you have completed a set, pause for a minute or two and then do a second set.

For each of the lifts, do two sets of eight to ten reps for each exercise. The entire set of eight exercises should take you no more than forty minutes. If forty minutes is too much time to find all at once, you can divide your workout into two parts. One part consists of the leg exercises, which are done with the ankle cuffs on. This should take about twenty minutes. Then you can do the other half, the arm exercises using dumbbells, at another time. It will also take twenty minutes. It is important that you do not work out the same muscle groups two days in a row, because your body needs a day to recover between sessions—this is when muscle is actually built.

Adrenal Types who need to do two full sessions per week can either do a complete session of both upper and lower body on any two nonconsecutive days; or you can do upper body one day, lower body the next day, for four days.

Gonadal Types who need to do two complete sessions per week, plus a third session of upper body only, can do a complete session on Monday and Wednesday, and arms alone on Friday, or you can do arms only on Monday, Wednesday, and Friday, and legs only on Tuesday and Thursday.

Thyroid and Pituitary Types who do three complete sessions per week can do their full sessions Monday, Wednesday, and Friday, or can do arms alone on Monday, Wednesday, and Friday, and legs alone on Tuesday, Thursday, and Saturday. Remember, each half-session is only twenty minutes, and since you don't work up a sweat you won't need to shower or change. Strength training is extremely easy to fit into your schedule and can even be done in smaller sessions (just one single exercise) and squeezed in at odd moments in your day, without any loss of benefits.

Part I: Leg Exercises (with Ankle Cuffs)

The first three exercises work the major muscle groups in your legs: the quadriceps (the large muscles in front of your thighs); your hip abductors (the muscles on the outside of your thighs); and your gluteus maximus (the large muscle of your buttocks).

1. Knee Extension (to strengthen your quadriceps). Wearing your ankle weights, sit back in a chair with your feet shoulder-width apart. Slowly raise your right leg until your knee is as straight as possible. Pause, then slowly lower your leg to the starting position. Pause for a breath, then repeat the lift with your left foot.
2. Side Hip Raise (to strengthen your hip abductors). Wearing your ankle weights, stand behind a chair, holding the back lightly for support. Slowly lift your right leg out to the side until your foot is five to eight inches off the ground. The knee of the supporting leg should be relaxed, not locked. Pause, then slowly lower your leg to the starting position. Pause for a breath, then repeat the lift with your left foot.
3. Hip Extension (to strengthen your gluteus maximus). Wearing your ankle weights, stand about eighteen inches behind a chair, holding its back lightly for support. Bend forward forty-five degrees at the waist, keeping your legs straight. Keep your neck and head in line with your torso. Slowly lift your right leg straight out behind you until your leg and torso form a straight line. Your foot will be eight to fourteen inches off the floor. Keep both feet pointed straight ahead during the entire lift. Pause, then slowly lower your leg to the starting position. Pause for a breath, then do the lift with your other leg.
4. Back Extension (to strengthen your back extensor muscles). Still wearing your ankle weights, lie on the floor facedown with two firm pillows under your pelvis. Your hipbones should be in the center of the top pillow. Your arms should be on the floor in front of you with your elbows bent so that your shoulders and arms form a U. Keeping your chest, head, and arms in line, slowly lift your chest about four or five inches off the floor. Pause, then slowly lower your chest, head, and arms to the starting position. Pause for a breath, then repeat. Do two sets, eight reps each.

Part 2: Arm Exercises (with Dumbbells)

You will be doing three exercises to work the major muscle groups in your arms: your biceps (the muscles in the front of your arm); your triceps (the muscles in the back of your upper arms); the deltoids (shoulder muscles); and the trapezius (upper back muscles).

5. Biceps Curl. Sitting in a chair, hold your dumbbell in your right hand with your arm hanging at your side. Slowly bend your arm at the elbow, lifting the weight to your shoulder without moving your shoulder or upper arm. Pause, then lower your arm to the starting position. Pause for a breath, then repeat with the same arm. When you have done your first set, do a set with your left arm. Do two sets with each arm.

6. Triceps Curl. Sitting in a chair, hold your dumbbell in your right hand. Raise your right arm over your head and bend the elbow so that your wrist is resting behind your neck. Slowly raise the weight until your arm is straight up over your head. Pause, then lower your arm to the starting position. Pause for a breath, then repeat with the same arm. When you have done your first set, do a set with your left arm. Do two sets with each arm.

7. Upward Row (to strengthen your deltoid, trapezius, and biceps). Stand with a dumbbell in each hand, with your arms hanging down in front of your thighs, palms toward your thighs. Slowly pull the dumbbells upward along your torso until they are just below your chin. At the top of the lift, your elbows will be at shoulder height and pointing out at your side. Pause, then lower your arms to the starting position. Pause for a breath, then repeat.

8. Abdominal Curl (to strengthen your rectus abdominus and obliques). This important exercise uses no weights—your head is actually the weight that you are lifting with your abdominal muscles. Be sure that when you do this you hold your abdominal muscles in, pushing them toward your navel. There is a tendency to push out on the abdominals while doing this exercise, but this will make the muscles protrude outward—somewhat defeating the purpose!

    Lie on your back with knees bent and feet flat on the floor. Place your hands on top of your thighs. Slowly lift your head and shoulders, sliding your hands up your thighs. Your chin should be slightly tucked under, but not touching your chest. Pause, then lower your head and shoulders to the starting position. Do two sets of eight reps.

At the conclusion of your strength training, you need to spend a few moments cooling down and stretching. The best way to do this is to go through each exercise two or three times without weights, holding the fully extended position for fifteen to thirty seconds each time. Don't bounce—just hold the position and relax.

SUPPLEMENTATION FOR YOUR BODY TYPE

Of all the areas of health and balance that make up the Body Type Program, the two that have seen the most advances since 1983 are exercise and supplementation. In the previous chapter you saw the significant advances in exercise research, which confirm that if you don't exercise regularly, you greatly reduce your chances of keeping off the weight you lose. In this chapter, you will see that the new discoveries in nutritional supplementation are just as important to the success of your long-term weight loss and health goals.

If you have read my 1985 book, *Dr. Abravanel's Body Type Program for Health, Fitness, and Nutrition,* you know that it contains supplement recommendations for each body type. By 1985 research had already confirmed many of the benefits of nutritional supplementation. Today, science has given us an even clearer idea of these benefits, as well as a better understanding of how much of each supplement everyone needs. Because of my particular focus on body types, I have been able to use the research in an even more precise way to address the special supplement needs of each of the four types.

You should be aware that the recommendations that follow are *not* the same as those I made back in 1985. If you still have your copy of *Dr. Abravanel's Body Type Program* and have been following those recommendations, you should change to the newer recommendations you will find in this chapter. If you have questions about your supplements or about changing over from the earlier recommendations, and wish to contact the Body Type Institute, we will certainly try to help you.

Despite the revisions, the basic rationale for taking supplements has not changed. I believed then and I believe now that taking the right supplement formulation for your body type serves a number of important purposes. First, supplements help to close up windows of vulnerability in each body type. Second, they provide a kind of nutritional insurance, especially for people who are very busy or under a lot of stress, or those who are eating less in order to lose weight. Third, they help maintain balance in your system. Fourth, they help control cravings, which I have found to be partially caused by certain key nutritional deficiencies. Finally, supplements play an important role in weight loss by helping to maintain your energy. I'd like to illustrate how these benefits come into play with the example of a patient of mine, Judith P.

STRESS, ENERGY, AND NUTRITIONAL SUPPORT

Judith P. sat across from me in my office looking like who she was—a T-Type with a problem. When I had last seen her, several months before, she had wanted to lose just five pounds. I put her on the Thyroid Type Diet, and she had lost the pounds easily. They'd been gone for a month, but Judith still wasn't happy.

"It's my energy level," she complained. "It's a lot better than it was before the diet. I can jump out of bed in the morning feeling pretty good now—that's progress for me. But I can't keep going. By the time I've made breakfast for my three kids, gotten them off to school, done a load of wash, battled traffic to the office, and straightened out the five or six emergencies that have blown up in my advertising business overnight, I'm exhausted. And it's still only nine-thirty in the morning!"

She looked so desperate it was almost funny—except, of course, that it isn't funny at all. It's the plain, grinding truth of modern life. Like Judith, most of us are living our lives at such an incredible pace, subjecting ourselves to so much pressure, and making so many demands on ourselves, that it's surprising we have any energy left at all.

I told Judith that the T-Type Program would give her everything a diet could possibly give, but she had to realize that she probably needed more nutritional support than any modern diet could provide. After all, she had two full-time jobs, both of them difficult and demanding. Her next scheduled vacation was in four years. She was demanding a lot from her body, and she needed to make sure it had *everything* it needed to perform at capacity. She also had certain risks that were part and parcel of her T-Type metabolism. Between her lifestyle and her risks, she didn't need just nutrition, she needed ultranutrition. What she needed was additional help from nutritional supplements—especially particular supplements designed with her body type in mind.

Supplements: Yesterday and Today

The human body needs ninety-one essential nutrients every day, and those are only the ones we know about. There may be many more we have yet to learn of that prove to be equally essential. Yet there was a time when taking nutritional supplements—pills or powders providing extra vitamins and minerals, amino acids, herbs, and glandular substances—was not quite the norm. The average person might take a once-a-day vitamin pill from the supermarket, or might not. Most people didn't.

Even today, taking supplements is still not completely routine but there have been changes. Today, more and more physicians are recommending supplementation to their patients and even taking supplements themselves. But that doesn't mean that there is general agreement as to exactly what, and how much, to recommend. Do you take only those nutrients whose effect has been studied in long-term clinical trials? Do you add those where the research suggests, but has not proved, benefits? Do you just take the supplements you've heard of, or do you try to keep up with the latest substance in the health food store? Do you take the RDA (Recommended Daily Allowance) or the ODA (Optimum Daily Allowance)?

Nutritional supplements are big today: big business (six *billion* dollars in 1997), big news, and for many people, a big question. As a consumer, you are bombarded with ads on TV and in print telling you to buy this pill because it has zinc, selenium, vitamin E, or folate, or is for your "special needs" as a woman, as an older person, as an athlete, or (with astonishing frankness) as someone who simply does not plan to ever eat fruits or vegetables. So how do you decide? You want the maximum benefit from your supplements, but you don't want to be sucked into spending your money on dubious or even harmful items. How do you know the truth?

Know This: Not Everything Is Known

I'd like to digress on one thing here, because there's a topic no one really talks about and yet it's central to everything we do in medicine and the health fields. It's simply this: *In the last analysis, we do not really know how the body works.* Nobody really has a *complete* understanding of why it's structured the way it is, why it gets sick, why it stays well, and how it makes use of things that seem to make it well, or encourage it to recover, or remind it of how it's supposed to work.

What's strange about the body is that many influences seem to have the ability to remind the body how it's supposed to be when it's well. I'm thinking about certain modalities from alternative medicine that, as a scientist, I have a hard time accounting for. Take aromatherapy, as an example. It's pretty big at this writing in 1998. Yet there is no one who can give you a clear explanation of aromatherapy who isn't either begging the question or talking through his hat. Yet it does seem to do something. Sure, people will tell you about olfactory pathways to the brain and so on, but it's total conjecture. And certainly we are all familiar with the powerfully evocative ability of smells to remind us of experiences and activate powerful memories. But this doesn't explain how smells affect our health. Could it be that they are "familiar" to the physiology and remind it how to function? Maybe.

But aromatherapy is only one example. Take glandular therapy. I'm going to be recommending some glandular substances a little farther on in this chapter. I know that on an emotional basis it may make some sort of sense that if you eat some desiccated thyroid it will help your thyroid. But speaking as a physician, I have to say that it's total mojo. On the surface, that is. Ultimately, no one really knows.

Or take homeopathy. In this modality, which is quite well respected in Europe, you take a few drops of a liquid that contains absolutely no molecules of the supposed active ingredient. Yet the body somehow gets a message and changes its functioning, aligns its energies, recovers. Homeopathy has been studied in peer-reviewed journals; the results even work in agriculture, where there shouldn't be a placebo effect, yet it still doesn't change the fact that there are *no molecules* in the juice. All is not known.

We know, in a sort of gross way, what the body is made of. We have some sense of its composition at the material level. Yet, in the same way that we can't measure the soul, so too we have not been able to measure the energetic identities of the body that give rise to and sustain the physical body. Besides, in many areas we don't have a good sense of even its material construction. The trace minerals are a good example. Exactly which and how much we need, no one is sure. And their synergy with all the other nutrients, hormones, and chemicals of our body—that area is also mostly shadow right now.

This being so, the best we can do is to make available what your body needs, and let it choose. In states of weakness, avoid that which weakens further and add that which may strengthen. This goes for vitamins, minerals, herbs, actions, thoughts, postures, foods, and friends. I'm serious about this; it's important. Don't take these remarks with too many grains of salt.

For all the foregoing reasons the Body Type Supplements may seem a little unusual to those of you who read up on these things. They are unusual because they are more complete and are constructed as formulas to make the most of the synergy of the nutrients, to make them better, and to enhance their effects in making the body recover its memory of how to work best. The same goes for food. The foods in the Body Type Diet are there to remind the body of its best nature. That's why it's important to eat the best food you can find. Smell it, taste it, chew it, digest it, absorb it, transform it. Let it uplift you.

Supplement Research

All this notwithstanding, most of us like to think of ourselves as rational creatures (even if our spouses are only half convinced). We'd like to base our decisions on facts. That turns out to be not so easy, even when you're trying to look only at the research. If the research isn't flawed in some way, oftentimes it is inconclusive or contradictory. For instance, a study done in 1966 showed that 200 mcg a day of the mineral selenium cut the risk of colon, prostate, and lung cancer in half. Encouraged, researchers did follow-up studies, but failed to find *any* link between selenium and cancer. Yet, other follow-ups showed there was a link after all, and so on.

Contradictory results are not at all uncommon. You may have read about a recent beta-carotene study. While this nutrient appeared to lower the risk of many cancers, when smokers were given high doses of the substance, their cancer rates actually went up.

And that's the good research! If you look closely at many studies on newer or more controversial nutrients like ginkgo or DHEA, you'll find that many of them are seriously flawed. They study just a few subjects for too short a time, or they fail to take into account other factors that might also explain the results. Yet, with so much money at stake, it's not surprising that supplement manufacturers are tempted to exaggerate favorable studies even if flawed, and ignore contradictory or negative ones.

However, there is some very conclusive research on some supplements. For at least two nutrients, vitamin E and folic acid, the evidence is so strong that even conservative physicians, the kind of doctors whose only previous supplement recommendation was for a prenatal vitamin during pregnancy, are actually taking supplements themselves. "I have high LDL cholesterol myself," Dr. Wayne Callaway, associate professor of medicine at George Washington University, explained in print. "I'm watching my diet, exercising, and taking medication, but I also take vitamin E on the presumption that the data are sufficiently suggestive to think it might be worthwhile." Dr. Andrew Weil, an authority on alternative medicine, wrote, "I strongly recommend taking supplements because they seem to provide optimal protection from heart disease and cancer, *but only at levels that would be almost impossible to obtain from diet.*" I added the italics to Dr. Weil's statement, because I agree with it strongly. For instance, the research on vitamin E indicates that to get its protective benefits, we need at least 50 IU (international units) and perhaps as much as 400 IU per day. Vitamin E is found in wheat germ, nuts, seeds, greens, and sweet potatoes, but its primary dietary source is oils (safflower, corn, and olive oils). To get even 200 IUs a day you'd have to drink a cup or two of olive oil— glug, glug—and that's not on anyone's list of good dietary recommendations. Clearly, a supplement is the way to go.

Another nutrient where the research is very strong is vitamin D. Your skin makes vitamin D when exposed to sunlight, but we are learning to avoid sun to cut the risk of skin cancers. And unless you live in the south, there is not enough sun available in the winter months to make vitamin D at all. Again, a supplement is definitely the way to go.

The same is true with folic acid, which is actually the synthetic version of folate, a B vitamin found in greens, legumes, citrus fruits, and organ meats. Having enough folic acid during pregnancy has actually been *proven* to greatly reduce the risk of neural tube defects such as spina bifida. Evidence is also mounting that folic acid offers protection against heart disease. The FDA is now requiring manufacturers to add folic acid to enriched flour and other grain products; but for a woman to fulfill her folic acid requirements from this source she would need to eat a loaf of bread a day. The experts say bluntly, "Take a supplement."

I'll discuss just one more supplement: calcium. Research clearly shows that by consuming enough calcium you will reduce your risk of bone fractures, as long as you also have enough vitamin D present to help you absorb the calcium. Could you get enough calcium from food? Yes, but it's hard. You need to eat three servings a day of dairy products; but what if you're allergic to, or hate, dairy? What if you're a P-Type and dairy is your most unbalancing food? You will certainly need to take supplementary calcium.

These nutrients—vitamins E and D, folic acid, and calcium— have an abundance of solid research behind them. What about the other vitamins and minerals found in a multivitamin/mineral pill? When you're squinting at the tiny print on the bottle, you can see that there are many more nutrients listed. While there may not be evidence strong enough to convince a conservative physician, there is plenty of good reason to know that these supplements are important to the total health of your metabolism. Besides, most conservative physicians rarely give enough attention to nutrition to have a strong base of knowledge. My dentist told me he now takes vitamin E. But when I asked him about the other ninety, he just blinked at me. He barely knew what I was talking about.

I feel that it does a disservice to my patients to withhold my recommendations until there are controlled clinical trials, the gold standard of scientific research. I prefer to use my own clinical observation backed up by good, if not perfect, research. Using this standard, I have no hesitation in recommending a program of nutritional supplementation. Will you get everything you need in your food? It's basically impossible, so don't kid yourself. You want the best for your body. A good program of nutritional supplementation ensures that you will get it.

THE NEEDS OF THE FOUR BODY TYPES

I explained my thinking to Judith P. and then handed her my supplement recommendations for her as a T-Type. She asked me how I had arrived at the recommended amounts, and whether they were different for each body type.

I told her that for some nutrients (folic acid is an example), I recommended the same amount for all body types. But for the majority of nutrients, my experience told me that each of the four body types has somewhat different needs. For example, she as a T-Type needed more trace minerals, especially magnesium, manganese, chromium, and zinc, and the ultratrace colloidal group, than either Adrenal or Gonadal Types.

On the other hand, the T-Type metabolism is at less risk for heart disease than A- or G-Types, so her need for antioxidants was not as great. She does need A, E, C, and selenium, but not as much as her husband, who I knew happened to be an Adrenal. My body type recommendations are based on the best research available today, combined with my clinical experience with the different body types and my understanding of their needs. In addition, I base my recommendations on my experience with the tens of thousands who have used Body Type Supplements since 1985.

What Your Supplements
Should Do for You

The experience I gained with my patients and my knowledge of the needs of the four body types have now joined together fully for your benefit. My Body Type Supplement recommendations take into account the typical cravings of your body type, as well as your metabolism's particular nutritional needs.

In terms of the quantity of specific supplements, the Body Type Supplement Program falls somewhere between the extravagant (where you take so much of every nutrient, you have to buy vitamin powders in bulk) and the very conservative (the RDA). I am convinced that the right amount of a given supplement may be very valuable, but you don't have to spend a hundred dollars a week to get the benefits. The Body Type Supplement Program recommends the adroit, personalized use of supplements to satisfy your needs safely, effectively, and realistically.

My recommendations to patients like Judith, who are living lives of noisy desperation, consist of a list of nutrients with the ideal quantities of each. The total package works together and does many things at once, which means that you can't think about the supplement program in bits and pieces.

In other words, don't think to yourself, "T's need minerals, and A's need antioxidants." That would be an oversimplification of your magnificently complex metabolism. We all need some of all the vitamins and minerals, and we also need some additional nutrients, including certain amino acids and glandular support substances, to give maximum support to that metabolism.

So what differences will you notice if you haven't been taking supplements before? After a week or two you will probably find that your energy will be better. You should feel more resistant to stress. You'll be better able to keep going if you have a long, demanding day. Your cravings, if you still have trouble with them at fatigue or stress times, will definitely be much reduced.

After several months on the program many people will find significant health benefits, although this depends on your taking care of yourself in other ways as well. Supplements can't undo the results of eating badly, being inactive, or undergoing extreme stress. Yet there is a great deal they can do. Many of my patients tell me that when they take the right supplements for their body type they have fewer small illnesses—colds, sore throats, flu—and you may find this as well. This is a sign that the supplements are helping to balance your metabolism, and are working to optimize the functioning of all parts of your body.

What about long-range benefits—reduction in major illnesses, less aging, longer life? With the lack of long-range studies, it's unscientific to make claims. Yet the effects of these nutrients on the factors that accelerate aging—cross-linkage and superoxidation—are known, and it's reasonable to assume that if they improve health in the present, longevity will be part of the effect. Certainly, if you reduce your risk of a major, life-threatening disease, you would expect to find that you would be increasing your chances for a longer, as well as a healthier, life.

To me, taking nutritional supplements is certainly a worthwhile investment. There is no danger, that we know of, as long as you don't go above the recommended amounts. And you're taking the better course: giving yourself every opportunity to feel better and live longer. It's the choice I've made—I take the entire T-Type Supplement Program and feel better than I ever have.

Three months after our first conversation about supplements, Judith told me, "It's working. I'm making it all the way through the morning without collapsing. I don't even feel the need for a cup of coffee at eleven anymore. I haven't had a cold since we talked, and there haven't been any of those awful days when I truly understand why some people abandon their children. One more step toward Superwoman!"

Recommendations for All Body Types

I tell my patients that everyone needs to take three or four main types of supplements, depending on their situation. These are:

1. A vitamin-and-mineral supplement, including ultratrace minerals
2. An amino acid supplement
3. A combination of glandular support substances, herbs, and/or homeopathics
4. Specific extra nutrients to help control cravings

All the recommended supplements should be taken at least twice a day, preferably three times, because they are continually being washed out of the body.

Each of these types of supplements has its own role to play in balancing your metabolism. In the discussion that follows, I go over the main ingredients in each from a body type perspective. This isn't intended to be a complete course in nutritional supplementation; there are many good books that you can study if you're interested in exactly what each vitamin, mineral, or amino acid does. Rather, it's to let you know what special needs each supplement fills in balancing your particular metabolism.

At the end of this section I'll give you my specific recommendations for each of the four body types.

BODY TYPE SUPPLEMENT ANALYSIS: WHO NEEDS WHAT, AND WHY

Vitamins

Vitamin A is a powerful antioxidant. One of the reasons for aging is that our metabolism produces "superoxidants," chemicals that actually burn our tissues. This produces mutations in our genes and ages our tissues. Antioxidants are chemicals that help reduce this burning. Vitamin A is also used in vision, and helps maintain cell integrity. It is important in maintaining the immune system. All body types need vitamin A, but Adrenal Types are given an extra quantity because of their increased vulnerability to superoxidation.

Vitamin B_1 (thiamin) aids in the digestion of carbohydrates. People who don't digest carbohydrates well, who get gas, may be deficient in vitamin B_1. Also, and this is very important, it is used in brain functioning. It reduces the stressful influence of experiences on the brain. Alcohol tends to wash Vitamin B_1 out of the system, so A- and G-Types, who are most attracted to alcohol, have been given extra. But caffeine also washes it out, so T's benefit from this supplement as well.

Vitamin B_2 (riboflavin) is the most commonly deficient in the United States. It is important in digestion. Very few vitamin formulas have enough of it. All body types need much more than the RDA.

Vitamin B$_3$ (nicotinic acid or niacin) has been found to reduce blood cholesterol levels by up to 30 percent or even more. The "niacin flush" that people sometimes get comes from the sudden release of cholesterol into the system; if you get this your body will adjust to it quickly. A-Types need extra B$_3$. It is also an antioxidant.

Vitamin B$_5$ (pantothenic acid) is an antistress vitamin; it increases your stamina and your ability to utilize energy in your body. P-Types have extra B$_5$ because you need to increase your ability to get energy from your body.

Vitamin B$_6$ (pyridoxine) is important in the production of antibodies. It is also a natural diuretic and reduces nausea (pregnant women take it for this). A- and G-Types have extra B$_6$ because it works against cardiovascular disease.

Vitamin B$_{12}$ is a strange vitamin; it produces a huge effect from just a tiny amount. One milligram by injection has great effects in rejuvenating the nervous system. It increases mental energy. Thus, P-Types require extra B$_{12}$. You need a functioning thyroid gland to utilize B$_{12}$, so T-Types need to be on the entire T-Type Program to revive their thyroid in order to get any benefit from B$_{12}$.

Beta-carotene is a precursor of vitamin A, and is called "provitamin A." It protects the system by stabilizing all membranes. A's and G's have more of it for its antioxidant effects. All body types have a large amount for its general protection against cancer.

Vitamin C is the most vital stress vitamin. It protects the brain from free-radical formation, a process that is part of aging. Like superoxidation, free radicals burn the tissue. Vitamin C is able to get through the blood-brain barrier and reduce aging in the brain. It also reduces cholesterol, and thus A's and G's require the most. Some experts feel that you need even larger quantities of C, but I feel that the amounts I suggest are a good baseline amount. If you would like to take more, vitamin C powder is an easy way to do so.

Vitamin D helps maintain calcium and phosphorus in the bones. All body types have at least 400 IU, the amount needed to help fight the risk of some cancers. P-Types have even more, to help strengthen the typical underdeveloped P-Type body.

Vitamin E is the "vitamin C of the fat-soluble vitamins." It is a powerful antioxidant and also fights free-radical formation. Being fat soluble, it is able to go to the fatty areas of the body where C, a water-soluble vitamin, cannot. I've already discussed the research showing vitamin E's value in protecting against heart disease, stimulating the immune system, and increasing longevity. A's have the largest amount because of its value in protecting against heart disease. P's also have extra, for strengthening the immune system. All body types benefit from extra E.

Vitamin K is a fat-soluble vitamin crucial in blood clotting. Without a sufficient supply of K, any wound would bleed uncontrollably. It also appears to be crucial in preventing bone fractures. A significant percentage of the vitamin K you need is produced by the bacteria normally present in your gut. The body type soups are rich in vitamin K, and your supplement makes up any possible deficiency.

Choline and inositol are chemicals used by the brain. Choline is a neurotransmitter precursor, and inositol is a chemical used in brain functioning. P's and T's have extra to increase their mental energy.

Minerals

The trace minerals are extremely simple, but very powerful, elements that are needed by the body in minute amounts. Literally a tablespoon of minerals may be all that is needed in a mixture that will produce 100,000 vitamin/mineral tablets. Yet a deficiency of any of these minerals has a domino effect through the system, causing all kinds of disruption.

Vitamins are "coenzymes," which means that they work with the enzymes in your body that catalyze chemical reactions. The assistance of the vitamins enables these reactions to take place more efficiently at body temperature. So vitamins assist your enzymes, while minerals actually assist the vitamins! They are called co-coenzymes, which means that they help the vitamins help the enzymes. As I said, you need just a very minute amount. Yet isn't it fascinating to realize that just a tiny amount of dirt (which is what minerals are) is absolutely vital for your body to work properly?

Chromium is a constituent of Glucose Tolerance Factor and is an important part of carbohydrate metabolism. It helps insulin do its work. Sweets cravings are often associated with chromium deficiency. Without enough chromium, sweets are not digested well, and so they do not give you the feeling of satisfaction you were looking for when you reached for them. Without satisfaction, your craving just continues. T's and P's have more chromium to help fight their sweets cravings.

Magnesium is important in nerve and brain function and also in preventing heart disease. Extra magnesium is also vital in controlling cravings for sweets, so T's and P's have extra.

Manganese is also essential in carbohydrate metabolism, in the sexual system, and in the health of the adrenal glands. Deficiency in manganese gives rise to starch cravings. Therefore, T's and P's have extra.

Selenium is an antioxidant that fights aging and cancer. Smokers and people with high cholesterol (usually A's and G's) need extra selenium. It can make you sick if you take too much, but it would take ten times as much as is in the Body Type Supplements to do so.

Silicon (actually, this is sand) gives stability to connective tissue and helps deposit calcium in the bones. By stabilizing the connective tissue it helps with arthritis-type disorders, so A's and G's have slightly more of it.

Vanadium is involved in the stabilization of blood fats and in maintaining the chemical balance of the bones and teeth. It works with omega-3 fatty acids from fish oils to reduce cholesterol. This is why A's and G's have a little more of it.

Zinc is used in healing, especially in knitting of broken bones, and it also helps insulin respond to carbohydrates. T's and P's have more because of its role in carbohydrate metabolism.

Amino Acids

Amino acids are the building blocks of protein. Like vitamins and minerals, they help the body's chemical reactions go forward. But unlike vitamins and minerals, they don't just assist in the reactions, they also participate. At the end of a reaction, a vitamin or mineral will still be there, whereas an amino acid will have been transformed into something else.

When you're deficient in vitamins or minerals, it's because you didn't get enough of them or because they have been washed out of your system by stresses of various kinds. But amino acid deficiencies can also occur because the amino acids are actually used up by your body—consumed, like food.

Amino acids also give support to sexual potency, in the same way that Viagra does. A special formula actually produces very much the same effect.

Glutamine is a component of important neurotransmitters in the brain. The feeling of a tired brain may often be caused by glutamine deficiency. P-Types have the most because they are most prone to mental exhaustion, followed by T's, A's, and lastly, G's. Glutamine is the only amino acid taken by A's.

Arginine and ornithine, the other two I recommend, are growth hormone releasers that build muscle mass. A's don't need this. T's and P's both benefit greatly from arginine and ornithine. They will help your system lose fat and create muscle, and improve the effectiveness of your exercise program.

Glandular Support Substances

One of the most important goals of your supplement program should be to create balance in your system by restoring your tired, overstimulated dominant gland. You can help your body reach this goal through the adroit use of glandular support substances—highly purified glandular material taken in very small amounts—just enough to provide a gentle support to your own glands.

Note that these support substances do not contain any hormones per se. Thyroid Types, particularly, often take Synthroid or other thyroid hormones because their own thyroid functions poorly or not at all (a result of overstimulation in the past). Thyroid *glandular support substance* is completely different from thyroid *hormone* (and in any case thyroid hormone is a prescription drug, not a nutritional supplement). Taking glandular support substance does not interfere or conflict with taking hormone; but by restoring a depleted gland, it may over time reduce the need for taking the hormone.

It would be very irresponsible to state categorically that T-Types on Synthroid can eliminate their need to take supplementary hormones by following the T-Type Program, and I don't claim that by any means. However, it would also be irresponsible not to tell you that T-Types have indeed done so. Many T-Types have greatly reduced their thyroid hormone need, and some have eliminated it completely. This is a wonderful result when you consider that most physicians believe that once you start on thyroid hormone you must take it for your entire life.

If you are a T-Type who takes thyroid hormone, do not even think of reducing your intake on your own. Talk with your physician and arrange to have your thyroid level carefully monitored as you go through the T-Type program. It takes time, but depleted thyroid glands can be restored in many cases.

Each of the herbal/glandulars is unique and has been designed specifically for each body type.

Herbals

For each of the body types, I have found that certain herbs are helpful in restoring balance to the system. For example, Dong Quai, damiana, and black cohosh have traditional functions that are of great help to the G-Type metabolism. For the T-Type metabolism I recommend kelp (actually a sea "herb"). For Adrenal Types my herbal recommendation includes licorice root and buchu leaf, and for Pituitary Types I recommend sarsaparilla and ginseng.

The body type teas also function as herbal supplements. These are the main reasons I chose the body type teas:

Red clover is helpful in cleansing the female sex organs, and so is most useful to Gonadal Types.
Parsley leaf is a diuretic and kidney cleanser, and is much needed by Adrenal Types.

Raspberry leaf purifies and cleanses the thyroid gland, especially the substrate of the gland that produces thyroid hormone. This makes it very helpful to Thyroid Types.

Fenugreek seed soothes brain functioning, which is much needed by Pituitary Types.

Special Anti-Craving Supplementation

According to your body type, you have characteristic cravings for foods that drive your dominant gland. T-Types tend to crave thyroid-stimulating sweets, starches, and caffeine; P-Types tend to crave pituitary-stimulating dairy foods and fruit; A-Types crave adrenal-stimulating fats, salt, and alcohol; and G-Types crave foods that stimulate the ovaries—rich, spicy foods. While you are working to create balance in your system, you can also benefit by taking targeted supplements to help ease the pull of these dominant-gland stimulators.

For T- and P-Types, I recommend two different combinations of supplements. Both of these combinations work to curb the cravings for carbohydrates that can be so difficult for T-Types, and also to reduce the craving for sweets that P-Types have in combination with their craving for dairy foods (for example, in the craving for fruit or frozen yogurt).

The two formulations are different, and if you think carefully about your sweets craving you can decide which one would be best for you. The first is a combination consisting of two forms of the amino acid phenylalanine, the d,l– form and the l–form. Phenylalanine is a precursor of the neurotransmitter dopamine. When you have a sudden, very intense sweets craving at a particular time (at eleven in the morning or four in the afternoon, for example), it may come from a dopamine deficiency in your brain. Taking phenylalanine shortly before you usually have the craving helps restore your brain's dopamine level and reduce the craving.

On the other hand, you may not have one particular time when your sweets craving is so intense, but you may have a constant, nagging, low-grade desire to eat something sweet or to have a carbohydrate—like bread or pasta. This is another kind of craving and more commonly is related to tissue deficiencies of trace minerals. For this type of craving I recommend a supplement made up of the trace minerals related to this craving (magnesium, manganese, chromium, and zinc). This supplement does not work almost instantaneously, the way an amino acid can, but when the tissue deficiency of the minerals is restored the constant craving usually fades.

A-Types and G-Types may also have a craving that is related to mineral deficiency, whereas it is generally T-Types who have the more intense sweets craving. So I also recommend a mineral supplement for G's and A's; but I also strongly recommend another supplement to help control more persistent cravings for fats.

What I have found to be most helpful for fats cravings is actually a combination of the digestive enzymes amylase and lipase, which the body uses to digest fats. These enzymes are normally produced by the gallbladder; but A's and G's with cravings for fats very often have weakened their gallbladder by overstimulation, in much the same way that T-Types weaken their thyroid gland by overstimulating it with sweets and starches.

When you are low in the digestive enzymes needed to break down fats, the fats you eat are not digested well and your body does not gain a satisfied feeling. Fat is a highly concentrated food, very dense in caloric value. Normally just a small amount of fat is satisfying, and you really won't want to eat more. But if your gallbladder works poorly, your body does not recognize that it has eaten enough fat, and you continue to consume it. Thus, you can eat a tremendous amount of fat and still not feel satisfied.

With a digestive enzyme supplement, your ability to digest fat improves dramatically. As a result, a small amount of fat will satisfy you. The little bit of olive oil on your salad or cooked vegetables is all you really want—a tremendous relief to your overburdened system.

It is perhaps not surprising to note that many A-Types have actually had their gallbladders removed. That's what constant overstimulation can do; but with the gallbladder gone, fat cravings can be intense. If you have lost your gallbladder to surgery, you will probably need to take digestive enzymes indefinitely—an exception to my statement that anti-craving supplements need be taken only for the period of time it takes for your cravings to be controlled.

I also have one more supplement to recommend: a particular combination that helps support brain functioning. I saved it for last because it is such a valuable combination of nutrients that I recommend it for all body types. It consists of the amino acid glutamine, plus choline and inositol, plus the herb gingko biloba, in a base of lecithin. These nutrients work together to support and improve brain functioning—including short- and long-term memory and attention span. It reduces all cravings, because a tired and depleted brain is a major factor in every single craving. I firmly believe that everybody can benefit from such a supplement.

MY SPECIFIC BODY TYPE RECOMMENDATIONS

These are my recommendations for each body type, based on the research briefly outlined above and my understanding of the particular needs of each body type. I have found that supplementation at this level is safe, gives you the benefits I've outlined above, and may do much more. It's cost-effective insurance and I think it's well worth the effort.

To put together the supplements I recommend, you will have to do some careful label reading. *Not all supplements are alike* (to put it mildly). Though some of the supplements I suggest for each body type can be obtained in a really good multivitamin combination, you must get a first-rate supplement made by a responsible laboratory. The trace minerals, particularly, are very important, and many lower-end supplements simply do not contain them. To do a quick check, look on the label for molybdenum, vanadium, or silicon. If the pill you're looking at has these, keep reading—there's hope. If not, put it back on the shelf and keep looking.

The G-Type Supplement Program

These supplement recommendations work with the G-Type diet and exercise plans to offset your potential weaknesses and increase your strengths. Interestingly, I find that the G-Type supplement needs are a combination of the needs of the A-Type and T-Type metabolisms. This makes sense when you reflect that as a G, you are almost like two different people: one above the waist and one below. Above the waist, your slenderness gives you the needs of a T-Type: stability and strength. Below the waist, your body has the A-Type needs for flexibility and protection against superoxidation.

NUTRIENT	AMOUNT	RDA
1. Vitamin/Mineral Combination		
A	500 IU	5,000 IU
B_1 (THIAMIN)	25 MG	1.5 MG
B_2 (RIBOFLAVIN)	33 MG	1.7 MG
B_3 (NICOTINIC ACID)	66 MG	20 MG
B_5 (PANTOTHENIC ACID)	25 MG	10 MG
B_6	80 MG	2 MG
B_{12}	80 MCG	3 MCG
BETA-CAROTENE	20,000 IU	***
C	1,000 MG	60 MG
D	400 IU	400 IU
E	250 IU	30 IU
K	30 MCG	65 MCG
FOLIC ACID	400 MCG	400 MCG
CHOLINE	125 MG	***
INOSITOL	125 MG	***
RUTIN	2.5 MG	***
HESPERIDIN	2.5 MG	***
PABA	2 MG	***
CALCIUM	167 MG	1,200 MG
CHROMIUM	500 MCG	**
COPPER	2 MG	2 MG
IODINE	150 MCG	150 MCG
IRON	25 MG	18 MG
MAGNESIUM	75 MG	400 MG
MANGANESE	3 MG	**
MOLYBDENUM	35 MCG	**
PHOSPHORUS	50 MG	1,200 MG
POTASSIUM	15 MG	**
SELENIUM	20 MCG	**
SILICON	100 MCG	**

VANADIUM	10 MCG	**
ZINC	25 MG	15 MG
TRACE MINERAL		
COMBINATION	25 MG	

2. Amino Acid Combination

ARGININE	80 MG
ORNITHINE	40 MG
GLUTAMINE	160 MG

3. Herbal/Glandular Combination

OVARIAN SUPPORT	
SUBSTANCE	100 MG
ANTERIOR PITUITARY	
SUPPORT SUBSTANCE	10 MG
UTERINE SUPPORT	
SUBSTANCE	60 MG
DONG QUAI	50 MG
DAMIANA	150 MG
BLACK COHOSH	50 MG

Body Type Tea: RED CLOVER

4. Anti-Craving Recommendations

For fat cravings:

AMYLASE	200 MG
LIPASE	50 MG

For carbohydrate cravings:

CHROMIUM PICOLINATE	100 MCG
MAGNESIUM	100 MG
MANGANESE	30 MG
ZINC	10 MG

To support brain functioning:

L-GLUTAMINE	500 MG
INOSITOL	150 MG
GINGKO BILOBA	50 MG
CHOLINE BITARTRATE	400 MG

The A-Type Supplement Program

Your supplements work with your A-Type diet and exercise programs to reduce your tendency to congestion and stiffness. By stiffness, of course, I don't just mean not being able to touch your toes: I mean internal lockup as well: hardening of the arteries, stiffness in the joints, wrinkling, hard fat, coarsening of the skin. None of these are inevitable, but you do have the tendency, so you must be prepared to offset it with all your preventive health measures.

NUTRIENT	AMOUNT	RDA
1. Vitamin/Mineral Combination		
A	7,000 IU	5,000 IU
B₁ (THIAMIN)	33 MG	1.5 MG
B₂ (RIBOFLAVIN)	25 MG	1.7 MG
B₃ (NICOTINIC ACID)	100 MG	20 MG
B₅ (PANTOTHENIC ACID)	25 MG	10 MG
B₆	100 MG	2 MG
B₁₂	60 MCG	3 MCG
BETA-CAROTENE	20,000 IU	★★★
C	2,000 MG	60 MG
D	400 IU	400 IU
E	400 IU	30 IU
K	50 MCG	65 MCG
FOLIC ACID	400 MCG	400 MCG
CHOLINE	125 MG	★★★
INOSITOL	125 MG	★★★
RUTIN	2.5 MG	★★★
HESPERIDIN	2.5 MG	★★★
PABA	2 MG	★★★
CALCIUM	83.4 MG	1,200 MG
CHROMIUM	500 MCG	★★
COPPER	2 MG	2 MG
IODINE	150 MCG	150 MCG
IRON	18 MG	18 MG
MAGNESIUM	75 MG	400 MG
MANGANESE	3 MG	★★
MOLYBDENUM	35 MCG	★★

PHOSPHORUS	50 MG	1,200 MG
POTASSIUM	15 MG	★★
SELENIUM	20 MCG	★★
SILICON	100 MCG	★★
VANADIUM	10 MCG	★★
ZINC	25 MG	15 MG
TRACE MINERAL		
COMBINATION	25 MG	

2. Amino Acid Combination
ARGININE	0
ORNITHINE	0
GLUTAMINE	200 MG

3. Herbal/Glandular Combination
ADRENAL SUPPORT	
SUBSTANCE	100 MG
ADRENAL CORTEX	
SUPPORT SUBSTANCE	25 MG
LICORICE ROOT	50 MG
BUCHU LEAF	50 MG

Body Type Tea: DRIED PARSLEY LEAF

4. Anti-Craving Recommendations
For fat cravings:
AMYLASE	200 MG
LIPASE	50 MG

For carbohydrate cravings:
CHROMIUM PICOLINATE	100 MCG
MAGNESIUM	100 MG
MANGANESE	30 MG
ZINC	10 MG

To support brain functioning:
L-GLUTAMINE	500 MG
INOSITOL	150 MG
GINGKO BILOBA	50 MG
CHOLINE BITARTRATE	400 MG

The T-Type Supplement Program

The T-Type Supplement Program is designed to offset your greatest weakness: your energy swings. Physical steadiness and freedom from mental and emotional swings are the main objects here. Your volatile energy produces tremendous stress and strain on your body. Cross-linkage and superoxidation are the results, but the right supplements can reduce the damage.

T-Types are very likely to become deficient in the water-soluble B vitamins. You have efficient kidneys and excrete all water-soluble vitamins rapidly. The caffeine you've drunk (in the past, hopefully) also contributes to this effect. B vitamins are crucial if your body is to make use of any of the vitamins you take.

NUTRIENT	AMOUNT	RDA
1. Vitamin/Mineral Combination		
A	5,000 IU	5,000 IU
B_1 (THIAMIN)	12 MG	1.5 MG
B_2 (RIBOFLAVIN)	26 MG	1.7 MG
B_3 (NICOTINIC ACID)	32 MG	20 MG
B_5 (PANTOTHENIC ACID)	20 MG	10 MG
B_6	40 MG	2 MG
B_{12}	128 MCG	3 MCG
BETA-CAROTENE	16,000 IU	***
C	1,125 MG	60 MG
D	400 IU	400 IU
E	160 IU	30 IU
K	56 MCG	65 MCG
FOLIC ACID	400 MCG	400 MCG
CHOLINE	200 MG	***
INOSITOL	200 MG	***
RUTIN	2 MG	***
HESPERIDIN	2 MG	***
PABA	1.6 MG	***
CALCIUM	167 MG	1,200 MG
CHROMIUM	600 MCG	**
COPPER	1.6 MG	2 MG
IODINE	120 MCG	150 MCG

IRON	20 MG	18 MG
MAGNESIUM	400 MG	400 MG
MANGANESE	12 MG	★★
MOLYBDENUM	28 MCG	★★
PHOSPHORUS	40 MG	1,200 MG
POTASSIUM	12 MG	★★
SELENIUM	16 MCG	★★
SILICON	60 MCG	★★
VANADIUM	8 MCG	★★
ZINC	28 MG	15 MG
TRACE MINERAL		
COMBINATION	50 MG	

2. Amino Acid Combination

ARGININE	125 MG
ORNITHINE	60 MG
GLUTAMINE	250 MG

3. Herbal/Glandular Combination

THYROID SUPPORT	
SUBSTANCE	60 MG
ANTERIOR PITUITARY	
SUPPORT SUBSTANCE	10 MG
KELP	5 MG
L-TYROSINE	100 MG
SPONGIA TOSTA 6X	10 MG

Body Type Tea: RASPBERRY LEAF

4. Anti-Craving Recommendations

For intense sweets cravings:

D,L–PHENYLALANINE	175 MG
L-PHENYLALANINE	175 MG

For constant carbohydrate cravings:

CHROMIUM PICOLINATE	100 MCG
MAGNESIUM	100 MG
MANGANESE	30 MG
ZINC	10 MG

To support brain functioning:

L-GLUTAMINE	500 MG
INOSITOL	150 MG
GINGKO BILOBA	50 MG
CHOLINE BITARTRATE	400 MG

The P-Type Supplement Program

Your supplement program is designed to stimulate your lower body—that is, everything below your head, but especially your adrenals and sex glands. The right supplements can actually work to increase your sense of integration with your body. You'll find some remarkable changes in about four weeks—improved body tone, muscle size, and strength—if you follow this program along with the P-Type exercise recommendations.

NUTRIENT	AMOUNT	RDA
1. Vitamin/Mineral Combination		
A	5,000 IU	5,000 IU
B$_1$ (THIAMIN)	13.5 MG	1.5 MG
B$_2$ (RIBOFLAVIN)	30 MG	1.7 MG
B$_3$ (NICOTINIC ACID)	30 MG	20 MG
B$_5$ (PANTOTHENIC ACID)	30 MG	10 MG
B$_6$	30 MG	2 MG
B$_{12}$	144 MCG	3 MCG
BETA-CAROTENE	18,000 IU	★★★
C	1,275 MG	60 MG
D	720 IU	400 IU
E	360 IU	30 IU
K	17 MCG	65 MCG
FOLIC ACID	400 MCG	400 MCG
CHOLINE	225 MG	★★★
INOSITOL	225 MG	★★★
RUTIN	2.25 MG	★★★
HESPERIDIN	2.25 MG	★★★
PABA	1.8 MG	★★★
CALCIUM	167 MG	1,200 MG

CHROMIUM	600 MCG	★★
COPPER	1.8 MG	2 MG
IODINE	135 MCG	150 MCG
IRON	22.5 MG	18 MG
MAGNESIUM	400 MG	400 MG
MANGANESE	13.5 MG	★★
MOLYBDENUM	31.5 MCG	★★
PHOSPHORUS	45 MG	1,200 MG
POTASSIUM	13.5 MG	★★
SELENIUM	18 MCG	★★
SILICON	90 MCG	★★
VANADIUM	9 MCG	★★
ZINC	31.5 MG	15 MG
TRACE MINERAL		
COMBINATION	50 MG	

2. Amino Acid Combination

ARGININE	150 MG
ORNITHINE	60 MG
GLUTAMINE	350 MG

3. Herbal/Glandular Combination

ADRENAL CORTEX	
SUPPORT SUBSTANCE	25 MG
WHOLE PITUITARY	
SUPPORT SUBSTANCE	50 MG
THYMIC SUPPORT	
SUBSTANCE	25 MG
SARSAPARILLA	50 MG
SIBERIAN GINSENG	100 MG

Body Type Tea: FENUGREEK

4. Anti-Craving Recommendations

For intense sweets cravings:

D,L–PHENYLALANINE	175 MG
L-PHENYLALANINE	175 MG

For constant carbohydrate cravings:

CHROMIUM PICOLINATE	100 MCG
MAGNESIUM	100 MG

MANGANESE	30 MG
ZINC	10 MG

To support brain functioning:

L-GLUTAMINE	500 MG
INOSITOL	150 MG
GINGKO BILOBA	50 MG
CHOLINE BITARTRATE	400 MG

STRESS REDUCTION FOR YOUR BODY TYPE

In my years of working on metabolic balance with my patients, I have had periodic reminders that the single most important factor in creating *imbalance* in the system is stress. Sometimes these reminders are very striking indeed. I remember a patient, a Thyroid–Type woman named Candace, with whom I worked for four months after she had been through a divorce. It was a difficult time for her, and not knowing the potential weakness of her T–Type metabolism, she had used sweets and diet cola as stimulants to help her get through her days. Her thyroid had been worn down by the overstimulation, and she had gained over thirty pounds. I put her on the T–Type Diet, and we had both been extremely pleased with the results—as her thyroid gland recovered, she regained her energy and her weight returned to normal.

So it was with great surprise that I found her in my office several years later. Instead of the strong, balanced woman of our last visit, here was the tired, depleted, and overweight T–Type I first saw when she originally came to me for help. If anything, Candace looked *more* exhausted and stressed than she had on that first visit— and she had put back every one of those thirty pounds.

This was surprising because it was so unusual. I see very little weight rebound in my practice, because the principles of Body Type Dieting are so strong and give my patients the tools to maintain long-term weight loss. Of course, my patients tend to stay in touch with me or with a Body Type Counselor and check back if they find they are getting even a little out of balance. But Candace had not been to see me in the three years since our last visit, and obviously something had happened. I needed to know what it was.

The answer turned out to be stress of the first order. Candace had been through several job changes, a death in the family, and some serious problems with her children, with one thing following another, without giving her time to recover in between. As balanced as her system had been, she hadn't been able to maintain that balance in the face of these repeated blows. Cravings for her old comfort foods returned; she turned to sweets and soda; and once again her thyroid gland was overstimulated and exhausted. The weight gain that followed was inevitable.

Fortunately, I was able to help Candace regain metabolic balance with the T-Type Diet. This time we also worked more extensively with exercise and supplementation, to help her build a better set of defenses against stress. But it was from her experience and the experiences of several other patients who developed their balance and then lost it due to stress that I realized that I would have to make stress reduction an integral part of the Body Type Program.

The truth is that stress—which I define as any experience that is too intense for you to absorb without a negative effect on your system—can overwhelm your body and reawaken your cravings for foods that stimulate your dominant gland. And since the result of overeating these foods is dominant-gland exhaustion and overweight, an understanding of how to control stress is in fact a vital element in long-term weight control.

DIFFERENT BODY TYPES, DIFFERENT STRESS

You'll notice that my definition of stress is related to the individual. It defines stress as anything that a particular individual cannot absorb without harm. Clearly, something that is quite stressful for one person—rock climbing, motorcycle racing, giving a speech or a dinner party for twenty-five, let's say—might simply be exhilarating and challenging for someone else.

It has been fascinating for me to discover that beyond these differences are distinct classes of experiences that are *particularly stressful for each of the four body types.* Knowing this, I have been able to design a program of stress reduction for each of the body types that is not only an important part of my weight loss program but has enormous health benefits as well.

Let me give you an example of the way people with different body types experience stress. A few years ago a friend of mine decided to fulfill a long-standing desire to take a fishing trip to Florida. A busy man, he went through a lot of trouble to arrange the vacation: He put his professional life on hold, put together a group of his sports-loving buddies, negotiated many small deals with his wife, and took off.

The way I heard it, the trip was a disaster. My friend spun me a tale of a bunch of guys out on a boat with acute sunburn, bloodthirsty blackflies, horrible seasickness, and, worst of all, no fish. I was about to sympathize when I caught the rapt, contented expression on his face. "You know," he concluded, "I'd have to say it was just about the best week of my entire life." And he went on to urge, with great sincerity, that I go and fish the Florida Keys.

I think I would die first. To me, his trip sounded incredibly stressful. I'd rather row back to California through the Panama Canal than sit in a rocking boat under the broiling sun, to be chewed up alive by bugs while waiting in vain for something, anything, to happen. But I'm a Thyroid Type, and he's an Adrenal; for him the trip was complete and utter bliss. What it required from him, he had. Therefore, it wasn't stressful.

So you see how relative stress is. One man's restful vacation is another man's nightmare. One woman's challenging business day is another woman's pressure-filled burnout. A day taking the kids to the beach, which Dad handles easily, makes Grandmother want to bury her head in the sand—forever. No experience is stressful in and of itself—stress lies in the relationship between what's happening out there and the response we can or can't give. The same goes for disease. No virus or other agent is a disease by itself. If you're susceptible and you catch it, then it's a disease for you. But not necessarily for someone else.

So if stress is relative to you as an individual, so is stress reduction. To reduce the wear and tear of stress on your system, it's important to be aware of what sorts of experiences are stressful to you, and then to find ways of dealing with them and turning stressfulness into challenge and even enjoyment. Sound impossible? It isn't. It requires real understanding of your own range of responses, and for that you need the insights that come from an understanding of your body type.

"I Love My Stress: It Makes Me Strong"

Do you really believe you love your stress? Don't be embarrassed if you do; it's certainly not an uncommon belief, but it's based on a profound misunderstanding of what stress really is. Men, particularly, tend to have this idea—I guess men are supposed to be able to "handle anything"—but many women also believe that stress is a terrific stimulant to life.

"I wouldn't want to live without stress," I remember one of my patients telling me. He was an overburdened T-Type executive with terrible bags under his eyes, twenty extra pounds, and an ulcer. "Yes, you would," I responded. "You just don't know how. If you think you love your stress, you won't believe how much you would love your life if it was truly stress-free."

What my patient was really worried about, in all fairness, was the idea that without stress his life would be boring. He pictured something like a child's idea of heaven—you know, sitting around in a robe, playing the harp. We can only hope it won't really be like that, for who wouldn't be wild with boredom within a day? For me, anyway, that kind of heaven would be hell and a half.

The thing is that boredom, lack of stimulation, is also a stress. If you think you love stress, what you really love is experience, activity, richness, life. Yet you *can* have lively experiences without the stress. In fact, that's one big secret of an interesting and fulfilling life.

Stress comes in many packages; too much input can be stressful, and so can too little. As a matter of fact, there are psychological studies showing that students taking examinations (a stressful situation to most of us) do best when there is *just the right amount of pressure*. If there's too much anxiety, the students "clutch" and forget what they know. If there's not enough, they don't do well, either, perhaps because they aren't challenged enough.

What we all need, in fact, is enough challenge to make what we're doing feel exciting, but not so much that we get anxious and overwhelmed. Stress occurs at precisely the point where the pressure we need for motivation goes critical and becomes, simply, too much. This point varies for different people, and for the same person at different times. But we all have such a point, and it's important to be aware of it, because it is at precisely that point that stress begins to occur.

Depending on your body type, it can also happen that certain stresses are perceived as direct stimulants and give a kind of illusory "lift" to your system, in the same way that a food stimulates your dominant gland. For example, Thyroid Types are stimulated by extremely frantic and pressure-filled situations, which call on an extra effort from the thyroid gland. Adrenal Types sometimes get this kind of stressful stimulation from watching violent movies or a boxing match: The "fight or flight" syndrome, aroused by scenes of violence, gives stimulation to the adrenal glands. According to your type, you can actually come to crave certain stresses, just as you can crave certain stimulating foods. But these cravings tend to disappear as you improve the balance of your system.

Stressability: Where Are Your Reserves?

Stress is actually overload of the system. It occurs at the point where any experience overtaxes our reserves and becomes too much to handle. But precisely how much is too much? At what point does excitement turn into stress? This depends upon you and upon the extent and nature of your reserves.

If you take a moment to think about yourself, you'll find that there are reserves you can rely on—responses of yours that you can count on to be there when you need them—and other areas in which your reserves are small or nonexistent. Where you have low reserves, you have what I call "stressability." But to determine your stress and nonstress areas, you must really think hard about yourself, because most people take their strengths for granted and don't focus on them as they do their weaknesses.

I once complimented a patient of mine, a woman named Mary L., who had been waiting for some time to see me (sometimes, unfortunately, this happens in a medical practice) with her two young boys. As I looked into the overwhelmed waiting room periodically,

I noticed that she was handling her children beautifully. The kids were frustrated with waiting but she was helping them stay cool, dignified, and respectful. This is something many people have a hard time managing, and I mentioned it to her when she and her boys finally were in the examining room.

"Oh, well," she replied. "They're good kids." I could tell she really didn't realize she was extraordinary. A situation that for most people would have been very stressful, that would have resulted in bad temper and hurt feelings, and in general would have been a real downer, she'd taken totally in stride. She'd even used it to help her sons grow in maturity. But if I'd asked this woman to describe her strengths, she probably wouldn't have even thought of it!

We all have reserves of strength like this. But we also have areas where our reserves are painfully thin. This same woman, to whom real mothering came so naturally, told me how difficult she found dealing with any kind of tension in social situations. Parties where she didn't know the people well were agony for her. In this area she lacked reserves; she'd feel overloaded by a situation that wouldn't bother most people very much at all.

When Good Things Feel Bad

Interestingly, stress isn't confined by any means to "negative" occurrences. It's true that negative situations are more apt to overload our capacities, but intensely positive situations can also tax our reserves.

Thomas H. Holmes, M.D., has compiled a list of stressful events called the "Social Readjustment Rating Scale," which assigns relative values to various life events. The higher the number, the more stressful the event. The most stressful occurrence, "death of spouse," is given 100 points; "divorce," 73; "foreclosure on a mortgage," 30; "minor violations of the law," 11. But on the same scale Dr. Holmes assigns 45 stress points to "marital reconciliation"; "outstanding personal achievement" is given 28; "vacation," 13; and "Christmas," 12. Evidently, according to Dr. Holmes's research, reconciling with your spouse, while not as stressful as getting a divorce, also carries a considerable toll of stress.

This is important to keep in mind, because the consequences of stress are very real. Every physician is aware of this fact; those of us in family practice are especially alert to clues revealing the stress behind the disease. Whenever I hear that a patient is undergoing more stress than usual, I introduce the stress reduction techniques for his or her body type because I've learned that stress and sickness go hand in hand.

Dr. Holmes's research verifies this. He found that people who had more than 300 "stress points" on the Holmes Stress Scale in a single year had an eighty percent chance of getting a serious illness within two years. Now, getting 300 stress points in one year means going through a lot of changes, more than most of us experience all at once, but the point applies to us all. Stress produces increased vulnerability; it reduces our ability to repair our bodies, to "bounce back" after exertion; it makes us slower, less agile and flexible in all our responses. It shortens life. Reducing stress isn't just something we should do to become more "mellow"; it's a vital part of getting and keeping balance.

BODY TYPE STRESSABILITY

Dr. Holmes's scale rates various stresses and relates them to our chances of getting sick; but as with all scales designed to measure everybody on a single yardstick, it's apt to leave out some vital information. That information is *you*. All stresses are not the same, and according to your body type, they will have a greater or lesser impact on you, and greater or lesser consequences for your health.

Your body type, as you know, is a description of the response pattern of your entire system. Whichever your type, you will tend to respond to stress with a burst of energy from your dominant gland. As long as your dominant gland remains strong and active, it provides you with your main area of proven reserves, the response patterns you can count on to bring you successfully through a crisis. A challenge to your dominant gland will be far less stressful than one that challenges your less active glands.

For example, say you're a Pituitary Type. The pituitary gland gives mental energy, a coordinated response of the entire metabolism, but one without a strong physical component. When faced with a stressful situation, your response is to use your pituitary *and think of something*. Your proven reserves are mental, and you have confidence that you'll be able to come up with an idea that will get you through the crisis. But when faced with a physical or emotional challenge, where your less active glands are needed, you will feel far more stressed and less confident.

For each body type, the dominant gland gives an area of confidence and competence, where stress is at a minimum and challenges are welcomed, not feared. On the other hand, each type has its less developed areas—the response areas associated with the less active glands. These are the areas of body type stressability.

So Holmes's stress scale is only valid up to a point. According to your body type, you'll find that some events are more stressful for you, and some less, than they are for other people. The first five events on Holmes's list are "death of a spouse" (100 points), "divorce" (73), "marital separation" (65), "jail term" (63), and "death of a close family member" (also 63). These traumatic events are terribly stressful for all body types. But after that the variation begins.

The next most stressful item is "personal illness or injury" (53 points). But if you're a Pituitary Type, and your stress comes when you are challenged physically, this item deserves a much higher rating on your scale. An extremely unbalanced P-Type patient of mine was in a minor car accident: a rear-ender on the freeway under stop-and-go conditions. It wasn't much of an accident; but it was *totally stressful* for this P-Type woman, and she nearly fell apart. Even the cure was stressful. Coming in for the physical therapy she needed was very difficult for her—so much focus on her body!

It just so happened that her husband, an Adrenal Type, was in the car with her when the accident happened. Like most A-Types, his robust physique and level of comfort with his body allowed him to take the event in stride. For him, the stress quotient of the accident was probably down in the 20s, while for his wife it was at least in the 60s. If this A-Type man were fired from his job, on the other hand, it would be much more serious for him. "Fired at work" rates a 47 from Dr. Holmes, but it's a major A-Type stressor and would give him at least 60 stress points, if not more.

Before I go on to provide specific, practical techniques for your body type to reduce your stress areas, I want to be sure you're clear about the stress areas for each type.

Pituitary Type Stress:
Problems of Physicality

Pituitary Types, as I mentioned, can usually cope confidently with mental challenges. If a coworker throws out a statement such as "Where on earth did you get these figures?" or "I don't follow your thinking on this report *at all,*" it couldn't bother you less. Not only isn't it stressful, you're secretly rather pleased to have an excuse to go through the report, justify the figures, make your reasoning clear. You go home from work thinking that you had a good day, more interesting than usual.

At home, maybe your spouse tells you that you've got a complicated mix-up on your credit card billing. No problem! Your pituitary is still working; you rise to the challenge and sort out the difficulty. A good, stress-free day all around.

Your P-Type stress arrives in situations when mental energy won't help. All physical problems are stressful to a Pituitary Type—and that means almost anything to do with the body. Cooking and eating are stressful: You rarely cook, and mealtimes make you anxious, so you snack instead. Doctor's visit? Panic time: You'll put it off and put it off, even if you're really sick. The doctor, you know, might want to do a blood test, a big Pituitary-Type fear.

Sex is another P-Type panic-button pusher. It's not that you don't enjoy sex—you can, with the right partner—but any sexual difficulty at all is very anxiety-producing. What you doubt is your ability to deal with the difficulty, whatever it may be. Probably your least favorite thing to hear from your loved one is, "Honey, I feel like we should do something about our sex life." And your response, "Hey, let me go think about that," isn't really very helpful.

Animals are another big problem. You either hate animals or (in a sort of backfield switch) love them too much. Either way, animals are a source of anxiety to you. They are physical: You can't reason with them, so your proven reserves don't help you much.

And right up there with dogs and cats as stress-producers are strong feelings and heavy emotional confrontations of any kind. These cause physical sensations you're uncomfortable with. Your heart pounds, you get butterflies in your stomach. You'd rather avoid such sensations altogether. Your idea of dealing with feelings is to read a book about them. Which, let's face it, means they are going to continue to be stressful for you because you'll never resolve them.

Adrenal Type Stresses:
The Stress of Change

Adrenal Types are a contrast to Pituitary Types in all their stressful areas. If you're an A-Type, your reserves—which are considerable—are in the body, not the head. Anything that can be handled by sheer power, force of will, persistence, or pure head-down, shoulder-to-the-wheel pushing is basically all right with you.

You can even withstand rejection—the most stressful of all events for other types—and manage not to take it personally. You're a good salesperson, and I mean that with the greatest admiration: Sales is, in essence, the art of making things happen, and in some ways it's the most difficult, unappreciated, and necessary work in the marketplace. You do what you must do to make things happen, and you do it well.

Stress comes in, for you, on the heels of change. Unpredictability is what makes an event go critical: that and the suggestion that your force of will may not be sufficient to make things go your way. Art makes you profoundly nervous, because it brings to your attention those forces in the world that you'll never be able to control. How many A-Types have frustrated their spouses by refusing to go to any movie they think is even remotely "arty," and by insisting on a predictable action flick instead?

Often you have difficult relationships with your children, unpredictable little beings that they are. As an A-Type patient of mine remarked, "At work, when I tell my secretary to do something, she does it. My son wants to know *why*. I like it better at work." Home life was often very stressful for him, and the only solution he could come up with was to work late and send his son to a military school in the hope that he'd become more like his secretary. His son, it just so happened, was a T-Type; he came back from military school more balanced than before, but he still didn't respond with total obedience and he still wanted to know why!

So many A-Types become workaholics for exactly this reason. Life at work is predictable (relatively, anyway), nonemotional, and responsive to the kind of pressure you're good at applying. It requires unflappability, endurance, and the ability to deal with repetition and detail—all of which you have. I don't want to say that your approach to work is uncreative, because there is a kind of creativity involved in your single-minded application of power to problems; but in general you tend to believe that creativity is the province of women and underlings.

"Call in the creative people," says a typical A-Type executive I know. He gets their input and moves on, and in this way pretends that a stressful area for him is under control. He believes that the creative work can be done by the people who eat quiche. I didn't want to tell him that if the T-Types eat enough quiche, they may take over his job!

The same sense of vulnerability is behind A-Type alcoholism. Alcohol dulls the edges of unpredictability in social life. You're more comfortable telling jokes and stories than exchanging ideas and views. The convivial A-Types in the bar, who seem to be having such a good time, are often just waiting for their turn to tell a story.

The good news is that none of this is cast in cement. Whether you're a Pituitary Type who feels uncomfortable outside of your head, or an Adrenal Type who feels threatened by change, you're that way because of imbalance in your body type. You're relying too much on the energy of your dominant gland, on your proven reserves—yet you could be using all the potential of your three less active glands to reduce your stressability.

When you activate your balancing glands with the Body Type System, experiences you used to find extremely stressful become manageable, and ones that were merely trying are not stressful at all.

Thyroid Type Stress:
Powerlessness

For a Thyroid Type, as you might expect, the experiences that are stressful are not the same as those that are stressful for Adrenal and Pituitary Types. For T-Types, situations that require steadiness, strength, and endurance are the ones that are most likely to make you run for cover. At the same time, the sort of highly challenging experiences that are difficult for A's and P's, you take in stride because your dominant thyroid gland provides you with such different sorts of reserves.

Unpredictability, far from being stressful, is in fact the very breath of life to you. Change in general you perceive as a stimulant, and you know how much you love stimulants! The T-Types I know love the rush and excitement of starting new projects, but can become very stressed with the detail and repetition involved in finishing them.

I know a Thyroid-Type man who is a very successful surgeon. This man thrives on challenge and the unexpected. When he does surgery that challenges him with three or four unusual and unpredictable outcomes, he emerges from the operating room looking relaxed and exhilarated, and not particularly stressed. Another surgeon I know, an Adrenal Type, comes out of this kind of operation with a tense, unhappy expression. But not my T-Type friend; it's his great strength, and he is justly valued for this ability.

I know that if I ever needed the kind of surgery that requires flexible thinking and the ability to change course in midoperation, he's the one I'd want to perform it. But if it was a routine, repetitious procedure involving minimal challenge and lots of tiny, painstaking stitches, I'd just as soon the A-Type did it. I wouldn't tell him this, but it's true. I'd be afraid the T-Type would get bored doing it, and the stress could affect my outcome. Boredom, routine, repetition, waiting—and, of course, fishing—these are the stresses that get to T-Types every time.

More T-Type Stressability: Physical Challenges

T-Types are also, like Pituitary Types, easily stressed by physical problems, but with a difference. P-Types feel any intrusion of the body as a sort of affront to their pure, mental being. T-Types, on the other hand, experience stress from physical demands that require endurance and steadiness on their part.

For T-Types, the difficulty is that the dominant thyroid gland is so unsteady, so cyclic, that they can't count on their physical reserves being there when they need them. Pain, even minor pain—a cut, a tiny bruise, an injection—might be tolerable at any moment or it might not, and they never know in advance. From this they get a nervousness about pain that in fact makes their fears materialize more often than not. Hypochondria, a typical T-Type stress response, has its roots in this same nervousness.

The typically thyroidal nerviness also extends into personal relationships. If you're a T-Type, you know that you fear rejection terribly. You doubt that your physical reserves can handle being rejected, and you suspect (rightly) that it might actually make you ill. When a T-Type sits in my office complaining of nervous stomach, insomnia, headaches, or other such stress symptoms, I ask about his or her personal life; you'd be amazed how often T-Types are reacting to some real or perceived rejection.

"My daughter hasn't called me in three weeks," a T-Type patient might tell me, and that's exactly how long she's had the gnawing sensation in her gut. Yet she rarely has alleviated her feelings of rejection by making a call herself. Without confidence in her physical reserves, this T-Type has been unwilling to face the challenge of verbalizing her feelings, or of taking the risk of asking for something better. Where an Adrenal Type might have dealt with this situation by attempting to force her daughter to call, a T-Type will either resort to elaborate stratagems or, more often, withdraw and take the stress in the pit of her stomach.

Anorexia and bulimia are other examples of this T-Type response taken to an extreme. I've practiced medical weight control for many years and have seen large numbers of anorexics and bulimics, and almost every one has been a Thyroid Type. The disease is truly a syndrome involving every aspect of thyroidal stressability. Feelings of rejection, unwillingness to confront problems, lack of a secure sense of personal power, and a profound feeling of boredom coming out of an unchallenging, unchanging environment: These are the ingredients I've found in the T-Type patients I've treated for eating disorders.

Getting through to an anorexic or bulimic T-Type involves understanding that this person is struggling for feelings of self-control and self-worth. Confrontation and intense involvement are the keys to breaking up this pattern. In most cases professional help is needed to make it happen. Then, once you've broken through the ice, the T-Type Health and Weight Maintenance Program is vital so that the ice won't form again.

If you know a lot of T-Types or are one yourself, you might think that they are the most easily stressed of all body types. It's a mistaken impression, but it seems true because T-Types are so irritable under stress and complain so much more than any other type. But the other side of it is that T-Types can reduce their stressability more dramatically than any other type by improving the balance in their metabolism. I've provided a list of specific options for T-Types on page 277, but they're all designed to add a feeling of personal strength and power to your repertoire of responses. I'm not saying you'll ever be able to wait more than fifteen minutes without losing all hope, or miraculously gain the ability to do the same thing more than twice without existential despair, but they will help more than you'd think anything ever could.

Gonadal Type Stress:
Why Some Women Like to Stay Home

Statistics indicate that the number of women with outside jobs and those who work inside the home is now about equal. It would be interesting to know whether in fact there are more Gonadal-Type women in the second group, because the G-Types of this world have an impressive way of making a success out of working in a traditional home environment. If you possess a G-Type metabolism, your unique set of reserves helps you to withstand the very real stresses of homemaking better than any other type, while your stressability is usually higher in a marketplace situation.

I hope this doesn't appear sexist; it's difficult to make this sort of statement, which recognizes a distinct characteristic, without giving that impression. The G-Type metabolism exists, and it's important to be aware of its strengths and stressability. It doesn't mean that a G-Type "must" stay home; stressability is no binding limitation. Look at Hillary Clinton: a G-Type woman who is by all accounts a fine mother, but a mover and shaker outside as well. But if you're a G-Type woman and work outside the home, or want to, or need to for economic reasons, wisdom suggests that you take positive steps to minimize your stressability and get what you need to function at your best.

The proven reserves of the Gonadal Type are found in responsiveness, patience, persistence, and warmth unequaled by any other body type. This gives you the ability to withstand the stress of child-raising and turn it into a joyful challenge. Like Mary L., my patient I told you about at the beginning of this chapter who handled her sons so well, your metabolism gives you the physical, mental, and emotional reserves to do all the never-ending educational and psychological work that is the backbone of mothering.

You also have tremendous reserves against the stress of tedium and lack of stimulation: G-Types are rarely bored, even in situations that would drive other body types wild with boredom. It's certainly not that they're dull; it's that they have the inner resources to find rhythms and delight in small changes that others don't even notice. Routines that would exasperate Thyroid Types beyond bearing, that Pituitary Types would simply not do, and that Adrenal Types would try to change into something else, G-Types use in their own way.

As Mary L. told me on another occasion, when I asked her if she ever got tired of the routines of being with young children, "It's not that I like doing things over and over, it's more that I never feel that I'm repeating anything. I'm always aware of the development, in my kids and in me." These are reserves of a high order, and while raising children isn't the only task that uses them, it's perhaps the most important one there is.

Where G-Types are stressed, by contrast, is in situations where these reserves feel exploited, or where they don't seem to produce any worthwhile results. The exploitation aspect is a highly stressful one. Many G-Types with jobs end up in helping professions—education, medicine, social work—but don't have the assertive qualities they need to resist doing too much and burning out. Many a boss has treasured the devotion of a G-Type executive assistant; many a department head has marveled at the attentiveness of a G-Type teacher. And, frankly, many of them have used it to their own gain.

Competition, also, is stressful for most G-Type women. It feels wrong, as if by competing you are doing something bad. The essence of competitiveness is to be strongly pro-self: It's at odds with the caring a G-Type wants to give to others. Superficial business relationships are also stressful. You like to form intimate, emotional bonds that may be inappropriate in most business situations.

STRESS: IT REALLY
COMES FROM WITHIN

The point, really, is that stress is not the same for everyone. For some people, physical discomfort is intensely stressful; for others, mental strain is far harder to cope with. For some women, stress is found in typical work situations; for others, stress begins at home.

For some men, change and unpredictability are stressful; for others, the exercise of power is what hurts. But for each person, stress-ability is an *internal* affair and comes from some lack of ability to respond to a challenge from the environment. How many points your life stresses are worth really does depend on you.

A practical approach to stress reduction must take this fact into account and must open up new ways of responding for each individual, according to the individual's needs.

Now let's go on to the specifics. You should now begin to apply what I've said to yourself. You know your body type, and you know what situations have been most stressful in your own life. You're ready to begin selecting, from the following sections, those techniques that will extend your proven reserves into a fuller range of strong, nonstressful responses.

STRESS REDUCTION
FOR PITUITARY TYPES

Your Stress Areas

Your body
Emotions (yours or others)
Sex
Food (cooking, eating, thinking about it)
Being sick (even having a checkup)
Animals
Any conflicts that can't be reasoned away

Stress Reduction Techniques

FOLLOW THE P-TYPE DIET to stimulate body awareness. P-Types often find the diet itself stressful at first. It is designed to direct your attention down to your body, which is the key to all your stress-reduction techniques. Stay with it.

FOLLOW YOUR BODY TYPE EXERCISE PROGRAM regularly, vigorously, in a totally physical way. You won't enjoy it at first, but it will do wonders for expanding your reserves against stress. See Chapter 12 for specific exercise programs designed to enliven your physical resources. Exercise will also make sex less scary.

CREATE REAL MEALTIMES, as relaxed and sensual as you can make them. Don't just snack. Think about what you want to eat (not what you crave), and either prepare it or go to a restaurant and order it. Then sit down, look at, smell, and taste your food. In fact, do this to each bite. You'll have reactions: Many P-Types have told me that food actually looks unappealing, gross. Keep going with this anyway. No matter what you think, food is good stuff. Once you understand the physical pleasure of food, you'll have taken a big step toward making friends with your body.

FIND A GOOD DOCTOR, one you feel comfortable talking to, and tell him or her your worst fears. Find out as much as you can about your physical self. Again, this is part of recognizing your body, making friends with it, and letting it also take care of you.

ACKNOWLEDGE CONFLICTS, taking this one step at a time. Realize that conflict situations are stressful for you, but don't run away from them. When reality is at odds with your preconceived ideas, compromise. This will get easier—and when you find you can handle conflicts without too much stress, your whole life will be less stressful in a very significant way.

STRESS REDUCTION FOR ADRENAL TYPES

Your Stress Areas

Unpredictability
Creativity ("the arts")

Situations you can't control with willpower
Your children
Emotional complexity
Vacations where you don't know what's going to happen

Stress Reduction Techniques

FOLLOW THE A-TYPE DIET to improve the flexibility and creativity of your responses to all stressful situations. You know in your heart that there's more to life than business, more to relationships than "Me Tarzan, you Jane" or "Me Wonder Woman, you Jim." But what, exactly, is this "more"? It lies waiting somewhere in the parts of life you now find stressful: emotional involvement, creativity, play. Your diet will help you move into these areas by stimulating the creative parts of you, and you'll be amazed to find how enjoyable they really are.

FOLLOW THE A-TYPE EXERCISE PROGRAM, which has been designed to complement the diet in increasing your ability to handle change. Most A-Types do exercise, but in the wrong way. You do some sort of mindless physical pushing, and you come in more stressed than you went out. You need to spend less time on exercise than you think, but what you do should involve bending, stretching, and coordination (see page 212).

SET ASIDE TIME TO "WASTE": Every minute of the day doesn't have to be Productive with a capital P. Give yourself some free minutes—not even for exercise or "self-improvement." Go for a walk, or just sit there (really!). You probably think this is a huge waste of time, but what's really going on is that you're afraid of what will happen.

STOP DRINKING: If you don't drink alcohol, that's great, but many A-Types do, and it's an influence that makes any attempt at stress reduction more difficult. I'd like you to experiment with not drinking for a week and see how you feel. If this seems very difficult, try an AA meeting. I'm not saying you're an alcoholic, but the people at AA can help you deal with even moderate alcohol use.

MAKE YOURSELF LISTEN to the people in your life. This means your spouse, your children, your subordinates at work, all the ones whom you tend to disregard because they aren't powerful enough to be interesting. Listening will help you understand that there are more kinds of power then the ones you're used to. Don't try to change them in any way. Just listen. Try to learn. There's a whole world you could be enjoying, and it's not as hard as you think.

STRESS REDUCTION
FOR THYROID TYPES

Your Stress Areas

Repetition
Continuing demands (from other people or your environment)
Details
Rejection
Pain (even minor)
Lack of change or stimulation

Stress Reduction Techniques

FOLLOW THE T-TYPE DIET to improve endurance, steadiness, and personal power. For most T-Types, the diet is a major change, one that you often want to resist. You know that all change is somewhat stressful, but as a T-Type you're basically adaptable and will get into this change quickly. The T-Type diet is designed to give you the ability to cope with the demands of real life, and you'll soon find how much less stressful it can be. And deep down you know you need a steadying influence.

FOLLOW THE T-TYPE EXERCISE PROGRAM for a whole range of benefits, both psychological and physical. Regular aerobic exercise gives you relief from your wound-up emotional nervousness, greater endurance to deal with long-range demands, a sense of your own physical reserves, and greater confidence in your ability to keep going when you want to.

GET ENOUGH REST: This is a vital stress reduction technique for any Thyroid Type. Your tendency always is to ignore your need to rest, and to choose stimulation instead. Take breaks. Accept your limits, even as they are expanding.

MAKE YOUR HOME AND WORKPLACE AS SOOTHING AS YOU CAN: Your inner life is so active that you need less outside stimulation than other body types. Ringing phones, bustle, pressure: You like these, but they're basically stimulants, like coffee and a pastry, and your creativity will be less dissipated and easily used up in a calmer, more relaxed environment.

TAKE LIFE ONE DAY AT A TIME: It's important for you to keep the perspective that your life is your own, and that you do whatever you want to with it, provided you keep your head and make changes one at a time. A major source of T-Type stress comes from the fact that you want to do everything all at once. The better way is for you to learn to pace yourself, alternate activity with rest, and come back to a stressful situation with your T-Type freshness and creativity revived. If you learn to do this, you'll find that there is truly nothing you can't accomplish in a satisfying and stress-free way.

STRESS REDUCTION FOR GONADAL TYPES

Your Stress Areas

Competition
Interruptions
Disorderliness
Changes in routine
Asserting yourself
Risks (physical, mental, or emotional)

Stress Reduction Techniques

FOLLOW THE G-TYPE DIET to increase your ability to handle risky, challenging, nonroutine demands. At first the diet will make you feel comparatively "spacy"; that is, not as solid and rooted as before. That, for you, is the best kind of change. Once you get used to it, you'll find you can handle all kinds of situations that previously seemed intimidating because they were unfamiliar. In fact, you'll find they're actually fun.

FOLLOW THE G-TYPE EXERCISE PROGRAM not only for physical conditioning, but also for safe practice in competition and self-assertion. Competition at play also makes competition in real life easier to handle. Your exercise routine is also planned to make you more adept at handling change and surprise. Not every exercise program will do this, so be sure to check page 210 for specific instructions.

CHANGE YOUR ENVIRONMENT OFTEN even if it's just rearranging the furniture. The more you can make little changes in the world around you, the more you'll feel in charge of your life, and the less you'll feel stressed by change that comes from the outside.

AVOID TOO MUCH ROUTINE. You can reduce your tendency to get stressed by life changes by keeping yourself feeling lively and stimulated. Start with baby steps, but keep on making changes and taking risks on your own. You'll be amazed at how great it feels.

WORK ON ASKING FOR WHAT YOU NEED FROM OTHER PEOPLE. You're good at nurturing, but you usually find it stressful when you don't receive the kind of care you give. You must realize that not everyone in this world is a G-Type. You can get the love and attention you need. And if you have to ask your T-Type, P-Type, or A-Type friends for it, what's wrong with that? You're just sharing with them the enjoyment of nurturing you already have. So go ahead; ask, enjoy.

A STRESS REDUCTION TECHNIQUE THAT WORKS FOR ALL BODY TYPES

Throughout this chapter I've written about expanding your areas of reserve and reducing your stressability. The basic principle I've utilized has been that the body's four glands give us resistance to stress in different ways. Since each body type has a different strong, dominant gland, each one can withstand some sorts of stressful influences while remaining vulnerable to others. Whichever body type you have, you use various parts of the Body Type Program to balance your system and stimulate your less active glands, and this turns out to make your more vulnerable areas far less easily stressed.

There is, however, something else that you can do to reduce

your stressability, and this is the practice of transcendental meditation. I recommend this strongly to all my patients, whichever body type they are, and I practice it regularly myself because I have come to believe that it is the most effective form of stress reduction available in the world today.

What transcendental meditation, or TM, does is to provide your mind and body with a state of deep rest, which many studies have shown to be deeper and more restful even than deep sleep. Rest is the potent antidote to stress of all kinds; if sleep knits up the raveled sleeve of care, the deep rest of meditation creates a new and better garment altogether.

However you are dealing with stress at present, whether well or badly, you still have been through stressful events in your life, events that inevitably leave their mark on your mind and body. TM gives you a way of actually recovering from the stresses of the past, and renews your strength to cope with the stresses still to come.

TM enjoyed a vogue in the United States in the mid-seventies. In the twenty or more years since, the TM movement has compiled more and more scientific studies (I'm talking about good, hard science) to back its claims of benefits. The technique is an extremely valuable one and has helped, and is still helping, many individuals. A great deal of scientific research now exists, clearly showing the relationship between the practice of TM and many improvements in physical, mental, and emotional health.

TM, like the Body Type Program, takes into account the fact that people are different, and certain aspects of the technique are taught according to the characteristics of the individual. For this reason actual instruction in TM has to be done in person. You learn TM through a four-day course that takes about an hour and a half each day. You then have the technique for life.

I recommend TM over any other form of meditation. It is not a flash in the pan. But if, for personal, family, or other reasons, you want to use another meditation technique, here are the guidelines you must use to see if the technique is good enough for you. It should provide:

1. Deep relaxation
2. Increased energy
3. Increased clarity of mind

4. A better feeling about yourself
5. Better functioning at work
6. Better relations with others
7. An easier and more enjoyable life
8. Increased resistance to disease

Benefits like this are hard to come by. If someone can teach you how to get them, or if you can learn something from a book, I have no complaint. If not, try TM. It's the choice way to get these effects, which is why I do it.

TM is taught in centers located throughout the country. To take the course, look in the phone book under "transcendental meditation" for the location nearest you. If you follow only one recommendation from this chapter, follow this one; there is no single thing you can do that will help you more.

CHAPTER 15

THE LONG WEEKEND
OF REJUVENATION

One of the things I have always found to be vital to my own health, balance, and spiritual well-being is to set aside specific time for personal rejuvenation, healing, and meditation. I have encouraged my patients to make this a priority in their lives, and I want you to have the same benefit as part of your Body Type Program.

As you know, my program is about much more than just weight loss. I would never devalue weight loss as a goal—I have seen too well how important it is to my patients to ever do that. But I believe that trying to control your weight without creating total balance in your system is simply impossible. The Long Weekend of Rejuvenation is one more tool I am putting at your disposal for creating total balance—and it is actually one of the most powerful tools I know. By relieving deeply rooted stresses and turning your body's clock back to a more youthful way of functioning, it actually enlivens your body's natural capacity for reaching and maintaining its own ideal weight.

Rejuvenation—which literally means bringing back your youth—is a wonderful feeling. Once you've tried this process I have a feeling you'll want to do it regularly. A good schedule is to do a Long Weekend once each season—at the beginning of spring, summer, fall, and winter. Do this for one year and I predict you'll be amazed at the way you feel.

In the previous chapter's discussion of stress reduction I told you about the value I place on my own practice of transcendental meditation for reducing stress and increasing my inner balance. I use TM as part of my Long Weekends, because I know I can rely on it to give me deep rest and relief from stress. Before embarking on your own Long Weekend, be sure you are comfortable with some form of meditation or technique of relaxation, so that you can get the most out of your rejuvenation period.

THE VALUE OF TOTAL IMMERSION: SPAS AND FASTING PROGRAMS

In the past several years I have found an excellent development taking place in health spas all over the country. Spas have always been places where people have gone for weight loss, rest, and rejuvenation. Increasingly, their emphasis has shifted away from strictly weight loss and moved toward total health, fitness, and inner balance. The Body Type Institute has played an active role in this development, and I have personally worked with spas to create health programs geared to the needs of each body type.

A weekend or longer at a spa offering body type programs is a great way to boost the effectiveness of your program. Total immersion has its benefits! But you don't have to go to a spa to get those results. This chapter will give you the guidelines for something just as good or even better. The Long Weekend of Rejuvenation is designed especially for you and your body type. If you'd like to get started on your Body Type Program with some tremendous momentum in the direction of balance and integration, that's what the Long Weekend of Rejuvenation is all about.

Fasting weekends have also become increasingly popular in the last few years. Works such as *3 Days to Vitality* (HarperCollins, 1998), by Pamela Surure and Donna Karan, make the connection between fasting and a cleaner body, a clearer mind, and spiritual rejuvenation. In my experience, a Long Weekend of Rejuvenation is even more effective than a fast, because it adds the benefits of specific balancing foods for your body type to the benefits of cleansing and rejuvenation offered by a fast. In addition, the deep rest created by the meditation schedule gives even more profound benefits. This is a safe, supportive program that you can do in your own time, at your own pace, and in complete privacy. As such, it brings you the very best of spa and fasting programs in an entirely personal way.

The Long Weekend of Rejuvenation Versus Your Usual Vacation

The Long Weekend I'm about to describe is rather different from just taking some time off from work. To appreciate the difference, you just need to think back to your last ordinary long weekend off. You were probably exhausted, ready for a break, but not quite sure how to make the best use of the respite. If your usual habit has been to go off on an exhausting, stressful outing to somewhere half the world is also going, or to spend the weekend catching up on work around the house, you have probably found that the only thing that really took a break was your energy. You end up feeling more tired than if you hadn't gone. You need an alternative.

This kind of vacation just doesn't seem to be enough—and it isn't, because it starts from the wrong premises. Perhaps in the past, when life was simpler and less stressful, it would have been plenty; but now we all need more respite, more rejuvenation, more rest out of whatever breaks we get in our incredible routines.

The thing is, to sustain today's pressured, incessantly active lifestyles, we need equally intense periods of rest. After punishment, there should be repair, not more punishment. The deeper the rest we are able to gain, the more resources we have to draw upon in our active life. Rest is absolutely basic—to effectiveness, to enjoyment, to our very survival.

Activity and Rest

Rest is terribly underrated in the modern world. Sleep deprivation is common (fifty years ago, the average person slept nine to ten hours a night; now it's six to seven, which is not enough). None of us rest enough, or deeply enough. In today's emotional climate, where success is measured by achievement no matter what the cost, "kicking back" seems a weakness, and is certainly not the way to get ahead in business.

Most of our heroes are workaholics. They enter the fray in three-piece suits or basketball uniforms. They're high-energy all the time, and if the fray seems to fray them, well, those are the breaks. But the cost is tremendous, to them and to society. The life of constant activity is grinding and wearing down our best people. Burnout is a major problem.

In my own profession of medicine, the ideal of constant work prevails. Doctors are supposed to *want* to work thirty-six-hour shifts. It's hip, it's macho, it proves dedication. It also guarantees mistakes. A recent study indicated that physicians in emergency rooms who have been up all night make seventy percent more mistakes in reading EKGs. I don't know about you, but the doctor I want reading my EKG is one who's had some rest lately.

How many fights have you had with your spouse late at night that seem absurd in the morning? How many times have you failed to see the answer to a problem at night that was perfectly apparent to you the next morning? What makes the difference is rest. Exhaustion degrades the quality of life and health at the same time. Fatigue reduces metabolic and mental efficiency, and rest improves it. Here personal experience and medical knowledge dovetail: Both indicate that *something must be done to reverse this trend and give rest its rightful place in our lives.* This chapter is about rest—the technology of rest, and how to use it for health and life.

The Rest of Your Life

I hate those ads where you see a guy on the beach sending faxes from his laptop computer. What a fool! It's a guarantee he'll have no new perspective when he gets back to his normal life. But if you're like many people, the idea of resting seems almost sinful. We never give ourselves permission to do absolutely zilch. A friend told me that as a child, she was actually forbidden to just sit, ever. She always had to be reading, or doing something, or else be up and about. These admonitions are still there in the back of the mind, but let me give you a new one to answer that inner voice with: You *need* to rest if you want to do anything worthwhile in activity.

The Body Type Long Weekend of Rejuvenation is a model of effective rest. It's a detailed, specific schedule for you to follow whenever you have a chance to spend some time purely on yourself. Actually, *this is not a luxury—this is a necessity.* The Long Weekend has the effects of a totally restful vacation, and the feeling of an exciting holiday. It's a refreshment for yourself and your idea of yourself. It will send you back to your active life with a flexibility and freshness you may not have known since childhood.

The Long Weekend is a schedule to follow whenever you have a Saturday through Monday available—Memorial Day, Labor Day, Presidents' Day, in the middle of the week between Christmas and New Year's Day, or whenever else you can arrange for a day off besides the weekend. What you do on the Long Weekend is give yourself an intense exposure to the Body Type Program. The Weekend puts together all the elements of the program: the diet and the nutritional supplements, the special body-type soups and herb teas, the exercises, the positions, the stress reduction techniques. It adds in some special extras especially for this luxury time. All this happens in the context of a focused and carefully scheduled time period. The result is that the elements reinforce each other to produce wonderful results. You go for the maximum in a short time. It is designed to decouple every aspect of mind and body from the outside world, and give each and every piece a rest.

The Long Weekend is a serious proposition, and should not be undertaken lightly. It's an intense experience that will actually change you. You must really have the time; don't think that you can just do the Saturday schedule, and jump back into your usual routines on Sunday. It doesn't work that way. The Long Weekend has its own rhythms. You must be able to do the entire schedule, or don't do it at all.

If your doctor told you to take a course of medication for a week, it would be absurd to take the pills he or she prescribed for three days and then stop, correct? If you change the oil in your car, you don't put back only half as much as your car requires. You wouldn't have half an operation. And so, you shouldn't do half of the Rejuvenation Program, either.

Most of us dig ourselves a well-intentioned rut and think we've found a groove. Getting out of the groove is what you'll be doing on the Long Weekend. I have done the Long Weekend of Rejuvenation at least twenty times over the years since I developed the schedule, and it has always worked. Frankly, I wouldn't want to function without it. Over the years I have improved it as new knowledge has come along, but the basic idea of structured rest has remained the same. I know that life is heavy at times, but the Long Weekend lightens the load, reduces the stress, and gets me attuned to myself—all the more reason I need it.

CAVEAT: You should be sure to check with your physician before starting the Long Weekend of Rejuvenation. Get his or her approval and make sure that he or she is aware of what you are up to.

Changes Need Company

I do not want you to do a Long Weekend of Rejuvenation alone. As I said, the Weekend is all about change, and when you're making rapid changes it's good to have another person around as a sort of reference point, or stable contact. You use a "buddy system" on the Long Weekend, because change is more comfortable in company.

Ideally, your buddy will be someone who is doing a Long Weekend, too. Choose someone compatible whom you find pleasant to be around, but not necessarily your best friend (you may just talk all weekend instead of sticking to the schedule). Spouses are fine, but don't choose to do a Long Weekend with your spouse if you're not getting along well. In the process of cleansing, when you feel unsettled, you may decide that the feeling is somehow your spouse's fault. Anyway, your problems will seem easier after you've gained the increased clarity and flexibility that comes from a Long Weekend.

Whomever you choose for your companion, it's best to have separate rooms, and to meet just at meals and for the "walk and talk" afterward. (You can eat alone at lunchtime if you wish, but do join your buddy for dinner.) If separate rooms are impossible to arrange, designate separate areas for yourselves and agree to ignore each other except at these times. You can sleep in the same room with your spouse if you wish, but sex should wait until the Weekend is over. You need to save that vital energy for repair.

Though preferable, it's not necessary that your buddy be on a Long Weekend. If you want to do a Long Weekend and your spouse can't join you, or you can't arrange to do one with a friend, interest a buddy in just taking a weekend of golf, shopping, or walks in the country. Again, join your buddy at meals. Having someone with you who is aware of what you are doing is very important for you to get the results you want from your Long Weekend. And by the way, nine times out of ten your nonparticipating friend will want to join you on your next Long Weekend of Rejuvenation. The process—and the results—are too exciting to resist.

The Elements of Rejuvenation

Rejuvenation is an extremely exciting concept. Just the thought of turning back the clock (not as far back as acne and adolescent angst, but back) is thrilling. The reality, you'll find, is even better than the thought. Rejuvenation has many elements, and by putting as many of these elements as possible together, we can make them work synergistically and increase the effectiveness of them all. Synergistically means, simply, making the whole greater than the sum of its parts.

Rejuvenation means becoming younger. Since aging can be defined in terms of fatigue, loss of flexibility, increasing imbalance, and the gradual deterioration of the entire physical mechanism, it is fair to say that rejuvenation must involve rest, purification, rebalancing, and repair, since it must undo all the aging influences. This seems so logical, but nobody else seems to follow this idea consistently. In the Long Weekend of Rejuvenation, the schedule enables you to work on all these factors, separately and together, in a controlled, simple, but remarkably profound manner.

Creating balance, of course, is the goal of all body type techniques. Offsetting the typical imbalances of your body type, increasing the flexibility of your responses, and broadening the base of support for your energy and vitality to include all your glands are what balance is all about. The Rejuvenation Weekend draws its rebalancing elements from the Body Type Program, using special features of the diet, positions, and exercise, and nutritional supplement programs for each body type. In addition, the Rejuvenation programs have unique features to give you deeper rest, purification, and mental and physical repair.

Deep rest is provided by periods of meditation and by the

schedule of the Long Weekend itself, which as you will see is incredibly tranquil and soothing. Purification comes with special breathing exercises, with meditation, and with other techniques I'll explain as we go through the schedule. Repair too is a function of rest. Meditation is the most efficient method of bodily repair that we know of today, and you'll find that the entire Rejuvenation period gives you a sense of ongoing repair that will be unprecedented in your experience. Life can be very punishing; you need repair.

Forget what you've already learned about rejuvenation—the Long Weekend is very different. It's innovative, exciting, logical, and time-tested. As my patients tell me, the Rejuvenation Program makes them feel as if they've been suddenly lifted from one level of functioning to another, much higher level. "When I come off a Long Weekend," one patient said, "it's like I've had a glimpse of the feeling of perfect health you're always talking about." This was after her second Long Weekend; I told her that by the time she'd done four or five, the glimpse of perfect health would be turning into a more complete impression. The Long Weekend creates new patterns in your body's responses that carry over into daily life to give you balance, poise, energy, and perspective. The Long Weekend really does set your body in the direction you want it to go, and it provides tremendous momentum toward your goal.

Getting Ready for Your
Long Weekend of Rejuvenation

A Long Weekend of Rejuvenation is a luxury in the truest sense of the word. It's a gift to yourself of time, the rarest and most valuable commodity that is yours or anyone's to command. So to make the most of it, you need to organize your time in advance, before starting your Weekend. That way all the time of the Weekend will be totally yours, to use for your own luxurious benefit.

This means, first of all, that you must familiarize yourself with every element of the Weekend. You must understand and be comfortable with the diet, exercise, nutritional supplements, and body positions. The diet you'll be following is the Last Five Pounds Diet, which is found in your Body Type Diet chapter. For now we'll call it the Purification Diet, because that is really what it is, when taken out of the context of weight control. You're not trying to lose your last five pounds on the weekend—you're trying for something much more profound. The exercise and positions for your type are found in Chapter 12, and the nutritional supplements for your type, in Chapter 13. There are some special additions to the supplements, but they are added to the regular Body Type Supplement Program, which you should follow precisely during the Long Weekend.

Finding the Time and Place

Once you've mastered all the elements of the Weekend, you need to organize the place and time to do it. Finding the time is usually the hard part. You need a full, long weekend or equivalent: a Saturday, Sunday, and Monday. Of course, if you can choose your own schedule, a Tuesday, Wednesday, and Thursday schedule is fine. You may need to take off a bit early on Friday, as well. Another way to do it is to take three days out of the middle of a more active vacation; say, the Tuesday, Wednesday, and Thursday of a week at the beach. A cruise could also be a possibility, although the superabundance of food on most cruises could be a bit of a distraction. Choose three days when the cruise ship is on the ocean and not in ports, take your walks around the deck, and enjoy the luxury of solitude the rest of the time.

But what is most important is that you really have the whole time free. You won't be able to combine the Rejuvenation Weekend with taking care of your kids, catching up on paperwork from the office, paying your bills, seeing a few shows, or indeed with anything. So don't even try to do it if you know you're going to have to deal with anything else besides your own rejuvenation process.

When you've chosen your time, you need to decide on a place. My recommendation, if it's possible, is to go to some place that combines beauty, tranquillity, and moderate seclusion. You needn't go to Nepal or Machu Picchu, but a friend's condo out on the lake, or a nearby out-of-season resort, is ideal.

The ideal place is close to nature, with peace and quiet and a place to walk or exercise. Avoid the kind of place where the eighteen-wheelers downshift outside your cabin window. Family-type resorts that have facilities for cooking and storing food are especially convenient. You can use the cooking facilities for making your Body Type Broth (see recipe on page 293) for your body type and preparing your herb tea. The broth can be made on a portable stove, and the herb tea can be made with a little immersion heater; but a stove and refrigerator will make your Long Weekend easier.

If you're at a place without cooking facilities and plan to take all your meals at a restaurant, you will have to use a little creativity when ordering, to stay on your Purification Diet. However, my patients have found it's not really difficult. Virtually every restaurant today offers green salads and/or cooked vegetables. You can request that chicken and fish be broiled without sauce, and you can make any substitutions you like on the vegetables. Use reason and common sense, and you'll be fine.

When you've found the time and place for your Long Weekend and have familiarized yourself with all the elements, all that remains to do on the Thursday before the Weekend is to go over the schedule and make sure you have everything you need. Check the menus and buy the food for any meals you plan to cook yourself. Don't forget the herb tea and the vegetables for your broth. Get any of the extra things that you don't have (NaPCA, a loofah sponge, mineral salts for your bath, an enema bag, extra vitamins as specified for your body type). Once Friday night arrives, your Long Weekend begins.

THE LONG WEEKEND OF REJUVENATION: SCHEDULE

The Day Before (Usually Friday)

1. Plan to arrive at your Long Weekend location by about 5 P.M. Unpack, arrange your belongings, explore and settle your territory.
2. Take a gentle, cleansing tap-water enema (see instructions, page 302).
3. Take a warm shower, and use your loofah to gently rub your whole body.
4. Take a twenty-minute tub bath, adding mineral salts to the water. (You may use any mineral salts you buy in a pharmacy or health food store.)

5. Dry yourself off gently and apply NaPCA to your entire body. (NaPCA, or NaPCA.2–pyrrolidone–5–carboxylic acid, is a chemical your skin produces to keep moisture in and keep itself supple. It tends to decrease with age. NaPCA in spray form replaces the skin's own element, is nonoily, and leaves open the path of elimination through the skin. It is available at most health food stores.)
6. Do your Body Type Positions all the way through, twice.
7. Lie down on your back for half an hour (no radio or TV).
8. Have your Body Type Purification Diet dinner with an extra serving of Body Type Vegetable Soup.
9. After dinner, take a slow, 15- to 20-minute walk.
10. Take the following supplements after your walk:
    367 mg L, and D,L Phenylalanine
    A multivitamin/mineral combination with the recommendations for your body type
    2,000 mg Vitamin C
11. Be in bed by 9:30, and rest even if you can't sleep. You may feel restless at this point, as your body shifts from sympathetic to parasympathetic mode. Don't worry if you do—just rest and take it easy. Whatever you're feeling at this point is a sign that your body is getting ready for the deep repair it will be undergoing when the Long Weekend proper gets under way.

The Two Full Days
(Usually Saturday and Sunday)

Follow this same schedule for both of the two full days of your Long Weekend. Do not get out of bed before 8:00 A.M., even if you awaken very early. Lie there and rest. Lying awake is not easy for most people, and it may not be easy for you. A-Types, particularly, will be longing to get up and get *busy rejuvenating;* A-Types seem to hear an inner whistle and a shout that says, "Okay, campers, hit the rejuvenation trail." Wrong: The way to rejuvenation is through rest, so stay in bed. Tossing and turning is okay and actually part of it. If the bed's a tangled mess when you get up, it's working!

THE MORNING PROGRAM

8:00   Shower.

8:15   Body positions all the way through once.

8:30   Breathing exercise (see page 301).

8:35   Twenty minutes of transcendental meditation, your own meditation, or lie down and rest.

8:55   Body positions again.

9:10   Two cups of Body Type Broth. (The Body Type Broth is made by taking the same vegetables as in your body type soup, cutting them up fairly fine, and boiling them in three cups of water for about eight minutes. Strain and discard the vegetables, and drink the liquid.) During this time you can read or listen to music if you wish. But read something inspirational, or listen to some soothing music—no wild rock, no bloodcurdling book.

9:45   Lie down and rest for fifteen minutes. This may not be easy to do. By this point you will probably feel either restless or very energetic, or totally exhausted. But what you are doing is breaking a cycle, and it's vitally important to do so. You may find that your body is full of unexplained tensions as you rest. If so, this is okay—don't think there's any particular way you "should" feel. Just lie there and feel the way you do. You will find it's an interesting sensation to lie down, experience many sensations and feelings, and not feel you have to do anything about it!

10:00   Breakfast from the Purification (Last Five Pounds) Diet for your body type.

11:00   Pituitary and Thyroid Types: half an hour of one of the aerobic exercises recommended for your body type, or an energetic walk. Adrenal and Gonadal Types: half-hour walk. Do this even if it's raining.

11:30   Breathing exercise.

11:35   Twenty minutes of transcendental meditation, your own meditation, or lie down and rest. If you happen to conk out, no problem, it just means you need sleep.

11:55   Body positions.

12:15   One cup Body Type Broth.

12:45   Lunch from the Purification Diet for your body type. Take
your Body Type Nutritional Supplements now.

How You'll Feel by Lunchtime

By the time you've finished your lunch, chances are you're going to
feel very unusual. The effects of the Rejuvenation Program are really starting to take hold now, and your body and mind are going
through intense purification. Until you have taken enough Long
Weekends to get some definite perspective, you won't be fully aware
that purification is what's happening right now. You'll just feel weird.
For one thing, you will have experienced several hours without TV.

Purification, which in this instance means rebalancing and re-
structuring of your system, is a sort of housecleaning process. It produces all kinds of temporary "dust" in your atmosphere, which tends
to settle on this or that piece of your mental furniture. What does
this mean? It means you might think you're mad at your mother, or
delighted with your son, or have any of an infinite variety of feelings. You feel emotional: perhaps upset, or out of sorts, or euphoric.
This is totally normal for this stage of the rejuvenation process.

Don't Worry About Anything Now

None of what you're feeling right now has any real meaning in
terms of your true inner state. Whatever you feel will pass soon; you
can take my word for it. If you feel angry at me and decide that the
Rejuvenation Program, and in fact the whole Body Type System, is
just some nonsense I've dreamed up to aggravate you, don't worry
too much about that, either (this has happened occasionally on
Weekends I've run for my patients, so I know the feeling's temporary). *All that's going on is purification;* by Tuesday you're going to feel
different. So let it go and just carry on with the schedule, no matter
how you happen to feel.

Some people find, at this point, that they feel extremely restless
and want more than anything to go out after lunch and shop, play
golf, or do a little work at the office. *Don't.* You can't fully realize
how relaxed and spaced-out you are: how nonpredatory, how open,

how vulnerable to sensory input. Even a trip to the grocery store right now will be too much. *Stay where you are,* and go on with the program.

THE AFTERNOON AND EVENING PROGRAM

2:45	Take an easy walk.
3:15	Back to your room. Rest, read, listen to music (no rock).
5:00	Shower (use loofah).
5:15	Body positions.
5:30	Breathing exercise.
5:35	Twenty minutes of transcendental meditation, other meditation, or lie down and rest.
5:55	Body positions again.
6:15	Rest.
7:00	Dinner from the Purification Diet for your body type.
8:30	Take another nice, easy walk.
9:00	Back to your room. Cup of Body Type Broth. Take the following supplements: A multivitamin/mineral combination with the recommendations for your body type 2,000 mg Vitamin C
9:45	Lights out. If you cannot fall asleep, just lie there awake, eyes closed. No television.

The Effects of Rest (After the First Day)

You will discover, by the end of your first day, how unused you are to resting. Most people feel very tired, much more so than at the beginning of the day. If you're one of these, you may be thinking that resting makes you tired, or that the Rejuvenation Program isn't restful. These thoughts are signs that your rejuvenation is under way. They're dust flying, nothing more. You have, in essence, released deep, stored fatigue from your body, in the form of toxins and other unwanted chemicals. They are now in circulation, and will be eliminated in the course of the weekend. It's working.

It's also possible that you may feel extremely restless or stir-crazy. I remember one patient telling me, "At noon on Saturday I was overwhelmed with fatigue. By Saturday night I was raring to go; I wanted to go dancing. Fortunately, I didn't. Sunday morning I was exhausted again—after an early night and eleven hours' sleep. It wasn't until Monday afternoon that I realized that what I thought was energy on Saturday night was just nervous restlessness, sort of like summer lightning."

The point to note here is that on the Long Weekend it's extremely hard to evaluate what you're feeling. These waves of fatigue or restlessness can be quite overwhelming, and it's usually not till the weekend is over that you get back your perspective.

Some people at this point feel wonderful. To be honest with you, much as I would like to take credit for a great result, euphoric feelings should be passed over just as much as tired or restless ones. All feelings at this point are the result of purification.

You Might Feel Something Negative— But It's Really Positive

Occasionally it happens that your body responds to the rejuvenation process with some slight physical or emotional side effects. The kind of things I'm talking about here are quite mild and not long lasting. You may experience a passing headache or some slight nausea, for instance—you won't get a migraine or a severely upset stomach. If you have any physical symptom that makes you very uncomfortable, or if you're alarmed for any reason, be sure to consult your physician.

The physical effects, like the emotionally stirred-up feelings, come from the toxins and other unhelpful chemicals temporarily in circulation in your system. You may not get any of them, but if you do it is important to be aware of what's happening to you. When you read the list, don't you feel amazed at how much badness is just waiting for an opportunity to be eliminated from your system? And aren't you impressed at how flexible and creative your body can be in getting it out, once you give it a chance?

Often a cup of your body type herbal tea will help relieve the feelings.

1. WEAKNESS: A feeling of weakness is not uncommon during the Long Weekend. There are three possible reasons: (a) you are releasing hidden fatigue; (b) you are releasing toxins; or (c) you are in a state of chemical imbalance occurring as part of the re-balancing process. The weakness comes from the body's way of turning its energies toward repair rather than activity.

2. STIFF MUSCLES: The reason here is usually that you have strained while doing your body positions, or you are simply un-used to stretching. *Never force any position past the point of comfort.* Go just as far as you comfortably can, feeling stretch but no strain, and hold for the time specified. Never try to match yourself against your friend, who may be more limber than you are. And resolve that when you get home again you'll do your stretching positions every day.

3. MILD HEADACHE: This, or feeling head pressure, can come from the same causes as weakness. You can also get a headache if you have been used to drinking a lot of coffee. This can feel like a migraine, but is rarely so intense and usually lasts only a day, at most a day and a half, and does not come back.

4. FUZZY THINKING: The best way to deal with this—which, frankly, almost everyone has on the Long Weekend—is to resolve in advance not to make any decisions at all while you are doing the program. Just follow the schedule and take it easy. Afterward, your thinking will be much clearer, so wait until then to decide anything.

5. BAD MOOD: A-Type anger, G-Type frustration, P-Type obses-sion, and T-Type depression are the most usual. If these occur, it's important to remember that they are far more closely related to the rebalancing in your system than to any circumstances in your life. This is not to say you may not have good reasons to be angry or depressed, but they aren't the main causes right now. It's a good idea not to do a Long Weekend with your spouse if you're in the middle of a feud; why take a chance of increasing your problems? Later, when your mind is clearer, you can better deal with it all. Meanwhile, on the Weekend, have an extra cup of your body type tea to cool you down.

6. WORRY: The rest you're getting is letting pent-up tensions come out; again, let them take their course.

7. FUNNY SMELLS: The release of toxins can give you various

funny smells: bad breath, body odor, urine and feces that are smellier than usual. All these are caused by the body using whatever channels of elimination it can to get rid of those same old toxins. A coated tongue is the same thing; so are hives (although this is extremely rare). If you remembered to bring your tongue scraper, be sure to use it. It will all pass. For any symptoms that you feel are of real concern, consult your physician. It is unlikely that you will have any.

The Last Day (Usually Monday)

Follow the morning program of the two full days (see page 293) up to 11:30. End with the exercise or walk. Then, at noon, lie down and rest for fifteen minutes. Then begin to pack up to go home.

At 1:00 (or so) have the Maintenance Diet lunch for your body type, either at home or on the road. After lunch, take a thirty-minute walk. Talk. Go somewhere where there are some people, but not a lot of noise—a quiet mall, for instance. What you're trying to achieve is a sense of contact with life, in a pretty nondemanding setting. A well-used park is another good place to walk. By letting your mind move around from one stimulus to another, you're regaining a sense of your usual reality.

Around 3:00, continue to your home. At home, you must take it very easy. There should be no business calls (tempting though it may be to go through the messages on your answering machine and deal with all the "crises"). Don't go to a loud party, either, or go dancing, and don't decide to take a long jog or do anything very strenuous at all. Have the dinner from your Health and Weight Maintenance Program, then watch TV or read a book. You can go out to a movie if you have an overwhelming desire to do something, but pick a reasonable (PG) one. Go to bed at your usual time.

The Day After (Usually Tuesday)

As you get up in the morning of the day following your Long Weekend of Rejuvenation, you should notice how you feel. I believe you'll be very surprised; most of my patients are. Nothing in the Weekend itself, which is often full of feelings of restlessness, stir-craziness, and funny bodily sensations, quite prepares you for the freshness you feel when the Weekend is over.

What most people report (and what I certainly find myself) is that the greatest gain is in mental and emotional expansion. My mind feels more capable and my heart more loving. Problems—personal, work, all kinds—seem not less challenging, exactly, but more soluble. Tension seems less necessary. I always have a sense that I'd been worrying more about my problems than was ever necessary.

Occasionally patients report that they thought at first that they were having a hard time getting back into their work, but then realized that what was actually happening was that they were working more efficiently and with less stress. This may well happen to you—it has happened to me after several Long Weekends. Other times it seems that the people you work with are trying to get you frantic again. Just realize that you don't need a mask of frenzy to feel as though you are functioning. Gauge effectiveness by results, not mileage.

DO IT RIGHT, AND ENJOY THE MARVELOUS RESULTS

As long as you go through your Long Weekend with care and attention, you're going to enjoy the most marvelous, delicious feeling of restfulness and freshness for weeks afterward. Problems that come up after the Long Weekend—any feelings that are not pure freshness and vitality—usually mean that you weren't careful about the schedule. If you feel any sort of strain in picking up the threads of your routine, it usually turns out that you changed the schedule in some important way. For instance, you may have meditated more times than was scheduled, or skipped a meal, or didn't do your body positions or your exercises.

Meditation and the breathing exercise are powerful tools that produce many changes in your system. Too much of either one can be, well, just too much. Exercise and body positions, by contrast, are stabilizing influences that you should never skip. Even if you feel as though you can't do the positions at all, it's better to approximate them without strain than to skip them one day.

You could also feel not quite perfectly fresh if you spent the evening following your Long Weekend at a disco or a loud, violent movie. You must take it easy on this evening for best results. You're still going through the purification process, and there's a lot going on in your system that demands rest to complete.

The Long Weekend of Rejuvenation is going to teach your body a better way to function. By taking the time to do it, you switch your approach from fight-or-flight to stay-and-play. And you'll find that when you get back to the dog-eat-dog world, your stay-and-play approach will remain with you. This is actually an expanded state of consciousness that you're experiencing, and bringing it back into the fight-or-flight world must be done carefully and correctly. So please follow all the directions accurately. The schedule of the Long Weekend is tried and true: It works. If you let it, it will work for you, too.

If You Have More Time

Sometimes patients who have done two or three Long Weekends ask me if it's possible to follow the schedule for a little longer time. Yes, you can, but only if you've already done at least two Long Weekends and are thoroughly familiar with the entire schedule and the results.

To extend the Long Weekend, you repeat the schedule for the two full days. You always end with the schedule for the final day, and begin with the schedule for the day before. For example, suppose you have five days free, beginning on a Monday. Monday would be like the Friday of the Long Weekend. Tuesday, Wednesday, and Thursday would be like the Saturday and Sunday of the Long Weekend; Friday, like the Monday of the Weekend.

Two important points. Never do the Rejuvenation Program for more than a week at a time, and be sure to have someone with you on the program whenever you extend your schedule. Finally, be doubly, triply sure to take it easy on the day, or even for two days, after your Rejuvenation period. You will be deeply involved in the balancing process, and it is very important that you give your system ample opportunity to get all the benefits through deep rest.

How to Meditate

The schedule for the Long Weekend of Rejuvenation calls for three twenty-minute periods of meditation on each of the two full days. In order to get the most out of these meditation times, I strongly recommend that you take a course in transcendental meditation before your first Long Weekend. The course in TM takes just days to complete, at the end of which time you will know how to meditate without further instruction being required. If you started TM in the seventies or eighties, as many people did, but haven't kept it up, it's a good idea to have a "checking" (a brief refresher on the technique, offered without charge by TM centers) before your Long Weekend.

More about some of the benefits of TM, along with how to locate a center for instruction, appears in Chapter 14.

How to Do the Breathing Exercise

This simple breathing exercise comes from the tradition of yoga. Yogis say it strengthens the heart and lungs, improves digestion, purifies the nervous system, and conserves energy. You are using it for all these reasons, and above all for its ability to balance your entire system. Though simple, it is amazingly effective.

It's a good idea to practice the breathing exercise a few times before beginning the Long Weekend. To begin, sit in any position that is comfortable for you in which your back is fairly straight. You could be cross-legged on the bed, in a comfortable chair, or wherever. You can even sit in the "lotus position" on the floor, if this happens to be comfortable for you.

Take your right thumb and press gently on the side of your right nostril, closing the nostril. Breathe out slowly and completely through the left nostril. Noiselessly breathe in through the same nostril. Then press gently with your ring and middle fingers of your right hand on the left nostril, closing it, while opening your right nostril to breathe out. Breathe out noiselessly, slowly, and completely through the right nostril. Breathe in again through your right nostril in the same way.

Continue in this way, alternately breathing out and in, then changing nostrils, for five minutes. Take it easy. There is no rush. Go slowly and don't hyperventilate, or you'll get dizzy or upset. The purpose of this breathing exercise is to settle and calm you, not to make you tense! You don't need to breathe in and out so slowly that you don't feel you're getting enough air—breathe comfortably. Once you get used to it, it's very pleasant.

How to Take an Enema

For many, the idea of an enema is kind of repulsive. They don't like to have anything to do with what goes on "down there" and especially don't want to think about it—or they remember it as a kind of punishment when they were kids. But we're going to think about it now just for a minute.

The intestines are the avenue for the absorption of nutrients and the elimination of waste. This elimination can be more or less efficient. Bad or toxic food, stress, fatigue, lack of exercise, and other bad habits all contribute to a disturbance in the efficiency of elimination. On the Long Weekend of Rejuvenation we want all the routes of elimination to be working as well as possible to get the most out of the program. Meditation, the Purification Diet, the positions, and all the rest contribute to improved cleansing and balancing of the body. This means that the routes of cleansing and elimination must work well.

The enema at the beginning of the Weekend is designed to cleanse one route that carries toxins from the blood, liver, and fat to the outside. The skin is another route of elimination, and this is the reason we also cleanse it carefully (the shower, loofah, and bath on the first day). The lungs eliminate as well, which is why your breath may become a bit strong.

So an enema is just really another form of cleansing that facilitates rejuvenation. It is not simply "icky"—it has a purpose.

Many people have never taken an enema. Others do take them, but for constipation rather than cleansing. The enema I want you to take is to cleanse your colon, stimulate the lining to allow toxins to be eliminated, and to remove toxins and feces that are currently accumulated.

Here is precisely how to go about it:

1. Buy any standard enema bag in a drugstore. Buy some petroleum or lubricating (K-Y) jelly.
2. Use the enema nozzle, which is the smaller of the two nozzles that comes with the bag.
3. In the bathroom, put a towel down. You will be lying on it. Find a place where you can hang the bag so the bottom is about three feet above the floor.
4. Fill the bag with tepid water and run it out so the tube is filled. Clamp the tube shut. Hang the bag and apply a small amount of petroleum or lubricating (K-Y) jelly to the tube tip.
5. Lie down on your left side and insert the nozzle as far as it will go. Be gentle. Don't hurt yourself. If you've never done this before, it will definitely feel weird. Don't let it pop out.
6. With one hand slowly undo the clamp so that water runs out of the bag. Let about half the water in the bag go in slowly. You may get an instant cramp and have to "run for it." Go ahead. If not, wait about two minutes and then expel the water into the toilet.
7. Refill the bag. This time, lie on your back. Slowly allow three-fourths of the water in the bag to flow in. With the clamp shut but still lying on your back, massage your abdomen gently from the lower left up to the bottom of your ribs, then right across the abdomen just below the ribs, then down the right side of the abdomen. You will hear the water gurgling around. You may have to stop or go to the toilet because of cramps. If you don't, massage back up the right side, across, and down the left side. Expel the water and toxins. It will look and smell very strange—these are the toxins.
8. Repeat the procedure using a whole bag of water if it's comfortable to do so. Do not at any time lie on your right side, only your left side and then your back.
9. Shower.

Some people find they are oddly invigorated after an enema; others feel tired. You are starting to get your elimination system going. Some people (men and women both) feel sexy, because toxin congestion affects sexuality (the ovaries and prostate are in this area, too). You may feel "airy" because of the cleansing effect. Whatever you feel, take it easy. Don't have sex. Follow the program—bath, NaPCA, body positions, rest. You are going to be using all your energy for rejuvenation, so remain focused. There's plenty of time for everything else later, after the Long Weekend of Rejuvenation.

ENTRAINMENT: WHY YOU'RE DOING ALL THIS

I want you to keep in mind—as you wonder, on reading through this section, how it will work to do all these things, some weird and some familiar, on the Long Weekend—that you're doing all this for a reason. I've spoken in terms of rebalancing, refreshment, and rejuvenation; another important feature of the Long Weekend is what is called *entrainment* of your total system.

Entrainment is a term that means bringing your various systems into step with one another, so that they work together in an integrated manner. Entraining your system means creating a synergistic effect—the whole becomes greater than the sum of its parts.

All the features of the Long Weekend contribute to entrainment. The Purification Diet entrains the glandular system. The meditation entrains the brain (there are fascinating studies that have been done on people practicing TM, showing that the various parts of the brain begin to work more coherently together). The breathing exercise works to entrain the spinal cord and the brain. The body positions entrain the nervous system and the internal organs. Nutritional supplements entrain the entire system at the biochemical level. Exercise helps entrain organs, glands, and the brain. Finally, the total rest of the Long Weekend allows all these entrainment effects to be coordinated for greatly increased harmony of functioning.

This is the technology of rest. Rest alone can enable these effects to occur; rest gives the quietness in which positive change can happen. The technology of rest explains how such profound changes can happen in such a short time. The improvements of the parts come together, and the improvement of the whole is assured.

SIGNPOSTS TO CHANGE: WHAT YOU CAN EXPECT, AND WHEN

I'm going to assume that you have finished reading through this book (or at least, reading the chapters that apply to your body type) and are now contemplating your first steps on the Body Type Program. If you're like most of my patients, you're intrigued and eager to get started. Perhaps you have already had a couple of "aha" experiences over your body type characteristics, or have felt a sense of relief at finally understanding why the last three times you've tried to lose weight made you wonder why you even bothered. This time, be sure, it's going to be different.

What I'd like to do now is give you an overview of what you can expect from the program—not just for the next few months, but over the course of your *lifetime*. This *is* a lifetime program, you understand, not a "diet" you'll be on for a little while but a permanent way of steering your metabolism through life. There are five very definite markers—what I call "Signposts to Change"—that you will encounter. When you read about them now they may not make a lot of sense, but I'd urge you to hold on to this book so you can look at this chapter again in a year or two, when they will probably seem quite obvious.

The Signposts to Change, along with the approximate time you can expect them, are:

Signpost #1 Control of cravings. You reach this signpost after two to four months on the Body Type Program. The more body type modalities (snacks, soups, teas, supplements, exercise program, diet) you actually use, the shorter the time it will take to reach this marker.

Signpost #2 Reaching your ideal weight. There is no definite time for this marker, as it obviously depends on how much you want and need to lose.

Signpost #3 Achieving stability at your best weight. For most people, this signpost is reached when you have been at your best weight for about a year.

Signpost #4 Achieving a fully adjustable system. Most people find themselves at this point when their weight has been stable for one to three years.

Signpost #5 Going beyond your body type to the "meta-body type." Again, for this one I cannot give you an exact time frame, as it depends entirely on you, or more accurately, on your state of consciousness. But don't worry, because once you are at Signpost #4 and have a fully adjustable system, you will be perfectly happy with yourself and perfectly content to wait for the next step.

Now I'd better explain what these signposts are all about.

The First Signpost: Control of Cravings

The first days on the Body Type Diet are usually a bit euphoric—you feel the excitement and hope that always comes with something new. This euphoria will carry you a certain distance, but then the program has to take hold and begin actually transforming your system. Cravings are, in part, the resistance of your system to the process of change.

Always remember that when you ate foods that stimulated your dominant gland, you did so because it carried a reward with it. There was also a cost associated with it (overstimulation and exhaustion of the gland, loss of energy, overweight) but the payoff was that you did get some energy, some boost, from those foods. Now, you are taking another path, learning to gently stimulate other glands and get your energy from other sources within your body. But until those glands begin to respond, you are going to feel cravings for the old way of eating. Every time you have a dip in your energy, it will be accompanied by a craving. It was what your body knew well before—and your body is conservative even if you're a liberal. It hates to give up what "worked" until it's sure the new way will be better.

The way to negotiate this period, when your body is adjusting to, and learning not to resist, the new mode of functioning, is to use as many of the tools of Body Type Dieting as you can—but use them in a reasonable, not an extreme, way. For example, if you are an A-Type cutting down on red meat, don't switch immediately to nothing but tofu—enjoy chicken and fish, and have meat once or twice a week. If you're a T-Type and just beginning a strength training program, get a trainer or a good book and start slowly—don't try to pump major iron the first week. Make the changes you need to make, but be kind to yourself. Change that is too rapid is actually weakening to your body, and leaves it far more open to cravings and even injury.

Your body suffers if it changes too quickly. You may feel you are flying high with your new program, but if you're too extreme you will "hit bottom" with a thud, like a seesaw on a playground. You will then bounce back in the other direction. If you eat less than the amount of food I recommend, you may drop pounds rapidly, but find yourself overeating afterward. Remember, you are steering your body, not zooming around maniacally. If you overexercise, you become stiff and fatigued, and stop exercising, sometimes forever! It's much better to make your changes in a measured way, so that your body can incorporate the changes; the seesaw-swings will become smaller and there will be no sickening thuds.

What this means is that you should follow the recommendations just as they are, and not try to speed things up by eating less, or doing more exercise. If you haven't exercised before, it's extremely important that you start slowly and increase your amount of exercise gradually—review the Body Type Exercise chapter for details. The supplements are extremely helpful, but in the amounts recommended; twice as much is definitely not twice as good.

When you take this easy, comfortable approach, you will soon notice a gradual shift taking place in the way you feel. You may have been very out of balance when you started, or only moderately so, or scarcely out of balance at all. Of course, the change will start from where you are. Remember, people really are different, and your friend is not the measure of *you*. Depending on how far out of balance you were, you will come to the first signpost in anywhere between two and four months.

The signpost begins with a general reduction in the *intensity* of your cravings. This usually happens within two or three weeks. But several months are usually needed before they disappear completely. A craving is gone when you can eat a little bit of the craving food and not long to eat more of it. The craving food is now no longer a drug; it is just a food like any other food. You may still like it, but you won't feel you *need* it, because you won't have that intense craving feeling associated with it.

The same goes for other body type compulsions, such as the compulsion P-Types sometimes have to run obsessively, or the A-Type compulsion to pump heavy iron. If you're a P and can run a reasonable amount each week, or an A who can lift moderate weights just twice a week, you are doing well. The intensity of these cravings, as well as cravings for food, is a good sign of the degree of your imbalance. Controlling them means you have shortened the seesaw swings a lot.

The Second Signpost: Reaching Your Ideal Weight

This next Signpost to Change is an important one for most people, because it is an outward sign of the inward transformation of your system. Overweight, as you know, comes from imbalance in your glandular system; specifically, from overstimulating and exhausting your dominant gland. In other words, obesity is an outcome. When your cravings come under control, it is an inward sign—apparent to you but not yet to others—that your dominant gland is starting to recover. When you reach your ideal weight, it shows that your dominant gland is no longer an exhausted, imperious tyrant, demanding that you eat food you don't even really want just to keep it happy. With this inward freedom from cravings, you were able to transform your system, burn off toxins stored in fat, and reach a weight that is comfortable, efficient, just right for you. This vibrant health is also an outcome. It's an important step and one you should feel justly terrific about.

Once your cravings are controlled, how long it takes you to reach your ideal weight depends (no surprise here) on how much you needed to lose (or gain). The speed at which it happens is ultimately determined by your metabolism. I urge you (though without a lot of hope that you'll do this) to be patient. Slower is actually better; but patience is part of a fully balanced system, and you probably won't be completely patient with your body until you reach Signpost #3.

Note that this second Signpost to Change is the end point of all other "diet books." Losing weight is their goal, and whatever transformation their recommendations are meant to accomplish ends there. They imply that you will remain stable, but do not give you the tools you need to do so. You know the usual outcome: You do *not* remain stable at your new weight, but almost immediately begin a slide back to the weight at which you began, or beyond. This is not the case with the Body Type Program, though. The transformation continues for the rest of your life. This is just the second signpost—there are three more to come!

The Third Signpost:
Stability at Your Ideal Weight

When you reach Signpost #2, your ideal weight, you naturally have to make an adjustment in your Body Type Program. What you do at this point is change to the Health and Weight Maintenance Program for your body type. This change is fully discussed in the chapter on your particular Body Type Diet. For most people, when you have been following the maintenance guidelines for about a year, your body settles into its best weight and acquires stability. It becomes as hard for you to gain weight as it was to lose it before you discovered the Body Type Diet. You simply do not have the impulses that led to weight gain anymore.

As you already know, the Health and Weight Maintenance Program is not a diet—it's a set of guidelines for you to keep in mind and use for yourself. The Plenty foods, Moderation foods, and Rarely foods are listed, but quantities aren't spelled out for you, nor do I give an exact definition of how much to eat from each category. At this point, you yourself determine how much you eat, by paying attention to your body and using the intuition of your own needs that you have developed on the earlier stages of the program. *You* chart the course, *you* steer.

Even so, the Health and Weight Maintenance Program does give you some guidance, by outlining the foods you can eat freely (Plenty foods), foods you can eat as long as you watch them a little bit (Moderation foods), and foods to save for special occasions only (Rarely foods). This guidance is needed because even at this stage your weight is not yet absolutely stable. It has some stability, but can still swing. The same goes for your energy.

Built into the Health and Weight Maintenance Program is a miniadjustment that allows you to reduce your swings even further. You learn from the maintenance stage how to make adjustments on your own. You don't necessarily think about it, but whenever you eat one of your Rarely foods, you are doing so because you sense some kind of need in your system. When you reduce the Plenty foods, or increase Moderation or Rarely foods, you are responding to that intuition that is the sum total of your body's feelings. The better your balance, the more accurate your feelings will be. This accurate attunement to your body's needs is one of the biggest bonuses of the Body Type Diet. It becomes hard to remember how out of touch with yourself you were before.

By this time, you are pretty much free of cravings, which allows you to reach a finer sense of yourself from the inside. This freedom of intuition is the exact opposite of the slavery to cravings. But note that I used the phrase "pretty much free of cravings," because under very stressful situations it is still possible for cravings to rear their heads. You still have the memory of stimulating your dominant gland. Your system remembers that in past emergencies, there were certain foods that gave you a burst of dominant-gland energy. This memory can insinuate a faint craving for a chocolate bar or a hamburger, but these cravings do not have the completely overwhelming character they had before. You know too much for that, thank goodness. And even if you do succumb to a craving food, your system now has the stability to absorb that food without losing its balance.

Getting to the Third Signpost:
The Key Factors

The year or so between Signposts #2 and #3—after you reach your ideal weight but before it is fully stabilized—are actually the most crucial phase of the entire program. You know this yourself if you have had the very common experience of getting to your weight goal, and then gaining back everything you have lost (usually even more). It is so common that it is actually considered the norm for all dieters—the famous 98 percent who are said to "fail" at dieting. It isn't really the norm, but I can understand where the reputation has come from, when so many people have failed during this crucial stage.

The reason why this stage is so tough for so many people is simply because they haven't learned how to eat right for their body type. So they have lost weight, but haven't created balance or harmony in their system. Their dominant gland is still exhausted (often more so than when they started) and their cravings for dominant-gland stimulators are intense. They haven't learned anything new about their metabolism and they don't know how to handle it when they have low energy and need a snack. In short, they're right where they started before the diet. I call these people the "temporarily nonoverweight." They are the 98 percent. They are weight rebound waiting to happen.

There have been several recent studies that have looked at people who have reached the third signpost; in other words, people who have lost weight and are still at their new weight after a year. The research is interesting, because it studied people who did not necessarily follow their Body Type Diet, yet who did make it to this particular goal. You, with your knowledge of your body type, have an advantage they did not have, and their "secrets" are also part of the Body Type Program. So your chances of reaching this signpost are outstanding.

The research brings out one comforting fact: People who succeed in keeping off lost weight do so in spite of the "risk factors" many of them shared. You may have heard that some people are genetically programmed to be overweight; you may be worried that you are in this group. It is true that there is a genetic component in overweight, as suggested by the fact that up to 70 percent of overweight people have at least one overweight parent. Yet many people whose entire families were overweight have succeeded in keeping their weight off. The same applies to people who were overweight as children, or people who lost weight when they were already in their middle years. It's good to know that even if you have all these things in your background, they do not mean that it is impossible for you to reach Signpost #3.

The Keys to Long-Term Success

There are two things that the research underlines as most critical for long-term success: staying active, and staying with an eating plan that's right for you. Staying active appears to be the most important single thing you can do to get through this crucial stage. You can see why my emphasis on the Body Type Exercise Program is so strong. Ninety percent of all people who have achieved stable weight loss are regular exercisers. In one study, some participants lost weight through diet and exercise, some through diet alone. Several months later, *only* the people who ate right *and* exercised had maintained their weight loss! THINK about it!

Chapter 12, The Body Type Exercise Program, is all about the exercises that are most balancing for you. Depending on your body type, you will have a slightly different emphasis among the three kinds of exercise: aerobics, weight training, and flexibility. But whatever your body type, you will be doing a program you will thoroughly enjoy. Let it become a wonderful part of your life.

Continuing with a healthy, enjoyable eating plan is the other important key. That means, of course, your Body Type Health and Weight Maintenance Program. It doesn't mean you have to be a hermit. You can and should eat out ("Garçon, the check . . . to my friend.") and you can and should enjoy eating. But you do need to remember the foods that are right for *your* type of metabolism.

People whose weight loss becomes stable and permanent don't deprive themselves, and aren't rigid, but they *do* limit specific types of food, and watch those foods regularly. For you, of course, that means that you'll watch your Rarely foods, and make sure that you don't let them become once again druglike in their influence.

Finally, the research shows that successful people *enjoy* their healthy life-style. Far from being miserable or deprived, they are overwhelmingly positive about their life changes. This will definitely be the way you'll feel at this stage. You'll be enjoying eating more than you did before, because you won't feel guilty about it. You'll know that what you eat is right for your body type. You will be enjoying your Body Type Exercise Program, and you'll be proud of your health improvements.

Also, of course, you'll be taking Body Type Supplements, which will help you feel even better. Continuing to take Body Type Supplements is an important key at this stage. Most people take their Body Type Vitamin/Mineral Combination, Amino Acid Combination, and Herbal/Glandular Combination. You will know best by this time what works for you.

Even if you are one of those people who began the program without having very much weight to lose, or if you began for other benefits than weight loss, it is still a significant signpost for you when your weight becomes stable and comfortable. Many people who believe they don't have a weight problem are actually maintaining their weight only through rigid self-control, constant dieting, and attention. Such vigilance isn't life after all, and it hardly can be called ideal! Fighting to maintain your weight is also a weight problem.

Once you have reached the stage where your weight is stable, you will continue at this stage for perhaps another year or two, possibly as long as three, before reaching Signpost #4. As I've said before, this doesn't mean that you'll still be "on a diet" for all that time. Remember, you are steering your own metabolism by the time you reach Signpost #3. You're in control, and this is a stage you'll enjoy very much. The comments I hear from my patients during this stage are all about how well they feel, and how much more energy they have. This is the experience you too will have when you reach this signpost.

The Fourth Signpost:
The Adjustable System

To tell you about this Signpost to Change, let me tell you about the experience of one of my patients, a woman named Lisa B. She was a P-Type who had been following the Body Type System for several years. She'd started with the Weight Loss Diet, which she alternated with the Last Five Pounds Diet until she had reached her ideal weight, 135 pounds. She then incorporated the Health and Weight Maintenance Guidelines into her life. The effects were profound.

She'd done some serious thinking about her health, and had gotten serious about the P-Type Exercise Program—a real first for her, since she'd always hated the idea of exercise. But the effects intrigued her. She felt in touch with her body for the first time ever, and she liked it. She even started to find sex interesting. So she continued with her program, even when her husband teased her for eating liver for breakfast. She did it because it *worked*—she felt more energetic, stronger, more in touch with herself, more attractive. She felt like a member of the human race, not like a race of one member.

After a year or so on the program, Lisa knew she had become a really exemplary, balanced P-Type. Then she got a new job. She'd been a computer programmer, but now she went into sales, where her earning potential was much higher. She met people's eyes, she sent vibes, and she made sales. Her new energy and drive paid off, and she reaped the rewards of change.

She'd been doing well for the last year and I hadn't seen much of her in the office. On this particular day I'd been quite busy and didn't focus on the way she looked until she was actually in my office for consultation. Then what she said caught my attention immediately.

"Dr. Abravanel," she said, "I've been playing with my diet a bit over the last year, and I think I'm doing the right thing, but I wanted your opinion. What I think is that I'm not a Pituitary Type anymore. I've been supporting my adrenals with your diet for so long that now I'm an Adrenal Type, and the P-Type Diet isn't right for me anymore. So I'm switching to the A-Type Diet some of the time. It seems right to me, but what do you think?"

I looked at Lisa closely. To the casual observer, there was something of the Adrenal Type about her. Her body was definitely sturdier and stronger-looking. The P-Type Exercise Program, which emphasizes strength training, had given her a more defined shape that was actually more feminine than the way she'd looked before.

The baby fat and cellulite on her knees were gone. Her face had a better color and a more focused expression. There was an aura of warmth and power about her that hadn't been there before.

Nevertheless, despite all this, *Lisa was not an Adrenal Type.* She was unmistakably a Pituitary. Existing right along with the aura of warmth generated by her now-strong adrenals was the classic P-Type coolness, intellectual detachment, and that childlike, almost angelic quality that sets P-Types apart from all the world. Clearly, Lisa was a P-Type who had successfully balanced her system with the Body Type Program, to the point where she had a fully adjustable system. She had reached the fourth Signpost to Change.

Like Lisa, *everybody who is on the Body Type Program for some time will find that his or her body changes, and that these changes mean that you will have to adjust the program to your changing needs.* But to know how exactly to make these adjustments, you need to understand what happens to your system over time.

STABILITY MEANS CHANGE

Life is dynamic. Your body is dynamic. The Body Type Program is dynamic, too. It is intended to make changes in your entire system, and it does. It takes you toward balance and integration, and away from imbalance, fixed tendencies, cravings, cellulite, and your typical body type windows of vulnerability. Of course, you know all this; I've told you about it in each chapter of this book. But it's important to emphasize yet again that using these techniques results in predictable changes, and that *your* changes require, in turn, changes in the way you use the body type techniques.

For each body type, the basic technique is to rest the overused functions, and to nourish and support the less active functions. So we use diet, supplements, exercise, stress reduction techniques, yoga positions, and the Long Weekend of Rejuvenation to reduce overstimulation of the dominant gland and to encourage stronger functioning in the less active glands.

For each type, we use specific methodologies to bring up the *balancing glands.* This means:

FOR PITUITARY TYPES: reducing stimulation of the pituitary, and supporting the adrenals and sex glands.

FOR THYROID TYPES: reducing stimulation of the thyroid, and supporting the adrenals primarily, the sex glands to a lesser extent.

FOR ADRENAL TYPES: reducing stimulation of the adrenals, and supporting the pituitary primarily, the thyroid to a lesser extent.

FOR GONADAL TYPES: reducing stimulation of the sex glands, and supporting the pituitary and thyroid glands.

After some time, usually between two and four years on this program, you will find that *your balancing glands become so much stronger and more active* that you experience these results:

Pituitary Types become more adrenal and/or gonadal.
Thyroid Types become more adrenal.
Adrenal Types become more pituitary and/or thyroidal.
Gonadal Types become more pituitary and/or thyroidal.

Certain basic characteristics of the balancing glands are now a permanent part of you. If you're a Thyroid or Pituitary, you'll find you now have the warmth of a G and the steadiness of an A. You'll also have developed more of the qualities of the gland more associated with your own: T's will have enlivened more of the lively, innovative intellect of the pituitary gland, and P's will have more of the creativity and outgoingness of the thyroid gland.

By the same token, if you're an Adrenal or a Gonadal, you'll find that you have become more like *your* balancing glands. You'll be livelier, less rigid, more creative, more communicative, more playful, and more introspective. These truly balancing qualities sneak up on you—they don't arrive all at once, and there may be no clearly defined moment when you "change," but you will gradually realize (or someone close to you may tell you) that it has happened.

Once you have reached this point, you have created an entirely new situation. You have made the necessary corrections, but you don't want to *overcorrect* and end up with imbalance again. So, to maintain your balance, you have to adjust your program to *reduce* stimulation to the glands that you needed at first to stimulate. You may even have to stimulate your dominant gland (though in a balanced way—not using the foods that you craved in the past but with the right kind of stimulation). Remember, we are talking about years from now—so be sure to keep your book!

What you will do is to take the same body type techniques that you used in balancing your system originally, but turn them around, adjust them, so as to maintain the balance you have now acquired. Just as you once used food, exercise, and the other techniques to quiet your dominant gland and encourage your less active ones, you will now use these same things to give a light amount of stimulation to your dominant gland. At the same time, you may have to reduce (but not entirely eliminate) stimulation of your balancing glands. Like that seesaw, you keep yourself in balance by adjusting the weights on each end.

In the roughly twenty-five years I have been using the body type balancing techniques with my patients, I have noticed that many of them begin making these adjustments to the program on their own, quite spontaneously. This is what Lisa had been doing when she began adjusting her diet to be more like the A-Type program. At other times, patients come to me with questions; they feel that it's time for them to make some changes, but they're wondering exactly what to do, and when.

I explain to them, as I did to Lisa, that although they may feel that they have acquired characteristics of another body type, they have not actually changed. Your basic nature is a given—inborn and not subject to alteration. But their metabolism has undergone some real changes, and they have become permanent. P-Types and T-Types will realize that they have become "adrenalized" or "gonadalized"; A-Types and G-Types will notice that they have become more "thyroidal" or "pituitarized." These words are strange ones, but they do describe a reality! And now, your system is capable of expressing its full potential. You have available to you the energy of *all four glands*. Now you can use the techniques of body type balancing to draw on any sort of energy, at any time. This is the meaning of having a "fully adjustable system." Do you need thyroid energy for a creative project today? It's available, and you know how to get it. Do you need adrenal drive and push? You know how to get that, too. Do you have some focused intellectual work to do? Your pituitary is ready and capable. What about gonadal warmth and nurturing? Your system has that available, too. Whatever kind of energy you want and need is there for you in your own fully developed system.

The Signpost to Freedom

When you do get to this point and are clearly aware of it, then you are at a Signpost to Change that is really a signpost to freedom. It means that you now have the freedom to adjust your system in any direction you want it to go.

You can use the principles of the Body Type Program to tilt your seesaw just a little bit in any direction; enough to get the kind of extra energy you need for whatever you want to do. I hope you realize what this means. It means that your body will be close to a perfect balance and very flexible. No job will be impossible, no sport will be impossible, no idea will be too hard to accept, no relationship will seem too difficult. It's the difference between steering a speedboat and a trawler.

For example: You're a T-Type who has been on the program for long enough to reach this signpost. You have nourished your adrenals very well, and they're working; you're steadier in your energy, less easily fatigued, less up-and-down in every way. But you're still a T-Type, and your creative genius is still formed around your original body type. So what do you do if you have a sudden, intense call on your T-Type creativity—such as a demand from your boss to produce a terrific, snappy report, yesterday? You stimulate your thyroid. You give yourself some thyroid-stimulating food and adjust your diet and your exercise just enough to create the kind of energy you need for the task at hand.

It's a tremendous relief to reach this signpost, as I can confirm, having become a balanced T-Type on my own program! Occasionally someone will see me having a cup of coffee or eating a roll or some such, and reads me chapter and verse from the Body Type Diet. Yes, these would be mistakes for an unbalanced T-Type, but I'm not one anymore. I lost my "jelly roll" and my sweets craving long ago, and my body has learned to keep its balance. After following the T-Type Program for more than twenty years now, I have a fully adjustable system and I know how to use it.

Suppose, on the other hand, that you're a Gonadal Type like Elizabeth King Morrison, my coauthor, who has lightened up by "pituitarizing" and "thyroidizing" her system for all these years. She still may use adrenal-stimulating or gonadal-stimulating foods if she has a physical challenge coming up, or if she just wants that G-Type energy for any reason. But when she has creative work to do, she sticks with thyroid or pituitary stimulants; she might even go on the G-Type Balancing Diet (full of thyroid-stimulating foods) for several weeks to get the effects she wants.

The Stability and Flexibility of Being in Balance

The balanced system, in other words, is now fully adjustable. You're in charge, and can do whatever you want with it. Of course it takes a real understanding of the principles of the Body Type System. You have to know what you're doing, but once you get to this Signpost to Change, it's actually easy to observe your body's reactions and gauge what you do accordingly. You can sense the seesaw clearly and alter its balance however you wish. Your increased sensitivity to your body's responses and inner workings are another big plus of improved metabolic balance. It is now much easier to know thyself than ever before.

Your metabolism is now in such good balance that it's both more stable and more flexible than it was when it was out of balance. It is more stable in that you don't disrupt it with small deviations from your diet, or by missing your regular exercise, or by unexpected stress or fatigue. Like a top that's spinning fast, it comes back to center when given a knock. A slow top falls over. As Lisa B. told me, "I find I can eat all kinds of food now—even the ones that I couldn't handle before. In fact, even dairy products work for me now. Last week I had to go back to my old programming group and help them with some coding for a new software product I'm producing. I had yogurt for breakfast because I knew it would help cool down my adrenals and kick up my pituitary. It worked! I guess I can still write code if I need to!" I was delighted, too, and pointed out to her the advantages of having a fully adjustable system. Before, writing code was just about all she could do. Now, she has a job that lets her use *all* of her innate abilities, without losing a thing from her "old" self.

And by the way, this is also the answer to the frightened question people always ask when looking over their Body Type Diet for the first time: "Will I have to stay on this all my life?" No, but you have to be patient and have the perseverance to get to this Signpost to Change.

PERFECT HEALTH AND THE META-BODY TYPE: THE LAST SIGNPOST TO CHANGE

Let's project even farther into the future for a moment. It's important to have a clear idea where you're going, even though the destination may seem remote. The future I want to talk about begins after your system has become fully adjustable, about two to three years from now ("now" being the time you start on the program). Whenever you start, you need to be aware of the final goal, which is to make your health the best it possibly can be.

When you get your system in total balance, however long that takes, your health will be the best it can be *with your particular physiology.* Your body's self-repairing mechanisms will be so much more effective, and they are extremely powerful, but the passage of time isn't stopping, either; there will be some deterioration, some aging, some possibility of disease. None of us, as the saying goes, is getting any younger.

What you will have now is very close to perfect health. It's the best health you can have, taking only the body into consideration. But the ideal of health goes beyond what can be achieved by attention to your body alone. A perfectly balanced system is a prerequisite. It's the foundation, but it's not the whole story. To create the full reality, you need to continue to take care of your body and your consciousness.

What is actually the ideal of perfect health? It's not just being free of disease. It's not just being resilient enough to stay up late and party and not feel hung over the next day, or to work hard and not burn out. These things are fine, and it's nice to have them—and you will. But ideal health is much more than this. It's not even what today is called "positive wellness," which carries with it the idea of constant improvement. You will have this with the Body Type Program, but again, the ideal of health includes even more.

In truth, I believe that perfect health is about the expansion of consciousness. I think we all instinctively feel that ideal health must include the quality of inner life, which means perfect inner balance: emotional, mental, spiritual, along with outer, bodily equilibrium.

I have had the privilege of observing up close this kind of inner and outer balance in a few individuals, and from a distance in a few more. Maharishi Mahesh Yogi, founder of the transcendental meditation movement, possesses an inner and outer equilibrium and radiance that is truly amazing. So does the Dalai Lama of Tibet. Pope John Paul II seems to me to have it also (even now, when his outer health is precarious). This state of balance has recognizable glow, a radiant power, that once seen is unmistakable. In such people their radiant physical health seems to act like a perfectly constructed edifice that is designed to support, nourish, and reflect the life within.

The Meta-Body Type

Interestingly, all the people I'm aware of who have reached this level of health appear to have gone *beyond* their original body type. They do have a discernible underlying metabolic body type, but their physiology appears to have a more general and more organized structure about it. There are a number of biochemical studies that suggest that the hypothalamus, the neuroglandular control center located in the brain, may be their "dominant gland." However, rather than refer to a "hypothalamic type," I have chosen to refer to them as having developed a "meta-body type." I want to set the highly developed individuals definitely apart from the four body types, yet give reference to the fact that there is an underlying genetic type present. In other words, I want to indicate that their dominant gland is still there, and has left its mark on their system, but it is no longer *dominating* it anymore.

The meta-body type is not a fifth body type; it is a development from *any* of the four body types. Pope John Paul II and Maharishi Mahesh Yogi both appear to have the underlying characteristics of

Adrenal Types; but they are not A-Types, nor have they turned into one of the other body types. Rather, they have gone beyond the A-Type metabolism to a new and more organized state.

I first saw Maharishi Mahesh Yogi in 1969, and he had a meta-body type then, and probably had one from the very beginning of his life. The pope appears to me to have acquired a meta-body type after the attempt on his life in 1976. I saw him go from being a healthy, glowing A-Type to an even more glowing and more spiritual meta-adrenal type. What made the difference? I would say that the evolution of his consciousness, as demonstrated in the act of forgiving his would-be assassin, was somehow responsible for the transformation.

The Dalai Lama appears to me to have the underlying characteristics of a Thyroid Type, but like Maharishi Mahesh Yogi and Pope John Paul II, he has evolved beyond any limitations of body type to the meta-body type. Yet his diet still takes his underlying T-Type body into consideration. Recently I read in his autobiography, *My Land and My People,* that the Tibetan people, though Buddhists and opposed to taking life, do eat meat. "It is very difficult to stay healthy in the rigorous climate of Tibet if you don't eat meat," the Dalai Lama writes. Yes, that's probably true if you're a Thyroid Type. I also read a recent *New Yorker* article describing a talk that he gave to some supporters of the Tibetan cause in New York. The talk was followed by an earnestly "healthy" luncheon involving tofu, cottage cheese, and raw vegetables. Did the Dalai Lama share this Adrenal-Type lunch? Not he. He nipped back to his hotel, where he had a steak. He's a meta-thyroid and he knows what's good for him! As Jesus said, it's not what goes into your mouth that defiles you, but what comes out of it.

There is certainly a logic about the idea that our health will continue to evolve, even from the excellent physical balance created with the Body Type Program, and that the further evolution of health is inextricably bound up with the development of consciousness. Research on the development of consciousness suggests strongly that the best definition of the goal toward which health might evolve is a "physiological state that can support fully developed consciousness."

Another way of saying it is that perfect health is simply a body pure enough to sustain a pure soul.

Meta-body types—people who have reached this final Signpost to Change—are rare, but they exist. Even if I knew of only a single living example in the world, I would still want to try for it in my own life, and it would still be the goal of the Body Type Program. The program I have created for each body type is designed to lay the groundwork: to develop such a refined state of balance and integration that further development is made easy and natural.

The Body Type Program is not the whole way to perfect health. Meditation, inner development, and the quality of your actions are all crucial, and of course, they are quite outside of my ability to give you guidance. But the Body Type Program does give you a vital key. It will enable you to think about your body's health and balance in an efficient and scientific manner, and to take practical steps starting right now to grow in the direction you want to go. Along with this process, attention to your consciousness and your spirit will still be absolutely necessary for this development to continue.

Until there are more people who have reached this goal, there is little more that can be said to describe it. There is no current theory, except those offered by religion, to account for the level of neural and physical integration the meta-body types exhibit. It appears that aging in the meta-body type, also, is on its own terms. They're not getting older, they're getting much better, effortlessly. Whole new theories of aging, and of health itself, will have to be developed for individuals like this.

And if this seems like a daunting goal, remember that consciousness has its own momentum. There is in all of us something that wants to live, grow, and evolve, and this is consciousness in its purest state. This factor deserves all our attention; it is what makes individual life work, family life work, the whole of society work. It is the most precious value in human life, and it is my hope that the Body Type Program, by creating the most perfect physical health, will enable all of us to reach our highest goals.

RECIPES FOR GONADAL TYPES

G-Type Stir-Fried Chicken

1 whole chicken breast, skinned
and boned
1 cup fresh asparagus (if available)
or 1 cup frozen asparagus,
thawed and cut into 1-inch
lengths
1 teaspoon vegetable oil

MARINADE:
2 teaspoons soy sauce
1 teaspoon cornstarch
1 slice fresh ginger, minced
2 sliced green onions
1 teaspoon dry sherry (optional)

Cut boned chicken breast into $1/2$-inch-square pieces. Place in a bowl with the marinade. Heat $1/2$ teaspoon oil in a wok or frying pan, add the vegetables, and cook, stirring, 3–4 minutes or until just tender. Remove from the pan. Add the other $1/2$ teaspoon of oil. Drain the marinade from the chicken and save it. Add the chicken to the hot oil and cook, stirring, about two minutes or until it turns white. Add vegetables and marinade and toss together 1 minute, until the sauce thickens and the vegetables are hot. Serves two.

Salmon Steak Florentine

2 4-ounce salmon steaks
1 bunch of fresh spinach (or use
    package of frozen spinach)
$^1/_2$ teaspoon dried dill or
    1 teaspoon of fresh, if available
1 lemon, cut into wedges

2 teaspoons vegetable oil
$^1/_2$ medium onion, chopped
$^1/_8$ teaspoon salt
Pinch of pepper

Wash the spinach carefully and shake off water. Cut into 1-inch strips. Wipe fish with a damp cloth and arrange in a single layer on a broiler pan. Broil about 4 inches from the heat for 5 minutes. Turn, sprinkle with salt and pepper, and brush the tops lightly with 1 teaspoon of oil. Sprinkle on the dill. Return to the broiler and broil 5 minutes more. Meanwhile, heat the remaining oil in a skillet. Cook onion until soft. Stir in the spinach, cover pan, and cook, stirring occasionally, over high heat for 3 minutes, or until spinach is wilted and bright green. To serve, spoon spinach onto a warm platter and lay salmon steaks on top. Garnish with lemon wedges.

Marinated Fish with Vegetables

1 $^1/_2$ pounds of white fish fillet
    such as flounder or sole
2 tablespoons lemon juice
2 small carrots
$^1/_4$ cup of white wine vinegar
$^1/_8$ teaspoon of pepper
$^3/_4$ teaspoon of salt
$^1/_2$ cup of water

2 teaspoons dried thyme
$^1/_2$ large onion
2 celery stalks
2 teaspoons of vegetable oil
1 bay leaf
$^1/_2$ teaspoon of paprika
Lettuce, parsley, lemon wedges

Wipe fish with a damp cloth and cut into serving-size pieces. Sprinkle with lemon juice and set aside. Julienne (cut into thin, 1-inch strips) the onion, celery, and carrots. Combine vinegar, water, thyme, pepper, bay leaf, and $^1/_2$ teaspoon of salt. In a large skillet, heat oil and cook fish over medium heat for five minutes, then turn and cook 3–5 minutes more, or until fish flakes easily with a fork. Remove from the skillet and place in a shallow pan. In the same skillet, cook the carrots for two minutes. Add onion and celery and cook, stirring, two minutes more. Pour in vinegar mixture, cover, and simmer 1 minute. Spoon vegetables and sauce over fish and let cool. Cover and refrigerate four hours or overnight. Serve cold fish on a lettuce-lined platter, garnished with parsley and lemon wedges. Serves six (a large recipe good for a party).

Chicken Salad with Yogurt

2 whole chicken breasts
$^1/_2$ cup plain yogurt
1 green onion (optional)
$^1/_2$ teaspoon dried dill or
    1 teaspoon fresh dill

$^1/_3$ teaspoon salt
Lettuce leaves and tomato wedges

Cook chicken breasts in water to cover 25–30 minutes, until just tender. Cool in broth, remove fat, and save broth for another recipe. Remove the cooked chicken from the bone and cut into chunks. Mix with yogurt, salt, dill, and green onion. Cover and chill. Serve on lettuce leaves garnished with tomato wedges. Serves four.

Stir-Fried Fish Fillets

$^1/_2$ pound of firm white fish fillets
1 teaspoon soy sauce
2 teaspoons water
2 teaspoons vegetable oil
1 bunch broccoli, cut into florets

$^1/_2$ teaspoon sesame oil (if
    available)
$^1/_2$ teaspoon cornstarch
1 slice fresh ginger, minced

Heat 1 teaspoon of oil in a skillet or wok. Add the fish and ginger and cook, stirring very gently so that fish cooks evenly but does not come apart. When fish starts to turn white, remove from the pan. Precook the broccoli by placing it in a small amount of boiling water for a few minutes. Drain. Heat the remaining teaspoon of oil in the skillet and add the broccoli, stir-frying 1–2 minutes until just crisp. Return fish to the pan, add the soy sauce, water, and cornstarch mixed together, and heat through so that sauce thickens and coats the fish and broccoli. At the last minute, sprinkle on the sesame oil. This is not necessary, but gives an interesting, Chinese taste. Serves four.

Lemon Chicken Kabobs

2 whole chicken breasts   Dash of cayenne pepper, if desired
2 teaspoons vegetable oil   1 large lemon
2 small zucchini $^1/_4$ pound fresh mushrooms
$^1/_2$ teaspoon salt   1 teaspoon cider vinegar

Grate 1 teaspoon of lemon peel from the lemon, then squeeze juice into a bowl. Add lemon peel, vinegar, salt, and cayenne pepper. Bone and skin the chicken breasts and cut each breast into 4 or 5 roughly square pieces. Cut the zucchini into three pieces each. Add chicken, zucchini, and mushrooms to the lemon juice mixture and toss lightly to coat each piece. Cover and refrigerate at least 3 hours, stirring occasionally. To cook, thread chicken, zucchini chunks, and mushrooms alternately on 14-inch metal skewers. Place on a rack in the broiling pan, or over a barbecue, and broil 10–15 minutes, turning every few minutes. Brush several times with marinade mixture. Serves two.

Eggs Mornay

2 soft-boiled eggs   2 medium ripe tomatoes, peeled
1 teaspoon vegetable oil   and chopped
1 clove garlic, minced $^1/_4$ teaspoon salt
$^1/_4$ teaspoon dried basil   2 slices of low-fat Swiss cheese
2 slices of whole-grain toast   (totaling 2 oz. cheese)

Make tomato sauce by cooking the garlic and basil in the oil for a minute or two. Add the tomatoes and salt and cook just until the tomatoes are heated through. In the meantime, soft-boil the eggs by cooking them in boiling water for 6 minutes. Run them under cold water and peel them carefully. Wrap each egg in a slice of cheese. Divide the tomato sauce into two shallow baking dishes. Arrange an egg in the center of each. Broil about 5 minutes, until cheese is melted and slightly brown. Cut the toast into wedges and arrange around each dish. Serves two.

Herb Omelette

1 egg	2 teaspoons fresh herbs (basil,
1 teaspoon skim milk	parsley, tarragon, thyme) or
1 teaspoon vegetable oil	1 teaspoon dried herbs

Beat egg with milk in a bowl. Heat oil in a small skillet until hot, add egg, and sprinkle with herbs. Lower the flame under the skillet and cook, drawing cooked egg away from the edges of the skillet with a spatula and letting the uncooked mixture run out toward the edges, until mixture is set. Fold in half and slide onto a plate. Serves one.

Greek-Style Eggs

1 teaspoon olive or other vegetable oil	1 tablespoon feta cheese (Ricotta cheese may be used if feta is
$1/2$ cup tomatoes	not available)
2 eggs, beaten	

Cut up tomatoes into chunks and sauté in the oil 5–6 minutes. Add beaten eggs and feta cheese and cook, stirring, until eggs are set and cheese is slightly melted. Serves one.

Spaghetti with Cheese

2 ounces spaghetti, whole-wheat   4 ounces Parmesan cheese, grated
  or spinach   1 teaspoon butter

Bring water to a full boil in a large pot and add the spaghetti. Cook
7–9 minutes or until just tender but not soft. Drain. Add the butter
and the cheese and return to the pot, tossing together over low heat
until the cheese is melted and blended with the spaghetti. Serves
one.

G-Type Vegetable Soup

zucchini   watercress
beet tops   cucumber
romaine lettuce   parsley

Cut the vegetables into chunks, using as much as you wish but approximately equal amounts of each. Use about ¹/₃ cup of each vegetable per serving. Place in a pot with water or chicken stock from
which you have skimmed all fat. Cook for 5–10 minutes or until the
vegetables are tender. You may eat as is or puree lightly in a blender
if you prefer. A pinch of salt and pepper only is permitted. Eat as
much as you wish while on your Last Five Pounds Diet—even between meals. For convenience, you may prepare enough Vegetable
Soup for several days. It keeps well in the refrigerator, and you can
reheat it as needed.

Clear Diet Dressing for Salads

The commercially prepared diet salad dressings are acceptable provided you choose a clear one and not one of the creamy-looking
ones such as Roquefort. These may have fewer calories than *regular*
creamy dressings, but are still too high in calories for your diet. If you
want to make your dressing at home, use any of the following:
    In a small saucepan combine 1 cup red wine vinegar and ¹/₂ cup
chopped fresh herbs (try basil, parsley, tarragon, dill, thyme, or a

combination). Bring to a boil. Cool and pour into a jar with a tight-fitting cover and let stand at room temperature for several days. Strain and use over any vegetable salad.

You can also mix 2 teaspoons of plain yogurt with a pinch of fresh or dried herbs and use it as a salad dressing.

Finally, fresh lemon juice squeezed over a salad is delicious.

Preparing Whole Grains: Bulgur Wheat, Brown Rice, Millet, Amaranth, Kamut, and Quinoa

Whole grains are prepared in the same way as refined grains such as white rice, except that the cooking time is longer to allow the harder whole grains to be cooked through. To prepare brown rice, place washed rice in a saucepan with twice as much water as rice. Rice does not cook well in very small amounts, so it is a good idea to cook a minimum of $3/4$ cup rice at any one time, using $1 1/2$ cups water. Bring the water to a boil, lower heat, and cover tightly. Allow to cook for about forty minutes, or until all the water is absorbed. Fluff with a fork and allow to stand for a few more minutes before serving. To prepare the other whole grains, place in a pot with twice as much water as grain. Bring the water to a boil, cover, and cook twenty minutes. For a rich flavor, use defatted chicken stock instead of water.

RECIPES FOR
ADRENAL TYPES

Stir-Fried Flank Steak

8 ounces of lean flank steak, sliced thinly on the diagonal
1 teaspoon vegetable oil
$^1/_2$ cup of bamboo shoots, sliced
1 cup of green peppers, sliced into strips

MARINADE:
2 teaspoons soy sauce
1 teaspoon cornstarch
1 slice fresh ginger, minced
2 sliced green onions
1 teaspoon dry sherry (optional)

Place flank steak in a bowl with the marinade for 30 minutes before cooking. Heat $^1/_2$ teaspoon oil in a wok or frying pan, add the vegetables, and cook, stirring, 3–4 minutes or until just tender. Remove from the pan. Add the other $^1/_2$ teaspoon of oil. Drain the marinade from the steak and save it. Add the steak to the hot oil and cook, stirring, about a minute or until it looks brown. Add vegetables and marinade and toss together 1 minute, until the sauce thickens and the vegetables are hot. Serves two.

Chicken Vegetable Soup

1 whole chicken, cut up
3 celery ribs, cut into 1-inch
  pieces
3 large carrots, cut into 1-inch
  pieces

1 box matzoh-ball and soup
  flavoring mix

Cover chicken pieces (except wings) and vegetables with water to cover in a large pot and cook 30 minutes or until chicken is tender. Add soup seasoning mix to the pot. Meanwhile, prepare matzoh balls according to package directions, reducing oil to one tablespoon. Cook as directed. Chill soup in the refrigerator overnight, or until the fat is solid and easy to remove. Remove the skin from the chicken and all the fat from the soup. Serve as a family meal. Your portion is one piece of chicken, one matzoh ball, and as many vegetables as you like. Serves six.

Sole Provençal

1 pound of sole (or you can use
  sea bass, flounder, or other
  lean fish in season)
1 teaspoon of olive oil
1 clove of garlic (optional)

4 fresh tomatoes, peeled and
  chopped, or 11-oz. can of
  whole tomatoes
$^{1}/_{4}$ pound mushrooms, sliced

Preheat the oven to 400 degrees. In a frying pan, cook mushrooms in the oil 2–3 minutes or until limp. Stir in the tomatoes and garlic and heat through. Add pepper to taste (no salt). Cut fish into four serving-sized pieces and place in a shallow baking dish. Cover with tomato-mushroom mixture. Bake uncovered, until fish flakes easily with a fork—about 10–15 minutes. Serves four.

Red Snapper "Scallops"

8 ounces of red snapper, fresh or frozen	1 lime, cut into wedges
1 teaspoon vegetable oil	1 tablespoon cilantro ("Chinese parsley"), minced or
1 tablespoon dry white wine	1 tablespoon parsley, minced
1 tablespoon water	

Cut red snapper into "scallops"—approximately $1^1/_2$-square-inch cubes. Heat the oil in a skillet and add fish. Sauté for 2 minutes, then add wine and water and cover. Cook about 10 minutes or until fish is opaque. Remove cover and squeeze $^1/_2$ of the lime over the fish and sprinkle with the parsley or cilantro. Heat 1 minute more. Serve, garnished with the rest of the lime. Serves two.

Chicken Burgers

2 whole chicken breasts, boned and skinned (turkey may be substituted)	4 large mushroom caps (optional)
	1 egg
	$^1/_2$ teaspoon salt
2 tablespoons dried bread crumbs	1 teaspoon of vegetable oil
$^1/_2$ medium onion, minced	

Grind the chicken in a meat grinder or in a food processor (or buy ground chicken breast in the supermarket). Add the remaining ingredients except the mushrooms and oil. Blend and form into four patties. Heat the oil in a skillet and cook over medium heat, turning once. Meanwhile, place the mushrooms in a toaster oven or under the grill for 5 minutes. Serve the chicken burgers with a mushroom on each. Serves four.

Turkey Kabobs

1 5–6 pound frozen turkey breast, thawed
1/4 cup of soy sauce
1/4 cup dry sherry
1/4 cup Chinese plum sauce

1 tablespoon fresh ginger, minced
1 teaspoon salad oil
1/2 teaspoon crushed red pepper
1 bunch of green onions, sliced

Mix the soy sauce, sherry, ginger, oil, plum sauce, and red pepper in a large bowl. Cut the turkey from the bone and cut into 2-inch cubes. Add to the marinade and toss to coat well. Cover and refrigerate for several hours or overnight. Thread the turkey cubes on metal skewers, alternating with onion pieces, and grill on a barbecue or in the oven for about 30 minutes, turning occasionally and brushing with marinade. Serves six.

Ceviche with Melon

1/2 pound firm white fish (flounder, sole, sea bass)—*very* fresh
1/4 medium red onion, sliced
1 whole clove

Juice of 1 lime
1/4 teaspoon red pepper flakes
1 cup cantaloupe cubes
1 tablespoon chopped parsley

Combine fish in a small bowl with onion, lime juice, clove, and red pepper. Refrigerate, covered, for six hours or overnight. The lime juice "cooks" the fish so that it is opaque rather than translucent. Just before serving, toss with the cantaloupe and parsley. Serves two.

Eggs Mornay

2 soft-boiled eggs
1 teaspoon vegetable oil
1 clove garlic, minced
1/4 teaspoon dried basil

2 slices of toast
2 medium ripe tomatoes, peeled
2 slices of low-fat Swiss cheese (totaling 2 oz. cheese)

Make tomato sauce by cooking the garlic and basil in the oil for a minute or two. Add the tomatoes and cook just until the tomatoes are heated through. In the meantime, soft-boil the eggs by cooking them in boiling water for 6 minutes. Run them under cold water and peel them carefully. Wrap each egg in a slice of cheese. Divide the tomato sauce into two shallow baking dishes. Arrange an egg in the center of each. Broil about 5 minutes, until cheese is melted and slightly brown. Cut the toast into wedges and arrange around each dish. Serves two.

A-Type Vegetable Soup

green pepper	chinese peas (snow peas)
zucchini	tomato
celery	celery tops

Use as many vegetables as you wish, but approximately equal quantities of all. About $1/3$ cup of each vegetable should be used for each portion of the soup. Chop the vegetables coarsely and place in a large pot with water or chicken stock from which you have removed all the fat. Bring to a boil and cook 5–10 minutes, or until vegetables are tender. You may add a pinch of pepper, but no salt. Eat as much of this soup as you want while on your Last Five Pounds Diet—even between meals if you wish.

For convenience, you may prepare several days' worth of Vegetable Soup at once—it keeps well in the refrigerator and you need only reheat it as you wish.

Preparing Whole Grains: Bulgur Wheat, Brown Rice, Millet, Amaranth, Kamut, and Quinoa

Whole grains are prepared in the same way as refined grains such as white rice, except that the cooking time is longer to allow the harder whole grains to be cooked through. To prepare brown rice, place washed rice in a saucepan with twice as much water as rice. Rice does not cook well in very small amounts, so it is a good idea to cook a minimum of ³/₄ cup rice at any one time, using 1¹/₂ cups water. Bring the water to a boil, lower heat, and cover tightly. Allow to cook for about forty minutes, or until all the water is absorbed. Fluff with a fork and allow to stand for a few more minutes before serving. To prepare the other whole grains, place in a pot with twice as much water as grain. Bring the water to a boil, cover, and cook twenty minutes. For a rich flavor, use defatted chicken stock instead of water.

A-Type Stir-Fried Chicken

One whole chicken breast, skinned
and boned
¹/₂ cup green beans, sliced
1 teaspoon vegetable oil
¹/₂ cup celery, sliced

MARINADE:
2 teaspoons soy sauce
1 teaspoon cornstarch
1 slice fresh ginger, minced
2 sliced green onions
1 teaspoon dry sherry (optional)

Cut boned chicken breast into ¹/₂-inch-square pieces. Place in a bowl with the marinade. Heat ¹/₂ teaspoon oil in a wok or frying pan, add the vegetables, and cook, stirring, 3–4 minutes or until just tender. Remove from the pan. Add the other ¹/₂ teaspoon of oil. Drain the marinade from the chicken and save it. Add the chicken to the hot oil and cook, stirring, about two minutes or until it turns white. Add vegetables and marinade and toss together 1 minute, until the sauce thickens and the vegetables are hot. Serves two.

Seafood Veronique

1 pound seafood (flounder,
haddock, sole, or other firm
white fish—fresh or frozen)
1 egg
2 tablespoons chopped chives
3 tablespoons plain yogurt
¹/₂ pound seedless grapes

1 tablespoon grated Parmesan
cheese
1 tablespoon diet mayonnaise
¹/₂ clove garlic, crushed (optional)
2 tablespoons of lemon juice
1 lemon, cut into wedges

Preheat oven to 400 degrees. Slightly beat the egg, then blend in the plain yogurt, chives, diet mayonnaise, and a sliver of the garlic. Cut fish into 1-inch chunks and combine in a bowl with the lemon juice and the rest of the garlic. Add the grapes and toss together to combine. Spoon the fish and grapes into four individual baking dishes or one 8-inch square dish. Spoon plain yogurt mixture over fish and top with grated cheese. Bake 12–15 minutes, until top is hot and bubbly. Garnish with lemon wedges. Serves four.

Chicken Breast Piquant

1 whole chicken breast, skin removed	1 small can water-packed artichoke hearts
1 teaspoon vegetable oil	1 teaspoon tomato paste
$1/2$ clove garlic, chopped (optional)	1 tablespoon wine vinegar
1 ripe tomato, coarsely chopped	$1/2$ teaspoon dried thyme

Heat the vegetable oil in a frying pan and brown the chicken five minutes on each side. Remove it from the pan and add all the remaining ingredients except the artichoke hearts. Stir and heat to boiling. Return the chicken to the pan, cover, and cook over low heat 20–25 minutes or until chicken is tender. Add the artichoke hearts for the last five minutes and allow to heat through.

Fruit Ice

1 pound of ripe fruit (strawberries, mango, papaya, peaches—you choose)	$1/8$ cup sugar
	1 envelope unflavored gelatin
	$1/4$ cup lemon juice

Sprinkle gelatin over lemon juice, let stand. In a small pan, combine sugar with 1 cup of water. Stir over low heat until sugar dissolves; bring to boil and boil gently, uncovered and without stirring, five minutes. Remove from heat. Add the gelatin and stir until dissolved. Puree the fruit in a blender until smooth, and add gelatin mixture to it; blend until smooth. Turn into an 8″ × 2″ pan. Freeze about 2 hours. Turn into a chilled bowl and beat quickly with a mixer or rotary beater until smooth but not melted. Return to the pan and freeze several hours, until firm. Serves eight.

Chocolate Cookies

3 egg whites, at room temperature   ½ teaspoon of vanilla extract
6 squares of unsweetened   ½ cup sugar
    chocolate, melted and cooled

Preheat oven to 350 degrees. Grease 2 cookie sheets. In a small mixer bowl, beat egg whites until stiff. Add sugar, 1 tablespoon at a time, and continue beating until mixture is smooth and glossy and sugar is completely dissolved. Fold in chocolate and vanilla. Drop by teaspoonfuls onto the cookie sheet. Bake 15 minutes. Makes 60 cookies.

Clear Diet Dressing for Salads

The commercially prepared diet salad dressings are acceptable provided you choose a clear one and not one of the creamy-looking ones such as Roquefort. These may have fewer calories than *regular* creamy dressings, but are still too high in calories for your diet. If you want to make your dressing at home, use any of the following:

In a small saucepan combine 1 cup red wine vinegar and ½ cup chopped fresh herbs (try basil, parsley, tarragon, dill, thyme, or a combination). Bring to a boil. Cool and pour into a jar with a tight-fitting cover and let stand at room temperature for several days.

Strain and use over any vegetable salad.

You can also mix 2 teaspoons of plain yogurt with a pinch of fresh or dried herbs and use it as a salad dressing.

Finally, fresh lemon juice squeezed over a salad is delicious.

RECIPES FOR THYROID TYPES

Mexican Stuffed Chicken

2 chicken breasts, skinned and
    boned
1 tablespoon dried bread crumbs
1 tablespoon grated Parmesan
    cheese
2 tablespoons mild green chilis,
    chopped

$^1/_2$ teaspoon chili powder
1 egg, beaten
1 ounce Monterey Jack cheese cut
    into two slices, 3 inches by 1
    inch

Preheat oven to 375 degrees. With a kitchen hammer or the side of a cleaver, pound out the boned breasts to $^1/_4$-inch thick. On each one, place a tablespoon of the chilis and a Monterey Jack cheese slice. Roll up and place, seam side down, in a baking dish. Brush with beaten egg. Mix together the bread crumbs, Parmesan cheese, and chili powder, and sprinkle over the chicken rolls, patting into place to form a crust. Bake for about 20 minutes—cheese inside will be melted and the crust nicely browned. Serves two.

T-Type Stir-Fried Chicken

One whole chicken breast, skinned
and boned
1 cup green pepper, sliced
1 teaspoon vegetable oil
1/2 cup celery, sliced

MARINADE:
2 teaspoons soy sauce
1 teaspoon cornstarch
1 slice fresh ginger, minced
    (optional)
2 sliced green onions
1 teaspoon dry sherry (optional)

Cut boned chicken breast into 1/2-inch-square pieces. Place in a bowl with the marinade. Heat 1/2 teaspoon oil in a wok or frying pan, add the vegetables, and cook, stirring, 3–4 minutes or until just tender. Remove from the pan. Add the other 1/2 teaspoon of oil. Drain the marinade from the chicken and save it. Add the chicken to the hot oil and cook, stirring, about two minutes or until it turns white. Add vegetables and marinade and toss together 1 minute, until the sauce thickens and the vegetables are hot. Serves two.

Salmon Steak Florentine

2 4-ounce salmon steaks
1 bunch of fresh spinach (or use
    package of frozen spinach)
1/2 teaspoon dried dill or 1
    teaspoon of fresh, if available
1/2 clove garlic, chopped (optional)

1 lemon, cut into wedges
2 teaspoons vegetable oil
1/2 medium onion, chopped
1/8 teaspoon salt
Pinch of pepper

Wash the spinach carefully and shake off water. Cut into 1-inch strips. Wipe fish with a damp cloth and arrange in a single layer on a broiler pan. Broil about 4 inches from the heat for 5 minutes. Turn, sprinkle with salt and pepper, and brush the tops lightly with 1 teaspoon of oil. Sprinkle on the dill. Return to the broiler and broil 5 minutes more. Meanwhile, heat the remaining oil in a skillet. Cook onion and garlic until soft. Stir in the spinach, cover pan, and cook, stirring occasionally, over high heat for 3 minutes, or until spinach is wilted and bright green. To serve, spoon spinach onto a warm platter and lay salmon steaks on top. Garnish with lemon wedges. Serves two.

Barbecued Tuna

$^1/_2$ pound of fresh or frozen tuna
  (albacore, if available)
2 ounces of frozen grapefruit juice
2 teaspoons lime juice (use lemon
  juice if lime is not available)

$^1/_4$ teaspoon salt
$^1/_4$ teaspoon Tabasco sauce
$^1/_4$ teaspoon dried thyme
$^1/_4$ teaspoon mustard

Combine grapefruit concentrate, lime or lemon juice, salt, mustard, thyme, and Tabasco sauce in a bowl. Marinate fish for 30 minutes. Cook over barbecue grill, or in the oven broiler, for 15 minutes, turning several times and basting with marinade mixture. Fish is done when it flakes easily with a fork. Garnish with a sprinkling of paprika. Serves two.

Chef's Salad

2 ounces cold cooked chicken
Lettuce, tomato, cucumber, celery,
  sprouts, as much as you like
2 teaspoons of any clear (not
  creamy) diet dressing

2 ounces hard cheese (Parmesan or
  Romano)

Slice chicken and vegetables, toss together with dressing, and serve. Serves one.

Sesame Shrimp with Asparagus

4 ounces of shrimp
1 bunch of asparagus, sliced into
   1-inch pieces
1 teaspoon soy sauce
1 teaspoon vegetable oil

1 small slice of fresh ginger,
   minced (optional)
2 teaspoons sesame seeds
$^1/_2$ teaspoon cornstarch

Peel shrimp and make a cut up the back, removing the black vein along the back. Place the sesame seeds in a wok or frying pan without oil and toast 2–3 minutes, watching to see they do not burn. Remove from pan. Heat $^1/_2$ teaspoon of oil in the pan and cook the asparagus 2 minutes, until not quite done. Remove asparagus from the pan. Heat the remaining $^1/_2$ teaspoon of oil and cook the shrimp 3–4 minutes, until they turn pink. Add asparagus and cook $^1/_2$ minute longer. Stir together soy sauce, ginger, and cornstarch and add to the pan, stirring to coat shrimp and asparagus. Sprinkle with toasted sesame seeds. Serves one.

Herb Omelette

1 egg
1 teaspoon skim milk
1 teaspoon vegetable oil

2 teaspoons fresh herbs (basil,
   parsley, tarragon, thyme) or
1 teaspoon dried herbs

Beat egg with milk in a bowl. Heat oil in a small skillet until hot, add egg and sprinkle with herbs. Lower the flame under the skillet and cook, drawing cooked egg away from the edges of the skillet with a spatula and letting the uncooked mixture run out toward the edges, until mixture is set. Fold in half and slide onto a plate. Serves one.

T-Type Vegetable Soup

yellow squash or zucchini	green beans
celery	celery tops
carrots	carrot tops

Cut the vegetables into chunks, using as much as you wish but approximately equal amounts of each. Use about $1/3$ cup of each vegetable per serving. Place in a pot with water or chicken stock from which you have skimmed *all* fat. Cook for 5–10 minutes or until the vegetables are tender. You may eat as is or puree lightly in a blender if you prefer. A pinch of salt and pepper only is permitted. Eat as much as you wish while on your Last Five Pounds Diet— even between meals. For convenience, you may prepare enough Vegetable Soup for several days. It keeps well in the refrigerator, and you can reheat it as needed.

Chicken Stew

2 whole chicken breasts	1 teaspoon curry powder
2 cups water	$1/4$ teaspoon dried thyme
1 celery, cut into 2-inch pieces	Dash cayenne pepper
$1/2$ teaspoon salt	$1/4$ medium onion
$1/2$ pound zucchini	$1/2$ green pepper, diced
$1/2$ clove garlic, crushed	1 teaspoon vegetable oil
1 14-oz. can tomatoes, with juice	$1/2$ bay leaf

Place chicken in a medium pan with water, bay leaf, celery, and $1/2$ teaspoon salt. Bring to a boil, reduce heat, and simmer 30 minutes, or until chicken is tender. Cool chicken in broth in the refrigerator overnight, or until fat is fully solid. Remove every trace of fat. Cut up chicken into bite-sized pieces, discarding the skin. Save 1 cup of broth. In the same pot, sauté onion, peppers, garlic, and seasonings in the oil for a few minutes. Add tomatoes, zucchini, and broth and simmer 5 minutes, until zucchini is tender. Add chicken and heat through. Serves four.

Chicken Breast Piquant

1 whole chicken breast, skin
   removed
1 teaspoon vegetable oil
1/2 clove garlic, chopped (optional)
1 ripe tomato, coarsely chopped
1 small can water-packed
   artichoke hearts

1 teaspoon tomato paste
1 tablespoon wine vinegar
1/4 teaspoon salt
1/2 teaspoon dried thyme

Sprinkle the chicken breast lightly with salt. Heat the vegetable oil in a frying pan and brown the chicken five minutes on each side. Remove it from the pan and add all the remaining ingredients except the artichoke hearts. Stir and heat to boiling. Return the chicken to the pan, cover, and cook over low heat 20–25 minutes or until chicken is tender. Add the artichoke hearts for the last five minutes and allow to heat through.

Baked Halibut Steak

2 fresh or frozen halibut steaks, 4
   ounces each
1/8 teaspoon of paprika
3 teaspoons lemon juice

1/4 teaspoon salt
Dash pepper
2 green onions, sliced
1/2 teaspoon vegetable oil

Thaw fish steaks, if frozen. Sprinkle with lemon juice, salt, paprika, and pepper. Place in a shallow baking dish and let stand to marinate for 30 minutes. Cook the onions for 2 minutes in the oil, then spoon over fish. Bake, covered, 15–20 minutes in a 350-degree oven. Remove cover for last three minutes to allow onions to brown. Serves two.

Preparing Whole Grains: Bulgur Wheat, Brown Rice, Millet, Amaranth, Kamut, and Quinoa

Whole grains are prepared in the same way as refined grains such as white rice, except that the cooking time is longer to allow the harder whole grains to be cooked through. To prepare brown rice, place washed rice in a saucepan with twice as much water as rice. Rice does not cook well in very small amounts, so it is a good idea to cook a minimum of $^3/_4$ cup rice at any one time, using $1^1/_2$ cups water. Bring the water to a boil, lower heat, and cover tightly. Allow to cook for about forty minutes, or until all the water is absorbed. Fluff with a fork and allow to stand for a few more minutes before serving. To prepare the other whole grains, place in a pot with twice as much water as grain. Bring the water to a boil, cover, and cook twenty minutes. For a rich flavor, use defatted chicken stock instead of water.

Turkey Kabobs

1 5–6 pound frozen turkey breast, thawed
$^1/_4$ cup of soy sauce
$^1/_4$ cup dry sherry
$^1/_4$ cup Chinese plum sauce

1 tablespoon fresh ginger, minced
1 teaspoon salad oil
$^1/_2$ teaspoon crushed red pepper
1 bunch of green onions, sliced

Mix the soy sauce, sherry, ginger, oil, plum sauce, and red pepper in a large bowl. Cut the turkey from the bone and cut into 2-inch cubes. Add to the marinade and toss to coat well. Cover and refrigerate for several hours or overnight. Thread the turkey cubes on metal skewers, alternating with onion pieces, and grill on a barbecue or in the oven for about 30 minutes, turning occasionally and brushing with marinade. Serves six.

Clear Diet Dressing for Salads

The commercially prepared diet salad dressings are acceptable provided you choose a clear one and not one of the creamy-looking ones such as Roquefort. These may have fewer calories than *regular* creamy dressings, but are still too high in calories for your diet. If you want to make your dressing at home, use any of the following:

In a small saucepan combine 1 cup red wine vinegar and ¹/₂ cup chopped fresh herbs (try basil, parsley, tarragon, dill, thyme, or a combination). Bring to a boil. Cool and pour into a jar with a tight-fitting cover and let stand at room temperature for several days. Strain and use over any vegetable salad.

You can also mix 2 teaspoons of plain yogurt with a pinch of fresh or dried herbs and use it as a salad dressing.

Finally, fresh lemon juice squeezed over a salad is delicious.

RECIPES FOR
PITUITARY TYPES

Preparing Organ Meats: Liver, Kidneys, and Heart

All organ meats—liver, kidneys, and heart—are highly perishable. Buy only what you will be eating within the next two or three days at the most.

Liver: To prepare any kind of liver—beef, calf, or chicken—wipe it first with a damp cloth, then remove the thin outer skin and veining. The cooking method is the same for all types. To grill, place it 3–4 inches away from the heat source. Cook only long enough to cook through—about a minute on each side. Cooking too long, or too close to the heat, will toughen liver. The center should remain just slightly pink. Liver can also be sautéed in a frying pan in a teaspoon of vegetable oil.

Kidneys: Veal kidneys are surprisingly tasty; the English eat them for breakfast all the time. To prepare, wipe the kidneys with a damp cloth, then split them and remove the cores. The white membranes should be snipped away. Cut them in half and expose the cut side to the heat first. They may be pan-fried in a teaspoon of vegetable oil, or broiled in the oven. Cook them until the center is just slightly pink—about 5 minutes on each side.

Heart: Heart is a muscle, rather than a true organ meat, and tends to be somewhat tough. It is best prepared ground. Ask your butcher to do this for you, or put it through a meat grinder or food processor. Form into a patty and sauté in 1 teaspoon of vegetable oil, or broil in the oven, until meat is no longer pink, about 25–30 minutes.

Broiled Shrimp with Lemon

Peel the shrimp and, with a sharp knife, make a shallow cut along the back and remove the vein (actually the intestine). Sprinkle with lemon juice and a small amount of salt. Place the shrimp under the broiler about 3 inches from the heat. Broil 3 minutes, turn, and broil three minutes more. Do not overcook—shrimp should be cooked just until the flesh is opaque. Serve with more lemon juice if desired.

P-Type Stir-Fried Chicken

One whole chicken breast, skinned
   and boned
$^1/_2$ cup zucchini, sliced
$^1/_2$ cup mushrooms, sliced
1 teaspoon vegetable oil

MARINADE:
2 teaspoons soy sauce
1 teaspoon cornstarch
1 slice fresh ginger, minced
   (optional)
2 sliced green onions
1 teaspoon dry sherry (optional)

Cut boned chicken breast into $^1/_2$-inch-square pieces. Place in a bowl with the marinade. Heat $^1/_2$ teaspoon oil in a wok or frying pan, add the vegetables, and cook, stirring, 3–4 minutes or until just tender. Remove from the pan. Add the other $^1/_2$ teaspoon of oil. Drain the marinade from the chicken and save it. Add the chicken to the hot oil and cook, stirring, about two minutes or until it turns white. Add vegetables and marinade and toss together 1 minute, until the sauce thickens and the vegetables are hot. Serves two.

Chicken Breast Piquant

2 whole chicken breasts, skin
    removed
1 teaspoon vegetable oil
$^1/_2$ clove garlic, chopped (optional)
1 ripe tomato, coarsely chopped
1 small can water-packed
    artichoke hearts

1 teaspoon tomato paste
1 tablespoon wine vinegar
$^1/_4$ teaspoon salt
$^1/_2$ teaspoon dried thyme

Sprinkle the chicken breast lightly with salt. Heat the vegetable oil in a frying pan and brown the chicken five minutes on each side. Remove it from the pan and add all the remaining ingredients except the artichoke hearts. Stir and heat to boiling. Return the chicken to the pan, cover, and cook over low heat 20–25 minutes or until chicken is tender. Add the artichoke hearts for the last five minutes and allow to heat through. Serves four.

Lemon Chicken Kabobs with Mushrooms and Zucchini

1 chicken breast, skinned
1 teaspoon vegetable oil
2 small zucchini
$^1/_4$ teaspoon salt
$^1/_8$ teaspoon cayenne pepper

1 lemon
$^1/_4$ pound fresh mushrooms
1 teaspoon vinegar
$^1/_2$ clove garlic

Three hours before serving, marinate the chicken as follows: Grate 1 teaspoon lemon peel from the lemon, then squeeze juice into a bowl. Add lemon peel, oil, vinegar, salt, garlic, and cayenne pepper. Cut the chicken into 4 or 5 roughly square pieces. Cut the zucchini into 3 pieces each. Add chicken, trimmed mushroom, and zucchini pieces to the marinade and toss lightly to coat each piece. Refrigerate. To cook, thread chicken, zucchini chunks, and mushrooms alternately on 14-inch metal skewers. Place on a rack in the broiling pan, or over a barbecue, and broil 10–15 minutes, turning every few minutes. Brush with marinade mixture when you turn. Serves two.

Celery-Onion Omelette

2 eggs
1 teaspoon water
2 teaspoons vegetable oil

$^1/_2$ cup sliced celery
2 sliced green onions

Heat 1 teaspoon vegetable oil in a small frying pan. Sauté celery and onions 4–5 minutes, until tender. Remove from the pan. Beat the eggs together with the water until mixed. Heat remaining oil in the pan and add the eggs. Gently stir the eggs in the pan and tip the egg mixture toward the edge of the pan until set. Put the celery-onion mixture on one side of the eggs, fold the egg mixture in half over the filling, and slide onto a plate. Serves one.

Stir-Fried Green Beans

1 cup of green beans
$^1/_8$ teaspoon salt
1 teaspoon vegetable oil

Slice beans crosswise into 1-inch pieces. Heat the oil in a frying pan and add beans. Cook, stirring, 3–5 minutes or just until beans are tender. Sprinkle with salt and serve.

Poached Pear

Bring 2 cups of water to a boil and add 1 clove and 1 stick of cinnamon. Reduce heat. Simmer pear gently in the spiced water until tender—about 15–20 minutes.

Sole Provençal

1 pound of sole (or you can use
   sea bass, flounder, or other
   lean fish in season)
1 teaspoon of olive oil
¼ pound mushrooms, sliced

4 fresh tomatoes, peeled and
   chopped, or 11-oz. can of
   whole tomatoes
1 clove of garlic, crushed

Preheat the oven to 400 degrees. In a frying pan, cook mushrooms in the oil 2–3 minutes or until limp. Stir in the tomatoes and garlic and heat through. Add pepper to taste (no salt). Cut fish into four serving-sized pieces and place in a shallow baking dish. Cover with tomato-mushroom mixture. Bake uncovered, until fish flakes easily with a fork—about 10–15 minutes. Serves four.

Stir-Fried Fish Fillets

½ pound of firm white fish fillets
1 teaspoon soy sauce
2 teaspoons water
2 teaspoons vegetable oil
1 cup green beans

½ teaspoon sesame oil (if
   available)
½ teaspoon cornstarch
1 slice fresh ginger, minced
½ cup mushrooms

Heat 1 teaspoon of oil in a skillet or wok. Add the fish and ginger and cook, stirring very gently so that fish cooks evenly but does not come apart. When fish starts to turn white, remove from the pan. Precook the broccoli by placing it in a small amount of boiling water for a few minutes. Drain. Heat the remaining teaspoon of oil in the skillet and add the green beans. Stirring 3–4 minutes until just crisp, add the mushrooms and stir-fry 1 minute more. Return fish to the pan, add the soy sauce, water, and cornstarch mixed together, and heat through so that sauce thickens and coats the fish and vegetables. At the last minute, sprinkle on the sesame oil. This is not necessary, but gives an interesting, Chinese taste. Serves four.

Baked Sesame Fish

2 frozen fish steaks about 1 inch
thick, 4 ounces each (cod,
whitefish, or other firm fish)
or 2 fresh fish pieces, cut into
4-ounce steaks, 1 inch thick

2 tablespoons sesame seeds
1 egg, beaten

Preheat oven to 350 degrees. Brush fish on top with beaten egg and press sesame seeds firmly onto the surface to form a crust. (You will not need all the egg, so save for scrambled eggs at another meal). Place fish in a small baking dish and bake about 20 minutes, or until sesame seeds are browned and fish flakes easily when prodded with a fork. Serves two.

Cracked Crabs P-Type

4 whole cleaned crabs in their
shells
$^1/_2$ lemon, sliced

$^1/_2$ lemon, cut into wedges
Dashes of salt and pepper

Crab is so delicious by itself it needs no special preparation to make it enjoyable. Simply bring to a boil a large pot of water. Drop in the crabs and lemon slices and boil 15–20 minutes. Drain, crack shells with a hammer, and serve with lemon wedges, salt, and pepper. Crabs can also be bought in many fish markets already cooked. Serves two.

P-Type Vegetable Soup

beets
okra
green beans
celery

beet tops
mushrooms
zucchini
green onions

Use as much vegetable as you wish, but approximately equal amounts of each. Use about $^1/_3$ cup of each vegetable per serving.

Chop the vegetables and place them in a pot with water, or with beef or chicken stock from which you have removed every trace of fat. Bring to a boil and cook for 5–10 minutes or until the vegetables are tender. You may eat as is or puree lightly in a blender if you prefer. A pinch of salt and pepper only is permitted. Eat as much as you wish while on your Last Five Pounds Diet—even between meals. For convenience, you may prepare enough Vegetable Soup for several days. It keeps well in the refrigerator, and you can reheat it as needed.

Baked Halibut Steak

2 fresh or frozen halibut steaks,
    4 ounces each
$^1/_8$ teaspoon of paprika
3 teaspoons lemon juice

$^1/_4$ teaspoon salt
Dash pepper
2 green onions, sliced
$^1/_2$ teaspoon vegetable oil

Thaw fish steaks, if frozen. Sprinkle with lemon juice, salt, paprika, and pepper. Place in a shallow baking dish and let stand to marinate for 30 minutes. Cook the onions for 2 minutes in the oil, then spoon over fish. Bake, covered, 15–20 minutes in a 350-degree oven. Remove cover for last three minutes to allow onions to brown. Serves two.

Marinated Fish with Vegetables

$1^1/_2$ pounds of white fish fillet
    such as flounder or sole
2 tablespoons lemon juice
2 small carrots
$^1/_4$ cup of white wine vinegar
$^1/_8$ teaspoon of pepper
$^3/_4$ teaspoon of salt
$^1/_2$ cup of water

2 teaspoons dried thyme
$^1/_2$ clove garlic, crushed (optional)
$^1/_2$ large onion
2 celery stalks
2 teaspoons of vegetable oil
1 bay leaf
$^1/_2$ teaspoon of paprika
Lettuce, parsley, lemon wedges

Wipe fish with a damp cloth and cut into serving-size pieces. Sprinkle with lemon juice and set aside. Julienne (cut into thin,

1-inch strips) the onion, celery, and carrots. Combine vinegar, water, thyme, pepper, bay leaf, and $^1/_2$ teaspoon of salt. In a large skillet, heat oil and cook fish over medium heat for five minutes, then turn and cook 3–5 minutes more, or until fish flakes easily with a fork. Remove from the skillet and place in a shallow pan. In the same skillet, cook the carrots for two minutes. Add onion and celery and cook, stirring, two minutes more. Pour in vinegar mixture, cover, and simmer 1 minute. Spoon vegetables and sauce over fish and let cool. Cover and refrigerate four hours or overnight. Serve cold fish on a lettuce-lined platter, garnished with parsley and lemon wedges. Serves six (a large recipe good for a party).

Salmon Steak Florentine

2 4-ounce salmon steaks
1 bunch of fresh spinach (or use
　　package of frozen spinach)
$^1/_2$ teaspoon dried dill or
　　1 teaspoon of fresh, if available
$^1/_2$ clove garlic, chopped (optional)

2 teaspoons vegetable oil
$^1/_2$ medium onion, chopped
$^1/_8$ teaspoon salt
Pinch of pepper

Wash the spinach carefully and shake off water. Cut into 1-inch strips. Wipe fish with a damp cloth and arrange in a single layer on a broiler pan. Broil about 4 inches from the heat for 5 minutes. Turn, sprinkle with salt and pepper, and brush the tops lightly with 1 teaspoon of oil. Sprinkle on the dill. Return to the broiler and broil 5 minutes more. Meanwhile, heat the remaining oil in a skillet. Cook onion and garlic until soft. Stir in the spinach, cover pan, and cook, stirring occasionally, over high heat for 3 minutes, or until spinach is wilted and bright green. To serve, spoon spinach onto a warm platter and lay salmon steaks on top. Garnish with lemon wedges. Serves two.

Clear Diet Dressing for Salads

The commercially prepared diet salad dressings are acceptable provided you choose a clear one and not one of the creamy-looking ones such as Roquefort. These may have fewer calories than *regular* creamy dressings, but are still too high in calories for your diet. If you want to make your dressing at home, use any of the following:

In a small saucepan combine 1 cup red wine vinegar and ½ cup chopped fresh herbs (try basil, parsley, tarragon, dill, thyme, or a combination). Bring to a boil. Cool and pour into a jar with a tight-fitting cover and let stand at room temperature for several days. Strain and use over any vegetable salad.

A variation is to omit herbs from the preceding recipe and add 4 crushed cloves of garlic.

Finally, fresh lemon juice squeezed over a salad is delicious.

Preparing Whole Grains: Bulgur Wheat, Brown Rice, Millet, Amaranth, Kamut, and Quinoa

Whole grains are prepared in the same way as refined grains such as white rice, except that the cooking time is longer to allow the harder whole grains to be cooked through. To prepare brown rice, place washed rice in a saucepan with twice as much water as rice. Rice does not cook well in very small amounts, so it is a good idea to cook a minimum of ¾ cup rice at any one time, using 1½ cups water. Bring the water to a boil, lower heat, and cover tightly. Allow to cook for about forty minutes, or until all the water is absorbed. Fluff with a fork and allow to stand for a few more minutes before serving. To prepare the other whole grains, place in a pot with twice as much water as grain. Bring the water to a boil, cover, and cook twenty minutes. For a rich flavor, use defatted chicken stock instead of water.

INDEX

ELLIOT D. ABRAVANEL, M.D., is known as a founder of holistic medicine. He received his B.A. from the University of California, Berkeley, and his M.D. from the University of Cincinnati in 1969. For many years he served Maharishi Mahesh Yogi as head of medical staff and as Professor of Medicine at Maharishi European Research University, where he pursued research on the relationship between consciousness and ideal health. In 1975 he opened a private medical practice in Beverly Hills, California, where he developed the Body Type System. He is the author of three books: *Dr. Abravanel's Body Type Diet and Lifetime Nutrition Plan, Dr. Abravanel's Body Type Program for Health, Fitness and Nutrition,* and *Dr. Abravanel's Anti-Craving Weight Loss Diet,* as well as numerous medical publications. He now divides his time between writing, lecturing, and research. He lives in Los Angeles with his wife, Weiyi Xu.

ELIZABETH KING MORRISON is a writer and educator who specializes in the creation of individual health and nutrition programs. She received her B.A. from Swarthmore College and her M.A. from the University of Texas at Austin. She is the author of two books on Transcendental Meditation in secondary education. She coauthored all three Body Type books with Dr. Abravanel, and has trained many health professionals in the Body Type System. She lives in Eureka, California, with her husband, the writer Ralph Morrison.

Other works on Body Types by Dr. Abravanel and Ms. Morrison include the *Body Type Counseling Modules, Body Type News* (a free newsletter now in its fourteenth year of publication), and an exercise video, "Exercise Right for Your Body Type." For more information about these publications or to subscribe to Body Type News, call 888-263-9897.